AF661476

BIOTECHNOLOGY RESEARCH IN AGE OF TERRORISM

BIOTECHNOLOGY RESEARCH IN AGE OF TERRORISM

A.K. Gaur

CYBER TECH PUBLICATIONS
4264/3, Ansari Road, Daryaganj, New Delhi-110002 (India)
Ph.: 011-23244078, 011-43559448 Fax: 011-23280028
E-Mail: cyberpublicationsdelhi@yahoo.com
Website: www.cybertechpublications.com

BIOTECHNOLOGY RESEARCH IN AGE OF TERRORISM

A.K. Gaur

© Reserved

First Edition 2010

All rights reserved. No part of this publication may be reproduced, stored in a retrieval system or transmitted, in any form or by any means, electronic, mechanical, photo copying, recording or otherwise, without the prior permission of the publisher.

Published by :

G.S. Rawat for **Cyber Tech Publications**
4264/3, Ansari Road, Daryaganj, New Delhi-110002 (India)
Ph.: 011-23244078, 011-43559448 Fax: 011-23280028
E-Mail: cyberpublicationsdelhi@yahoo.com
Website: www.cybertechpublications.com

Printed at: Asian Offset Printers, Delhi-53

Preface

The aim of this book is to set an agenda for critical inquiry, both the intellectual practice and the journal for which it is named, in the coming century. We want our diverse and multitalented editorial board to spend two days brainstorming about the possible, probable, and desirable futures of criticism and theory in the human sciences. What are the crucial topics, themes, and issues that will demand special attention and "special issues" of a wide-ranging interdisciplinary journal in the coming decade and beyond? What transformations in research paradigms are on the horizon? How will technology change the transmission and production of knowledge? What will be the fate of the humanities, of literature, the arts, and philosophy, in what is widely heralded as a posthuman age? How will the very notions of criticism and critique change in the epoch and in the current state of perpetual crisis and emergency? What will be the relation of the coming criticism to politics and public life?

The first thirty years of *Critical Inquiry* witnessed the emergence of structuralism and poststructuralism, cultural studies, feminist theory and identity politics, media and film studies, speech act theory, new historicism, new pragmatism, visual studies and the new art history, new cognitive and psychoanalytic systems, gender studies, new forms of materialist critique, postcolonial theory, and discourse analysis, queer theory and (more recently) "returns"to formalism and aesthetics, and to new forms of public and politically committed intellectual work. These critical and theoretical movements (and this is only a partial and unsystematic list) have spawned whole new schools of thought, new educational and research institutions, new journals and collectivities of knowledge production. Have we now reached a plateau in which the future is likely to be one of consolidation, refinement, and continuity? Or are we at the threshold of new developments, whether reactive rollbacks to earlier paradigms or dimly foreseen revolutions and emergent innovations

Just as crucial as cagey predictions are utopian declarations of purpose. What, in your view, would be the desirable future of critical inquiry in the coming century? If you were able to dictate the agenda for theory and criticism in research and educational institutions, and in the public sphere, what would you imagine as the ideal structure of feeling and thought to inform critical practice? And, above all, what steps do you think need to be taken in the present moment to move toward this desirable future? What, in short, is to be done?

—*Author*

CONTENTS

1

INTRODUCTION

The great achievements of molecular biology and genetics over the last 50 years have produced advances in agriculture and industrial processes and have revolutionized the practice of medicine. The very technologies that fueled these benefits to society, however, pose a potential risk as well—the possibility that these technologies could also be used to create the next generation of biological weapons. Biotechnology represents a "dual use" dilemma in which the same technologies can be used legitimately for human betterment and misused for bioterrorism. Events over the 1990s focused growing attention on this balance of risks and benefits, part of a larger concern about the proliferation of weapons of mass destruction (WMD)—chemical, nuclear, or biological. In early 1992, President Yeltsin acknowledged that, despite being an original signatory and State party to the Biological and Toxin Weapons Convention (BWC), the Soviet Union had maintained a major clandestine biological weapons program into the early 1990s.

Yeltsin ordered the program shut down, but concerns about other possible secret programs remained. Policymakers in the United States became increasingly concerned that so-called "rogue states" would turn to WMD to counter the overwhelming U.S. conventional military superiority. Secretary of Defense Les Aspin launched the "Defense Counterproliferation Initiative" in December 1993 to develop additional means to address these threats. Official statements continue to cite at least a dozen countries believed to have or to be pursuing a biological weapons capability. The terrorist attacks of September 11, 2001 and the subsequent anthrax letters accelerated already existing concerns that terrorists would seek WMD capabilities as well. President Bush, in a speech at West Point in 2002, said: "The gravest danger to freedom lies at the perilous crossroads of radicalism and technology. When the spread of chemical and biological and nuclear weapons, along with ballistic missile technology—when that occurs, even weak states and small groups could attain a catastrophic power to strike great nations."3 States, groups, and individuals are pursuing a biological weapons capability—and the means for them to do so are widely available. U.S. and British concerns about Iraq's reported biological and other WMD programs in early 2003 were a primary reason for launching preemptive military action to find and destroy these weapons capabilities. Biological weapons have long been stigmatized as "indiscriminant agents of unnecessary suffering, [whose] use … contradict(s) the universal principles of war."5 As discussed below, since November 1969 the U.S. programs linked to biological weapons have been restricted to research and development on defensive measures only. Thus few biologists in the United States today have knowledge of our country's past offensive weapons programs or of the concerns of the national security branches of government. In this respect the life sciences community is in a different situation from that of the physics community, which in large part has been continuously involved in government-sponsored weapons research programs since at least World War II. The scientific community and the government jointly face a double challenge: (1) to establish a working relationship with the national security branches of government, and (2) to help craft a system that will minimize the risk of wrongful use of biological agents or technology without damaging the scientific infrastructure that has made biological research so vital to the health of the nation.

THE LIFE SCIENCES TODAY

The biological sciences have experienced enormous growth over the last century, fueled by a stream of discoveries—such as the principles of genetics, the structure of DNA, and the discovery of gene-splicing technologies. These have opened new fields of inquiry and provided the basis for myriad applications in industry, agriculture, and medicine. Among the technological breakthroughs in the life sciences, genetic engineering plays a particularly significant role.

Genetic engineering is a technique that permits the artificial modification and transfer of genetic material from one organism to another and from one species to another. This technology is used throughout the world to alter the protein produced by a gene and to design organisms with desirable traits for applications ranging from basic research and development activities to pharmaceutical and industrial uses. During the last 30 years, these recombinant techniques have spawned a vibrant biotechnology industry focused largely on the development of new pharmaceuticals to fight disease. By 2000 the annual investment in the biotechnology industry peaked at nearly $29 billion, while employment in the biotechnology industry reached 191,000 by 2001.

In response to the opportunities presented by these developments, the resources devoted to the life sciences have increased dramatically, making further discoveries possible. The government has funded biological research generously through the National Institutes of Health and National Science Foundation budgets, with few strings attached; private foundations and the pharmaceutical industry have also made major contributions. The number of PhDs awarded each year in the biological and agricultural sciences has increased steadily; 6,526 were awarded in 2001. This ever-expanding research activity has resulted in numerous new biopharmaceutical products that are transforming medicine. Examples include human recombinant insulin for the treatment of diabetes, a vaccine against hepatitis B, and medicines for diabetes, cancer therapy, arthritis, multiple sclerosis, cystic fibrosis, heart attacks, hemophilia, and sepsis. As knowledge of the human genome increases, it may even become possible to tailor pharmaceutical products not only to specific diseases but also to specific individuals. Throughout this process, the time between new discoveries and their applications has grown ever shorter. One example is the very short time it took the scientific community to identify the coronavirus as the causal agent of the newly emerging human disease, severe acute respiratory syndrome (SARS).

Biotechnology research is now a truly global enterprise. While industrialized countries such as the United States, the United Kingdom, Germany, Israel, and Japan may be the first to develop advanced research and technologies, other countries have a skill base that will enable broad domestic utilization of biological technologies. For example: China has an aggressive program in plant biotechnology, and as of 2002 plans to increase funding by 400 percent by 2005. This energetic investment also exists in the Chinese private sector, and the national scientific establishment is attempting to lure foreign-trained scientists to return with lucrative financial packages.

India is in the process of tripling funding to its national biotech center, and is promoting the development and use of genetically modified crops throughout Asia. Singapore has for many years made a practice of recruiting foreign scientists. Taiwan is investing large amounts in biotechnology and is seeking citizens to return home to build up biotechnology in academia and industry. A Brazilian coalition recently demonstrated sophisticated domestic use of biological technologies by successfully sequencing the plant pathogen *X[ylella] fastidiosa* in 2000.

In addition to the dispersed research enterprise, publications and personnel are also widely spread. Well over 10,000 journals in the life sciences are published worldwide. Biological Abstracts, an international database on biology, clinical and experimental medicine, biochemistry, and biotechnology, provides coverage of over 6,000 active international journals and 14,000 archival titles from over 100 countries; Medline, the online service of the National Institutes of Health, provides abstract information for more than 4,600 biomedical journals published in the United States and 70 other countries; and PubMed currently provides full-text web access to 4,058 journals. According to Medline, the total number of scientific articles published in the peer-reviewed biomedical literature increased from 449,109 in 1998 to 491,620 in 2001.

Given the global nature of the biotechnology research and development enterprise, it is unrealistic to think that biological technologies and the knowledge base upon which they rest can somehow be isolated within the borders of a few countries. The rapid advance of scientific knowledge and applications owes much to a research culture in which knowledge and biological materials are shared among scientists and people move freely between universities, government agencies, and private industry. Large numbers of foreign graduate students and postdoctoral associates have been an essential ingredient in the success of the biological research enterprise. The scientific workforce is increasingly international; at the National Institutes of Health, for example, approximately 50 percent of the technical staff are non-U.S. citizens. Research results have been widely disseminated, so that even high school students now routinely perform experiments involving recombinant DNA techniques. In short, a dynamic national and international research enterprise has evolved, with an extraordinary record of achievement at multiple centers of excellence. These are values that should be preserved in any sensible policy for minimizing the risks associated with the misapplication of the fruits of the biotechnology enterprise.

THE DUAL USE DILEMMA

The regulation of dual use biotechnology research is a highly contentious technical, political, and societal issue. In the language of arms control and disarmament, dual use refers to technologies intended for civilian application that can also be used for military purposes. Technology involves more than just products; it also encompasses a means to produce and use products in such a way as to solve a problem. Thus, technology comprises "the ability to recognize technical problems, the ability to develop new concepts and tangible solutions to technical problems, the concepts and tangibles developed to solve technical problems, and the ability to exploit the concepts and tangibles in an effective way." The "general purpose clause" of the BWC prohibits the development, production, and stockpiling of biological weapons, but permits States that are parties to the treaty to conduct research activities for peaceful purposes or in order to defend or protect against BW agents. Useful distinctions between permitted and prohibited activities at the level of basic research are difficult to make because biotechnology presents a classic example of the dual use dilemma. In the life sciences, for example, the same techniques used to gain insight and understanding regarding the fundamental life processes for the benefit of human health and welfare may also be used to create a new generation of BW agents by hostile governments and individuals. For the scientists and technicians involved in cutting-edge research and development in biology, biotechnology, medicine, and agriculture, this duality creates both uncertainties and ethical dilemmas. The duality between the purposes permitted and prohibited under the BWC is at the heart of this Committee's activities.

Current research programs in universities, government laboratories, and pharmaceutical companies include experiments directed toward such goals as discovering vaccines for major diseases such as influenza, AIDS, and cancer; new antibiotics for both bacterial and fungal diseases; new sources of genes to protect crops against pests and diseases; and treatments for diabetes, stroke, and Alzheimer's disease. These research activities also include an intense effort to discover vaccines, antibiotics, and detection systems that would provide the defense against each of the select agents. But many of the same methods for developing attenuated live vaccines against viral diseases can have offensive applications as well. The key issue is whether the risks associated with misuse can be reduced while still enabling critical research to go forward.

A BRIEF HISTORY OF MODERN BIOLOGICAL WARFARE

Of thousands of species of potentially pathogenic microorganisms, very few have been developed and deployed as biological weapons. As a society, we tend to think that biological and chemical warfare are recent threats to individuals and populations, but in reality, the offensive use of chemical and biological agents has its origins in antiquity (see Annex to this chapter). It has only been within the last century, however, that infectious disease agents have been seriously considered, on a continuing basis, as tools of war. Based on scientific discoveries during the late nineteenth and early twentieth centuries, biologists were able for the first time to identify, isolate, and culture disease-causing microbes under controlled conditions and use them to intentionally induce disease in a "naïve" host. "The foundations of microbiology pioneered by Louis Pasteur and Robert Koch offered new prospects for those interested in biological weapons because it allowed agents to be chosen and designed on a rational basis."

Germany was accused of using disease-causing germs during World War I by infecting horses and mules with glanders—a highly infectious animal disease—and cattle with anthrax. German spies were caught in 1917 allegedly trying to spread anthrax bacteria among reindeer herds in the far northern portion of Norway, near the border with Russia. These charges were confirmed when anthrax-laced sugar cubes—obtained from a Swedish-German-Finnish aristocrat arrested as a German agent in 1917—were found to be still viable after being stored in the archives of a Norwegian museum for the last 80 years. Over the past 60 years pathogens have been identified and perfected as strategic and tactical weapons. Every major combatant during World War II—including the United States, Great Britain, Canada, France, the former Soviet Union, Germany, and Japan—had some type of biological weapons program. During the Sino-Japanese War (1937- 1945), Japan repeatedly attacked China with the plague-causing bacteria *Yersinia pestis*, targeting some eleven cities. At least 700 Chinese reportedly died from plague alone, although the number of Chinese civilians killed between 1933 and 1945 by Japanese germ warfare may be much higher.

Japan's secret biological warfare program, Unit 731, officially referred to as the Army Anti-Epidemic Prevention and Water Supply Unit, was located in a remote, high-security area in Japanese-occupied

Manchuria, first in Harbin and then in Ping Fan. The Japanese perfected culture and dispersal techniques for a large number of biological agents. After the war the Japanese commander of Unit 731, General Shiro Ishii, traded research data, at the suggestion of his debriefers with the American occupation government in Japan, in exchange for a grant of immunity from war crimes prosecution. Information obtained from General Ishii later found its way to Camp Detrick, and is still held in the National Archives in the United States.

The United States' offensive biological weapons program also had its origins in World War II. Begun in 1942 within the Chemical Warfare Service at Camp Detrick in Frederick, Maryland, the program's primary mission during World War II was biological warfare research on the causative agents of anthrax and botulism. The main element for carrying out this program, the Special Projects Division of the Army Chemical Warfare Service, had at its peak 3,900 personnel, of which 2,800 were Army, nearly 1,000 Navy, and the remaining 100 civilian. The work was carried out at four installations. Camp Detrick was the parent research and pilot plant center. Field testing facilities were established in 1943 and 1944 in Mississippi and Utah, respectively, and a production plant was constructed in Indiana in 1944. All work, which was coordinated with Great Britain and Canada, was conducted under strictest secrecy.

From the end of World War II until the U.S. decision to renounce its biological weapons program in 1969, this program developed and perfected offensive weapons capabilities for the Air Force, Navy, and the Central Intelligence Agency (CIA), utilizing a variety of human, animal, and plant pathogens. "Between 1941 [sic] and 1969, the policy of the United States regarding biological warfare was first (to) deter its use against the United States and its forces, and secondly to retaliate if deterrence failed."

The largest biological weapons complex ever created was in the former Soviet Union. Two main groups of facilities were involved in the research and development, production, and testing of biological weapons: a military-controlled system, which started in the 1920s, and Biopreparat, a top-secret program operating under civilian cover from 1972 until at least 1992, despite the fact that the Soviet Union was an original signatory to and repository for the Biological Weapons Convention. As a result, the Soviet program not only caught up with but surpassed the U.S. program to become the most sophisticated biological weapons program in the world. Its size and scope were enormous; by the early 1990s more than 60,000 people were involved in the research, development, and production of biological weapons as well as the stockpiling of hundreds of tons of anthrax spores and tens of tons of other pathogens, including smallpox and plague. In addition, it is now known that other state programs were involved in aspects of this effort including those of the Ministry of Health, Ministry of Agriculture, Ministry of Defense, KGB, and the Soviet Academy of Sciences.

U.S. POLICY AND THE CREATION OF THE BIOLOGICAL AND TOXIN WEAPONS CONVENTION

After intensive debate in the United Nations and domestic interagency review, President Richard Nixon on November 25, 1969 renounced the first use of lethal and incapacitating chemicals and stated that he would seek ratification of the Geneva Protocol by the U.S. Senate. (The Geneva Protocol of 1925 prohibits the use of chemical or biological materials in war, although it does not proscribe their acquisition or possession.) President Nixon also renounced the use of lethal bacteriological (biological) agents and weapons as well as all other methods of biological warfare, and directed the Defense Department to make recommendations for the disposal of existing BW stockpiles. He further stated that the United States would confine its biological agent and toxin research to defensive measures, such as immunization and safety. On February 14, 1970, this policy was extended to biological toxins regardless of their means of production.

The United States decided to abandon its offensive biological weapons program, destroy its existing stockpiles of biological and toxin weapons, and convert the production facilities to other purposes because it was recognized that:

- Biological weapons could be as great a threat to large populations as nuclear weapons and that no reliable defense is likely;
- Biological weapons could be much simpler and less expensive than nuclear weapons to develop and produce; proliferation of biological weapons would therefore greatly increase the number of nations to which the populations of the United States and its allies [could] be held hostage;
- Our biological weapons program was pioneering an easily duplicated technology and was likely to inspire others to follow suit.

The United States concluded that its biological weapons program was a substantial threat to its *own* national security and that one of the best ways to reduce this threat was not only to renounce biological weapons in this country but also to strengthen the international barriers to their proliferation. The United States, the United Kingdom, and the former Soviet Union together were responsible for the effort to sponsor the Biological and Toxin Weapons Convention (BWC) of 1972—the first arms control agreement to ban outright an entire class of weapons. The U.S. Senate ratified the BWC in 1975. To date, 162 countries have signed and 148 countries have ratified the BWC.

THE NEW THREAT

The revolution in biotechnology was just beginning when the BWC went into force in 1975. With the advent of the biotechnology revolution and the apparent proliferation of countries desiring to have a biological weapons capability, its signatories must reexamine the efficacy of the Convention in governing the use of disease as a method to spread terror. The acquisition of biotechnology and biological weapons capability is considerably easier than was the case in the 1940s and 1950s. The explosion in biotechnologies and genetic engineering technologies—all of which have legitimate civilian applications—could empower a hostile agent. Gordon Oehler, director of the Non-Proliferation Center at the Central Intelligence Agency, testified before the Senate Armed Services Committee on March 27, 1996, and stated that there was "a continuing pursuit by many countries to acquire chemical and biological weapons and that [t]he chilling reality is that these materials and technologies are more accessible now than at any other time in history."

The information to conduct genetic engineering research is easily accessible on the Internet. Moreover, the equipment and expertise to use this information to create novel agents are available globally. The international diffusion of knowledge and capabilities in biotechnology means that the capacity to carry out beneficial as well as harmful research activities is widely accessible, both to nations and to terrorist groups. In this situation it is futile to imagine that access to dangerous pathogens and destructive biotechnologies can be physically restricted, as is the case for nuclear weapons and fissionable materials. The nature of the biotechnology problem—indeed the nature of the biological research enterprise— is vastly different from that of theoretical and applied nuclear physics in the late 1930s. The contrast between what is a legitimate, perhaps compelling subject for research and what might justifiably be prohibited or tightly controlled cannot be made a priori, stated in categorical terms, nor confirmed by remote observation. Matthew Meselson, a leading molecular biologist, gave a stark warning of the potential dangers posed by the destructive applications of biotechnology in May 2000: Every major technology—metallurgy, explosives, internal combustion, aviation, electronics, nuclear energy—has been intensively exploited, not only for peaceful purposes but also for hostile ones. Must this also happen with biotechnology, certain to be a dominant technology of the coming century? During the century just begun, as our ability to modify fundamental life processes continues its rapid advance, we will be able not only to devise additional ways to destroy life but … also … to manipulate it—including the processes of cognition, development, reproduction, and inheritance. A world in which these capabilities are widely employed for hostile purposes would be a world in which the very nature of conflict has radically changed. Therein could lie unprecedented opportunities for violence, coercion, repression, or subjugation.

These dangers cannot be eliminated entirely since the fundamental knowledge from which they emerge is available around the world and the potential benefits of biotechnology for health promotion and national defense are too great to contemplate efforts to prohibit or reverse such research. But the potential adverse effects associated with the malicious exploitation of these technological advances cannot be ignored. Because of widespread moral repugnance against the production and use of chemical and biological weapons (CBW), the involvement of scientists and engineers in CBW research, development, and production is widely condemned. History demonstrates, however, that without any military application in mind, research in biology may still contribute to the production of biological weapons. As discussed earlier, the discovery and elaboration of the "germ theory of disease" in the nineteenth century led not only to better sanitation and hygiene practices but also to the intentional development of disease as a weapon in the twentieth century.

1. In discussing modifications of microorganisms that might have significance for bioweapons, Nixdorff and Bender identified four classes of microbial manipulations that have been the subject of intense debate within and outside the scientific community: The transfer of antibiotic resistance to microorganisms,
2. Modification of the antigenic properties of microorganisms,
3. Modification of the stability of microorganisms to the environment, and
4. The transfer of pathogenic properties to microorganisms.

Regarding these manipulations, they observed that: All four kinds of manipulations are possible and are being carried out daily in research laboratories. Some of the most intensive research concerns the elucidation of the mechanisms of pathogenesis. This work is essential for combating infectious diseases. It is hoped that the production of more effective vaccines with [fewer] side effects, better diagnostics and new therapeutic drugs will result from this research. At the same time, it is feared that the advances in biotechnology can be misused to develop and produce biological weapons.

The National Institutes of Health's (NIH's) recently released research priorities for countering bioterrorism identified several categories of research activities in immunology and genomics that would be considered "provocative" if conducted by a hostile or rogue government. These include efforts to "identify pathogen-induced immunoregulatory and immunosuppressive effects" as well as to "analyze gene expression of agents of bioterrorism." John Gannon, former chairman of the National Intelligence Council and a former deputy director for intelligence at the CIA, observed that "the continuing revolution in science and technology will accentuate the dual use problem related to biotech breakthroughs in biomedical engineering, genomic profiling, genetic modification, and drug development.... Responsible scientists will have an extraordinary opportunity to improve the quality of human life across the planet. At the same time, terrorists and other evildoers may develop a powerful capability to destroy that life."

RECENT EXAMPLES OF "CONTENTIOUS RESEARCH" IN THE LIFE SCIENCES

Biological weapons differ from other weapons systems in a number of important respects. They generally are based on naturally occurring pathogens that have coevolved along with their hosts to possess features such as high infectivity, ease of transmission, and virulence. As a corollary, however, the effects of naturally occurring pathogens are limited by the evolutionary advantage gained by not eliminating their hosts. Among the many implications of the anticipated progress in biotechnology is the presumption that it may be feasible to create novel biological agents that are far more predictable and dangerous than any of the naturally occurring pathogens that have been developed as biological weapons in the past. It may be difficult to engineer a more successful pathogen than those already present in nature that have been perfected by evolution for their niche in life. However, application of the new genetic technologies makes the creation of "designer diseases" and pathogens with increased military utility more likely. There have been several recent examples of what Gerald Epstein of the Defense Threat Reduction Agency refers to as "contentious research" —experiments that resulted in the creation of organisms or knowledge with "dual use" potential. The Australian *ectromelia* virus (mousepox) experiment; total synthesis of the poliovirus genome and recovery of infectious virus, and the comparison of the immune response to a host defense function from *vaccinia* and smallpox have all attracted the attention of the scientific community, the media, the defense community, and policy analysts. Each is elaborated below.

The Mousepox Virus: A Case Study in Preconsideration

The mousepox virus: a case study in preconsideration. Probably the most celebrated recent case involving the dissemination of research with the potential for bioterrorist uses was the report of an unexpected effect of the bioengineering of a strain of *ectromelia* virus (mousepox) that was intended to help eradicate mice in Australia. The authors of the paper had originally set out to make an infectious immunocontraceptive for wild mice by incorporating an ovary specific antigen, the mouse zona pellucida 3 (ZP3) glycoproteina gene into the genome of *ectromelia* virus. The authors subsequently sought to alter the ectromelia by adding an immunomodulator with the hope that this would increase the immune response of the infected mice to their fertilized eggs and thus make them permanently infertile. They drew upon previous published work by others with recombinant *vaccinia* virus in mice in which it had been shown that incorporating the gene for the immunomodulatory cytokine IL-4 into the viral genome and thus overexpressing it *in vivo* enhanced the virulence of *vaccinia* virus in mice. The increased virulence is probably due to suppression of the antiviral immune response mediated through competing cytokines like IL-2, IL-12, and interferon gamma, which work by stimulating immune effector cells to kill virus-infected cells and thus control the virus infection.

The authors of this study used standard and quite simple procedures for incorporating the IL-4 gene into the mousepox genome. They then demonstrated that this engineered mousepox virus was more virulent than the parent virus and killed 60 percent of infected mice, even if the mice were from a genetically resistant strain. Even more unexpected was their observation that mice that had been vaccinated and were completely resistant to the parent virus, and even to a more virulent strain of mousepox, were now killed by the IL-4 gene-expressing virus. Some have felt that the publication of this paper provides a blueprint or road map for terrorists to engineer a more virulent strain of smallpox that could overwhelm the human immune system in even well-vaccinated individuals. The methods section of the paper illustrates how easy it is to make an IL-4 expressing orthopox virus. It has been suggested that either the paper should not have been published, or at the very least the "materials and methods" section of the manuscript should have been altered or omitted entirely from the published article. The authors were sensitive to these issues and consulted with their peers in the Pest Animal Control Cooperative Research Center at the Australian National University in Canberra about whether the paper should be submitted for publication. The manuscript was submitted in July 2000 to the *Journal of Virology*. The reviewers and editors expressed no concerns about potential misuse of any information in the manuscript and the article was published in February 2001. A retrospective review by the editor-in-chief following concerns raised after the article was published concluded that the journal was correct in its decision to publish.

This example illustrates the difficulty of attempting to censor either the initiation of research or the publication of results. The initial goals of the mousepox research were directed to control the population densities of a rodent pest in Australia. The studies were done on mice, and the virus itself, while related to smallpox, is not of any danger to humans. Thus, these studies had desirable scientific and societal goals and there was no obvious reason not to undertake them. Even in retrospect, the decision by informed scientists who had no vested interest in the work to approve publication seems appropriate. There were numerous examples in the published literature demonstrating the effects of cytokines like IL-4 on immune modulation. The authors of this study, therefore, were building upon an established literature in this field that is filled with similar findings on the effects of the decreased or increased levels of IL-4 and other immunomodulatory factors on the virulence of other viruses and many microorganisms. As previously noted, the design of the mousepox study built upon previously published studies in which *vaccinia* virus engineered to express IL-4 was studied in mice. There is also a relevant preexisting literature in the field of oncology in which the increased expression of various cytokines incorporated into the fowlpox genomes and other orthopox viruses along with tumor antigens has been used to increase the immune response to tumors and decrease the immunogenicity of the viruses. The technique for incorporating new genes into the poxvirus genome had been published in many places. Thus there is little technical information that was not already abundantly available in the literature and well known to the scientific community.

The observation that even vaccinated mice were killed by the IL-4 expressing mousepox was a somewhat surprising finding that is of potential concern. However, since the ability of immunomodulatory factors to increase the virulence of this virus could have been predicted and the means to make such a virus were readily available, it was important to publicize that this strategy could overcome vaccination because it alerted the scientific community to such a possibility occurring either intentionally or spontaneously. First, knowledge of these experiments allows the scientific community to explore how to overcome such engineered viruses. It informs us of the fact that we should monitor cytokine levels in the blood of the initial cases of a highly virulent virus that is used in an attack.

Second, it suggests that we should be prepared to treat infections caused by such an engineered virus with antibodies that inactivate the relevant cytokine, with gamma interferon that would counter the effect of IL-4, or with both. Finally, it is worth noting that this work was done outside the United States and could have been published in an Australian or European journal, illustrating the limits of national policies to address dual use concerns and, in this case specifically, the need to have international guidelines for the publication of manuscripts containing "sensitive" information.

Total Synthesis of the Poliovirus Genome and Recovery of Infectious Virus

Wimmer and colleagues reported that they had reconstructed poliovirus from chemically synthesized oligonucleotides that were linked together and then transfected into cells. This report attracted considerable attention in the news media and concern in some segments of the public. The media treatment of the work suggested that this experiment proved that one could synthesize any virus from chemical reagents that can be purchased on the open market. This implication raised the public concern about bioterrorism because it suggested that the Wimmer experiment provided a recipe for terrorists to manufacture the virus. In response to the publication of this article in *Science*, in the 107th Congress, Representative Dave Weldon (R-FL) introduced H.Res. 514, which criticized the publication of this research because of its implications for compromising the national security interests of the nation.

The Weldon resolution, which did not pass, went on to state the concern of the House of Representatives regarding the potential of the poliovirus paper to enable terrorists to synthetically create a human pathogen to release on the people of this country and further called upon the publishers and editors of scientific publications and the scientific community to establish ethical standards and exercise restraint in the dissemination of information of potential use to terrorists in the development of bioterrorism agents. The Weldon resolution also called upon the Executive Branch to "examine all policies, including national security directives, relevant to the classification or publication of federally-funded research to ensure that, although the free exchange of information is encouraged, information that could be useful in the development of chemical, biological, or nuclear weapons is not made accessible to terrorists or countries of proliferation concern."

Many scientists concluded that the Wimmer experiment was neither a novel discovery nor a potential threat.

The general principle that one could make live poliovirus from a DNA template was already known in 1981, when Baltimore and colleagues reported that a DNA copy of the positive strand RNA genome of poliovirus could be taken up into living cells under appropriate conditions and result in the generation of encapsulated, infectious virus.

These studies led to the ability to manipulate DNA copies of RNA viral genomes to generate preselected genetic changes. This technology bypasses the technical problems of working with RNA molecules and allows subsequent recovery of infectious virus. Subsequent research has succeeded in extending this technology to RNA viruses with larger positive strand genomes, negative polarity RNA, or segmented genomes.

Several points should be emphasized, however. Like the mousepox IL-4 experiment discussed above, the technology for producing and manipulating the genome of RNA viruses has been available in the literature for a long time. The ability to synthesize a poliovirus genome and recover infectious virus was regarded as a foregone conclusion.

The Wimmer approach offers no technical advantage to a terrorist. And more importantly, in fact it is a very laborious and difficult way to accomplish this synthesis.

The interesting scientific results from the Wimmer experiment were not its highly touted potential for bioterrorism, but rather the fact that the virus synthesized had significantly weakened pathogenicity as compared to wildtype strains of poliovirus. The decreased virulence is likely due to thirdbase and noncoding changes inserted as supposedly neutral markers.

Comparison of the Immune Response to a Virulence Gene from Vaccinia and Smallpox

Variola major virus causes smallpox, which has a 30-40 percent mortality rate, whereas *vaccinia* virus, which is used to vaccinate humans against smallpox, causes no disease in immunocompetent humans.

In a paper that appeared in the *Proceedings of the National Academy of Sciences*, Rosengard and colleagues investigated a possible basis for the difference in the putative virulence factor between the virus that causes human disease and the one used to vaccinate against the disease.

Both viruses have an inhibitor of immune response enzymes—*vaccinia* virus complement control protein (VCP) and smallpox inhibitor of complement enzymes (SPICE). The authors focused on a comparison of the genes encoding this inhibitor. As live *variola* is not available for study, they used standard techniques to synthesize the *variola* SPICE gene.

They found that *variola* SPICE has a greater degree of specificity for human complement and is nearly a hundredfold more active than VCP at inactivating this component of the human immune system (human complement component C3b).

The authors suggested that the difference between VCP and SPICE could explain the difference in virulence between the two viruses and the restriction of *variola*'s host range to humans. Some might argue that the Rosengard study is of greater concern than the previous two examples because it provides information on how to increase the virulence of *vaccinia* virus, and thus on how to convert a readily available agent that has minimal virulence into a virulent virus.

A commentary written on this paper pointed out that it is very unlikely that *vaccinia* virus carrying SPICE in place of VCP would approach the pathogenicity of *variola.* Furthermore, publication of the article alerted the community of scientists to this mechanism for virulence.

This information should stimulate scientists in both the public and private sectors to identify compounds or immunization procedures that disable SPICE. These could form the basis for new treatments or vaccines both to immunize against the naturally occurring smallpox virus and to counteract the genetically engineered variety.

THE RESPONSE OF THE LIFE SCIENCES COMMUNITY TO PREVIOUS CHALLENGES

As the preceding examples make abundantly clear, there is an increasing awareness within and outside the scientific community of the dangers posed by the proliferation of biological weapons capabilities.

This heightened awareness has also increased the collective concerns of this Committee and the scientific community about preventing the destructive applications of biotechnology research. This is not a completely new issue. When gene splicing technology was first reported, the scientific community at the time raised concerns that the technology might deliberately or inadvertently be used to create organisms with increased virulence or novel characteristics. These possibilities eventually led to the 1975 Asilomar Conference, where scientists gathered to discuss the safety of manipulating DNA from different species.

The meeting resulted in the issuance by NIH of Guidelines for Research Involving rDNA Molecules (hereafter called the NIH Guidelines) in 1976 that regulated the conduct of NIH-sponsored recombinant DNA research and established a mechanism for reviewing proposed experiments in this field.

Just as the life sciences community with the Asilomar Conference stepped up to the challenge of responding to concerns that biology could set back rather than advance human welfare, so too the Human Genome Project created the ethical, legal, and social implications program to explore how advances in genetics intended to improve human health could proceed without undermining other dimensions of human well-being.

National commissions and Congress continue to debate whether certain advances in biology should be pursued and published. The initial fears about the inadvertent creation of virulent microbes by gene splicing techniques have abated because of overwhelming scientific evidence to the contrary. There have been no reported cases of disease caused by recombinant microorganisms despite the widespread use of gene splicing techniques in academic laboratories and in the production of pharmaceuticals.

In view of this experience, and the prospects for understanding the etiology of complex diseases and finding cures for them, the NIH has revised its Guidelines several times, with the net result being the elimination of the earlier prohibitions and the exemption from the Guidelines of essentially all recombinant DNA experiments except those that involve the molecular manipulation of human and restricted animal and plant pathogens.

COMMITTEE CHARGE AND PROCESS

Current policy at both the national and international levels may not be adequate to cope with the dangers inherent in the use and applications of genetic engineering.

As discussed in greater detail in the following chapters, the United States has enacted legislation to provide for the physical security of select agents and screening of personnel. The Committee's proposed system for reviewing research projects and publications would complement and strengthen this statutory regime. Internationally, however, protection against misuse of biotechnology is very uneven. The Biological and Toxin Weapons Convention, the centerpiece of biological weapons arms control, lacks effective verification and compliance measures.

Moreover, it addresses only the actions of states and was never intended to guard against the development of a BW capability by individuals or nonstate actors (although national implementing legislation required by Article IV of the Convention could constrain the actions of individuals and groups within the state).

In November 2001 the draft text for an international protocol covering compliance and verification measures was rejected by the United States. New, informal measures to strengthen the BWC being explored by expert groups and States parties are scheduled to continue over a period of three years (the first meetings were held in Geneva in August 2003).

The measures include enactment of national criminal legislation supplemented by an enhanced extradition regime; security standards for pathogenic organisms; genetic engineering oversight; and international adoption of professional codes of conduct. The hope is that these discussions will translate into coordinated action by the States parties, but at present only a few states have instituted security measures to protect against diversion and misuse of biotechnology.

The most elaborate treaty-based inspection procedures could not achieve effective restrictions at the level of basic research without severely restricting research in general. The inevitable diffusion of knowledge and capabilities has already demonstrated that the capacity to do harm is becoming globally available, both to state and nonstate actors. At the same time, developments in biotechnology are also capable of yielding great benefits, such as new treatments for many diseases.

The distinction between the great opportunities and great dangers of biotechnology turns on assessing whether the risk(s) associated with the benefits of fundamental research outweigh the potential for misuse. The challenge to the scientific community, therefore, is to develop formal and informal processes and procedures to mitigate or minimize the destructive applications of advanced biotechnology without unduly restricting legitimate biotechnology research activities.

Beginning the process of addressing these challenges is the purpose of this study. Specifically, the Committee was charged to:

1. Review the current rules, regulations, and institutional arrangements and processes in the United States that provide oversight of research on pathogens and potentially dangerous biotechnology research, within government laboratories, universities and other research institutions, and industry. The review would focus on how choices are made about which research is and is not appropriate, and how information about relevant ongoing research is collected and shared.
2. Use the review to assess the adequacy of current U.S. rules, regulations, and institutional arrangements and processes to prevent the destructive application of biotechnology research.
3. Recommend changes in those practices that could improve U.S. capacity to prevent the destructive application of biotechnology research while still enabling legitimate research to be conducted.

This report is part of a larger body of work that The National Academies have undertaken in recent decades on science and security issues, beginning with *Scientific Communication and National Security* in 1982 and continuing into the 1990s with the publication of *Chemical and Biological Terrorism: Research and Development to Improve Civilian Medical Response* (1999) and *Firepower in the Lab: Automation in the Fight Against Infectious Diseases and Bioterrorism* (2001). In response to the events of September 11th, the Academies undertook a comprehensive survey of the contributions that science and technology could make to countering terrorism; *Making the Nation Safer: The Role of Science and Technology in Countering Terrorism* was published in 2002.

The report of its panel on bioterrorism, *Countering Bioterrorism: The Role of Science and Technology*, was published separately. In addition, the Institute of Medicine's Forum on Emerging Infections convened a 3–day workshop on *Biological Threats and Terrorism: Assessing the Science and Response Capabilities*, which was released as a workshop summary late in 2002.

The 2002 report on *Countering Agricultural Bioterrorism*, a study already in progress prior to September 11th, enabled the Committee to focus its primary efforts on threats to human health. In the area of potential controls on information and data, the report on *Sharing Publication–Related Data and Materials: Responsibility of Authorship in the Life Sciences* (2003) is particularly relevant to the continuing concerns for ensuring the wide availability of the results of scientific research.

Committee Process

In creating the Ad hoc Committee on Research Standards and Practices to Prevent the Destructive Application of Biotechnology, the National Research Council (the operating arm of The National Academies) selected committee members representing a broad spectrum of backgrounds, expertise, and interests.

Areas of expertise included molecular and cellular biology, virology, medicine, laboratory safety, international and regulatory law, bioethics, and defense policy (see Appendix B for biographical information on the members of the Committee). In addition, the Committee relied on the expertise and advice of representatives from the Executive Office of the President, governmental and nongovernmental technical and policy experts, as well as educators and private consultants. Information available from the open literature and materials submitted by experts were reviewed and considered during the Committee's deliberations. Even though the Statement of Task did not require the Committee to consider information control regimes for dissemination of information in the life sciences that could be exploited for nefarious purposes, the Committee concluded that this issue was implicit in the larger task before it and needed to be considered along with the regulatory environment for biotechnology research.

An additional impetus for the Committee's consideration of information control regimes for unclassified research in the life sciences was the announcement by the White House shortly before the Committee's first meeting of its renewed interest in the application of "sensitive but unclassified information" control regimes for managing the dissemination of unclassified research that is financed by the federal government.

2

Biological Warfare in History

People figured out how to intentionally spread illnesses long before naturalists came up with the discovery that germs cause disease. Among the older military techniques that can be claimed as biological warfare is the use of corpses of humans or animals to befoul wells or other sources of drinking water. While the principal objective was thought to be the denial of clean water to the enemy, a secondary effect was to spread disease among people and animals that consumed the contaminated water. One of the earliest recorded instances of biological warfare occurred in 600 BC, when the Athenian leader Solon poisoned the water supply in the city of Kirrha with the noxious roots of the *Helleborus* plant—a primitive but effective biological toxin of plant origin. The Greeks and Romans may have used human and animal corpses to poison drinking water wells.

Alexander the Great is thought to have catapulted the bodies of dead men over the walls of besieged cities, possibly as a means of spreading disease and inciting terror among their inhabitants. A related technique, used in the Middle Ages, was to deliberately leave dead human or animal corpses behind in areas that would be occupied shortly by invading troops; catapults were used as well. In 1346, invading Tartars intent on controlling the Silk Road trade attacked the Black Sea port of Caffa—at the time occupied by the Genoese. The Tartar army, already exposed to the Black Death, hurled plague-infested cadavers over the impregnable walls of Caffa to infect the enemy population. It is usually reported that the fleeing Genoese brought the Black Death with them—via plague-infested rodents, along shipping routes to Sicily, Sardinia, Corsica, and Genoa—and from there it spread overland throughout Italy and Europe. It is considered equally likely, however, that the entry of plague into Europe from the Crimea occurred independent of this event. Over a four-year period, the plague eventually caused 25 million deaths—one-third of Europe's population at the time. Population losses were probably much higher in the French Mediterranean coastlands and in northern Italy.

During the seventeenth and eighteenth centuries, French and British soldiers and civilians are alleged to have deliberately infected North American Indian populations with European diseases. "(T)he use of smallpox as a weapon may have been widely entertained by British military commanders and may have been employed without scruple when opportunity offered, possibly on a number of occasions." During the French and Indian Wars, for example, Sir Jeffrey Amherst, commander-in-chief of the British forces, was concerned that his troops west of the Allegheny Mountains were in danger of being overrun by Indians. He wrote to the commander of the garrison at Fort Pitt on the Pennsylvania frontier and urged that smallpox be spread among the disaffected tribes. In June 1763, Captain Ecuyer of the Royal Americans met with two Indian chiefs under a pretense of friendship and gave them blankets that had been taken from a smallpox hospital. During the following months, according to historians of the episode, many Indians suffered and died as "smallpox raged among the tribes of the Ohio." During the 1800s, U.S. government agents were alleged to have deliberately infected the Plains Indians by giving them trading blankets infected with the deadly disease, decimating the population.

RESEARCH IN THE 21ST CENTURY

The regulatory environment for the life sciences has been developed over the course of five decades. Responsibility for regulation in the United States of various aspects of biotechnology research in the life sciences is shared among a number of federal agencies, ranging from the Department of Agriculture (USDA) and the Environmental Protection Agency (EPA) to the Nuclear Regulatory Commission (NRC). The National Institutes of Health (NIH), for example, sets standards and procedures for the research it funds on recombinant DNA (rDNA). Research on human gene therapy is a special case, with both NIH and the Food and Drug Administration (FDA) conducting reviews prior to the initiation of research. While review is mandatory for NIH-funded research, industry often seeks review voluntarily. The Centers for Disease Control and Prevention (CDC) sets standards for the handling and transport of some especially dangerous biological pathogens. The NRC has responsibility for regulations to control the receipt, possession, use, transfer, and disposal of radioactive materials by research institutions. The USDA has broad responsibility for biotechnology research related to plants and animals. Industries involved in biotechnology research generally have internal procedures to review potential research protocols, although these vary considerably within and between industrial and commercial facilities. Important aspects of their work such as clinical or field trials are also subject to regulation by federal agencies, in particular the FDA and the EPA. Universities have various methods for reviewing and approving potentially contentious research. Professional societies address questions of ethics and norms for research.

Until the mid-1990s the regulatory environment focused on protecting the public health and general environment from biological hazards associated with possible exposures to human pathogens via interstate transport, recombinant organisms, and containment of recombinants and their products so that inadvertent or deliberate releases of these materials to the environment would be within acceptable limits. The regulatory environment for microbial hazards also encompasses the importation of nonnative plant and animal pathogens.

Following the historic Asilomar Conference in 1975, the NIH, in 1976 published the Guidelines for Research Involving rDNA Molecules (hereinafter referred to as the NIH Guidelines or the

Guidelines). The NIH Guidelines described four levels of combinations of laboratory practices, containment equipment, and facility safeguards that were thought to be appropriate for the safe use and physical containment of rDNA molecules in research. The four levels, P1 to P4, provide increasing levels of physical protection against personnel contact with or accidental release to the environment of genetically engineered microorganisms.

The CDC and the NIH encouraged the life sciences community to participate in a collaborative initiative to develop consensus guidelines to safeguard worker safety and public health from hazards associated with the possession and use of human pathogens in microbiological and biomedical laboratories. This initiative resulted in the publication by CDC and NIH in 1984 of Biosafety in Microbiological and Biomedical Laboratories (hereinafter referred to as the BMBL). These consensus guidelines also established four ascending levels of physical containment using the terminology Biosafety Level 1-4. The combinations of standard and special microbiological practices, safety equipment, and facilities for each level are similar to those of the NIH Guidelines. Specific recommendations for appropriate practices, equipment, and facility safeguards are given in the BMBL for pathogens that meet one or more of three criteria: the pathogen is a proven hazard to laboratory personnel working with infectious materials; the potential for laboratory-acquired infection is high even in the absence of previously documented laboratory-associated infections; or the consequences of infection are grave. The recommendations are advisory and are intended to provide a voluntary guide or code of practice for investigators who possess and use human pathogens in their research activities.

The Recombinant DNA Advisory Committee (RAC) and the BMBL process have been highly successful. Laboratory-acquired infections from exposure to biological agents known to cause disease are infrequent. There are no reports that the possession and use of biological agents and toxins for research, education, and other legitimate purposes endangers the public health. The fourth edition of the BMBL states: "Experience has demonstrated the prudence of the Biosafety Level 1-4 practices, procedures, and facilities described for manipulations of etiologic agents and laboratories settings and animal facilities. Although no national reporting system exists for reporting laboratory-associated infections, anecdotal information suggests that strict adherence to these guidelines does contribute to a healthier and safe work environment for laboratorians, their coworkers, and the surrounding community." This experience indicates that compliance with voluntary guidelines can achieve safety in research and clinical laboratories and protect the public health without significantly restricting the pursuit of science.

Spurred by rising concerns about bioterrorism, we are now witnessing a transition from an environment based upon voluntary compliance with recommended practices to a greater number of statutes and regulations, particularly for control of biological materials and personnel. It took the United States three years to ratify the 1972 Biological Weapons Convention (BWC) and 17 years for the United States Congress to pass legislation making the provisions of the BWC binding on all Americans. Not much changed until 1996 when, with the passage of the Antiterrorism and Effective Death Penalty Act, new regulatory controls were enacted swiftly regarding transfers of dangerous pathogens. Less than a year following the terrorist attacks on September 11, 2001 and subsequent anthrax mailings, two major pieces of legislation were passed by Congress and signed into law—"The Uniting and Strengthening America by Providing Appropriate Tools Required to Intercept and Obstruct Terrorism of October 2001" (hereinafter, the PATRIOT Act), and "The Public Health Security and Bioterrorism Preparedness and Response Act" of June 2002 (hereinafter, the Bioterrorism Response Act).

The PATRIOT Act makes it illegal in the United States for anyone to possess any biological agent, including any genetically engineered organism created by using rDNA technology, for any inappropriate reason. The Act also prohibits the transfer or possession of a listed biological agent or toxin by a "restricted person." A "restricted person" is not permitted to ship or transport via interstate or foreign commerce, or possess, or receive any biological agent or toxin that has been shipped or transported in interstate or foreign commerce, if the biological agent or toxin is listed as a select agent.

The Bioterrorism Response Act added new requirements for the secretaries of the Departments of Agriculture and Health and Human Services to consider in listing agents and in preventing unlawful access to agents during transfers.

The statute also establishes new requirements for registration with the appropriate secretary concerning possession and use of listed agents and toxins, including "information regarding the characterization of listed agents and toxins to facilitate their identification, including their source; and safeguard and security requirements for registered persons." The law also requires the secretary to establish rules that provide appropriate physical security requirements for listed agents and for the Department of Justice—through the Federal Bureau of Investigation (FBI)—to conduct background investigations on individuals who are permitted access to select agents or who work in a facility where select agents are stored.

The security provisions in the Bioterrorism Response Act are radically transforming the life sciences research environment in the United States from one that is basically open to one that excludes, based upon criteria stipulated in the PATRIOT Act, certain individuals from access to and research on certain listed agents. The FBI provisions, which went into force without public notice and comment rulemaking, prescribe the collection of pertinent background information on individuals; who may access, use, receive or transfer select agents, and the release and disclosure of that information to other entities as described in Section IV in the FBI Information Form (FD-961). These provisions have raised concerns that qualified individuals may be discouraged from conducting biomedical and agricultural research of value to the United States because of the apparent infringement of these rules on individual liberties under the Fourth Amendment.

The next section of this report expands on the brief descriptions above to give a more complete picture of the current system of regulations and voluntary practices that govern research in biotechnology. It adds discussion of the growing web of controls over foreign nationals seeking to work, study, or participate in scientific activities in the United States and of the various codes of professional conduct that are a fundamental part of the self-governance of scientific practice. As noted at the beginning of this chapter, at present this system is focused on occupational safety and health and on environmental protection, but increasingly, additional efforts are being made to control access to biological materials that might be used by terrorists. With the exception of research involving human subjects, the system is not intended to provide oversight of research in the sense of making decisions about whether particular projects or experiments are appropriate.

THE U.S. REGULATORY ENVIRONMENT

Oversight of Genetic Engineering Research

Chapter 1 mentioned the response of the life sciences community in the mid-1970s to concerns about the potential unknown risks inherent in research involving the new field of genetic engineering. The Asilomar process led to the NIH assuming responsibility for promoting safe conduct of such experiments and to the subsequent publication of the NIH Guidelines. The Guidelines are designed to address the risks to public health and the environment associated with exposure to either rDNA molecules or organisms or viruses containing such materials. The NIH Guidelines are applicable to all rDNA research within or outside the United States or its territories where the research is conducted at an institution that receives any support for the research from the NIH, including research performed directly by NIH.

Institutions that are recipients of NIH support for rDNA research must establish an Institutional Biosafety Committee (IBC) as part of their compliance with the NIH Guidelines. Further, as part of documenting that they have established a properly constituted IBC, institutions must register the IBC with the NIH Office of Biotechnology Activities (OBA). IBCs are the cornerstone of institutional oversight of rDNA research. An IBC is a review body appointed by an institution to review and approve potentially biohazardous lines of research relating primarily to rDNA research. IBCs were originally established to provide local, institutional oversight of nearly all forms of research utilizing rDNA. On behalf of the institution, IBCs review rDNA research projects for compliance with the NIH Guidelines. Over time, the role of the IBCs at many institutions has been expanded to include review and oversight of a variety of experimentation that involves biological materials (e.g., infectious agents) and other potentially hazardous agents (e.g., carcinogens). While an IBC must consist of at least five members there is no upper limit on the number of members.

Every IBC is required to have two members not affiliated with the institution who represent the interests of the surrounding community with respect to health and protection of the environment. These may be officials of state or local public health or environmental protection agencies, members of other local governmental bodies, or persons active in medical, occupational health, or environmental concerns in the community.

It is also recommended that IBCs include: experts in biosafety and containment; persons knowledgeable in institutional policies and applicable laws; individuals reflecting community attitudes; and at least one representative member from the laboratory staff. Committee members cannot review a project in which they have been, or expect to be, involved or have a direct financial interest. Finally, the Guidelines provide that while opening IBC meetings to the public is suggested but not required, minutes of the meetings and submitted documents must be available to the public on request.

Because the NIH Guidelines require establishment of an IBC when research is conducted at or sponsored by an entity receiving any NIH support for rDNA research, even privately funded projects employing rDNA must adhere to the NIH Guidelines if they are being carried out at, or funded by, an organization that has any NIH contracts, grants, or other support for this kind of research. Additionally, some communities and real estate leases require compliance with the NIH Guidelines, making such compliance legally binding even for private companies. Adherence to the NIH Guidelines is mandatory and important because they stipulate biosafety and containment measures for rDNA research. Furthermore, they delineate critical ethical principles and outline key safety reporting requirements for human gene transfer research.

Most of the 400 or so IBCs registered with OBA are at institutions that are subject to the NIH Guidelines and for whom IBC registration is mandatory. While most of these institutions are academic, some industrybased IBCs are registered with NIH as a consequence of receiving NIH support for rDNA research (e.g., SBIR grants) and thereby becoming subject to the NIH Guidelines. In other instances, companies voluntarily comply with the NIH Guidelines as a means of observing the highest standards for safety practices; as part of that voluntary compliance, they register their IBCs with the NIH.

Several federal agencies including the USDA and the Department of Veterans Affairs (VA) have made compliance with the NIH Guidelines a condition of their support of intramural and extramural research projects. Furthermore, a number of federal IBCs are registered with NIH, including those at the NIH, the Department of Energy (DOE) laboratories (including the Lawrence Livermore, Los Alamos, Oak Ridge, Sandia National Laboratories) and various VA medical centers and military research institutes such as the Uniformed Services University of Health Sciences, the Walter Reed Army Medical Center, and the U.S. Army's Medical Research Institute for Infectious Diseases. Some of these facilities are registered with NIH because they receive NIH support for their rDNA research and others because it is the policy of the department or agency to comply with the NIH Guidelines. The responsibility for the "enforcement" of the Guidelines is shared by the NIH Office of

Biotechnology Activities, the Recombinant DNA Advisory Committee (RAC), IBCs at individual institutions, and by the principal investigators (PIs) themselves.

FRAMEWORK FOR IMPLEMENTATION OF THE NIH GUIDELINES FOR RDNA RESEARCH

The Guidelines provide an administrative framework that specifies the roles and responsibilities of various federal officials, research institutions, and individual scientists. Significant responsibility is shared among the NIH Office of Biotechnology Activities (OBA), the RAC, IBCs at individual institutions, the principal investigator (PI), the Biological Safety Officer (BSO) at the institution, and by investigators themselves. Scientific advice on the technical aspects of risk assessment is provided by technical experts on the RAC; public input is provided by experts in nontechnical subjects and by the right of the public to comment on major actions.

The system is based upon a tiered set of reviews that encourages experimental design to be well thought out and provides a means for catching potential problems. The Guidelines distinguish among experiments: those needing approval of the IBC as well as the RAC and NIH director before initiation; those involving human testing that need approval of the IBC and the Institutional Review Boards (IRBs) as well as the RAC; those that require approval of the OBA and IBC; those that only require IBC approval; those that merely require notice to the IBC at the initiation of the experiment; and exempt experiments.

The RAC is designated to consist of up to 21 voting members, including the chair. A majority of the voting members have to be knowledgeable in relevant scientific fields, such as molecular genetics, molecular biology, or rDNA research, including clinical gene transfer research. At least four members of the RAC have to be knowledgeable in fields such as public health, laboratory safety, occupational health, protection of human subjects of research, the environment, ethics, law, public attitudes, or related fields. Representatives of various federal agencies also serve as nonvoting members. Over time, the degree of centralized federal oversight has been substantially reduced. Many of the central functions of the RAC have been delegated to IBCs. Each institution (and the IBC acting on its behalf) has become responsible for ensuring that all rDNA research conducted at or sponsored by that institution is conducted in compliance with the NIH Guidelines.

The RAC is, however, still responsible for advising the NIH director on actions such as: (1) adopting changes in the NIH Guidelines; (2) assigning containment levels, changing containment levels, and approving experiments considered "Major Actions" under the NIH Guidelines; (3) promulgating and amending lists of classes of rDNA molecules to be exempt from the Guidelines because they do not present a significant risk to health or the environment; and (4) certifying new host vector systems. The RAC is also responsible for: (1) identifying novel human gene transfer experiments deserving of public discussion; (2) transmitting to the NIH director specific comments/recommendations about human gene transfer experiments; (3) publicly reviewing human gene transfer clinical trial data and relevant information evaluated and summarized by the NIH OBA in accordance with the annual data reporting requirements; (4) identifying broad scientific, safety, social, and ethical issues relevant to gene therapy research as potential Gene Therapy Policy Conference topics; (5) identifying novel social, ethical, scientific, and safety issues relevant to specific human applications of gene transfer and providing the necessary guidance.

All institutions subject to the NIH Guidelines are required to establish and register an IBC for the review of rDNA research. The IBC is designed to provide a quasi-independent review of rDNA work done at an institution. It is responsible for: (1) reviewing all rDNA research conducted at or sponsored by the institution and approving those projects in conformity with the Guidelines; (2) periodically reviewing ongoing projects; (3) adopting emergency plans for spills and contamination; (4) lowering containment levels for certain rDNA and recombinant organisms in which the absence of harmful sequences has been established; and (5) reporting significant problems, violations, illnesses, or accidents to the NIH OBA.

It is also the responsibility of the institution to appoint a Biological Safety Officer if it engages in large-scale research or production activities involving viable organisms containing rDNA molecules. If the institution engages in rDNA research at BL-3 or BL-4 (see below), the officer must be a member of the IBC. The officer's duties include: (1) conducting periodic inspections to ensure laboratory standards are rigorously followed; (2) reporting to the IBC and the institution any significant problems, violations of the Guidelines, and any significant research-related accidents or illnesses; (3) developing emergency plans for handling accidental spills and personnel contamination and investigating laboratory accidents involving rDNA research; (4) providing advice on laboratory security; and (5) providing technical advice to the PI and the IBC on research safety procedures.

Pre-initiation review of experiments by the RAC has been an important part of the oversight mechanism. Pre-initiation approval of experiments by NIH is required only for: (1) experiments that have not been assigned containment levels by the Guidelines; (2) experiments using new host-vector systems, which must be certified by NIH; (3) certain experiments requiring case-by-case approval; and (4) requests for exceptions from Guideline requirements. Prior to the initiation of these experiments the PI must submit a registration document to the IBC containing the following information: the source(s) of DNA; the nature of the inserted DNA sequences; the host(s) and vector(s) to be used; whether an attempt will be made to obtain expression of a foreign gene, and if so, the protein that will be produced; and the containment conditions that will be implemented as specified in the NIH Guidelines.

The initial RAC review process includes a determination as to whether the human gene transfer experiment presents characteristics that warrant public RAC review and discussion. The NIH OBA will notify the PI(s) about the results of the RAC's initial review. Two outcomes are possible: (1) the experiment does not present characteristics that warrant further review and discussion and is therefore exempt from public RAC review and discussion; or (2) the experiment presents characteristics that warrant public RAC review and discussion. Completion of the RAC review process is defined as: (1) receipt by the PI(s) of a letter from the NIH OBA indicating that the submission does not present characteristics that warrant public RAC review and discussion; or (2) receipt by the PI(s) of a letter from the NIH OBA after public RAC review that summarizes the committee's key comments and recommendations (if any).

TYPES OF EXPERIMENTS THAT REQUIRE IBC, RAC, AND NIH DIRECTOR REVIEW

At this time, only two categories of experiments are considered "major actions" that require decision by the NIH director after review by the IBC and the RAC. One category includes experiments that propose the "deliberate transfer of a drug resistance trait to microorganisms that are not known to acquire the trait naturally—if such acquisition could compromise the use of the drug to control disease agents in humans, veterinary medicine, or agriculture." The second category includes experiments that propose the deliberate formation of rDNA-containing genes for the biosynthesis of toxin molecules lethal for vertebrates at an LD of less than 100 nanograms per kilogram of body weight (e.g., microbial toxins such as the botulinum toxins, tetanus toxin, diphtheria toxin, and *Shigella dysenteriae* neurotoxin). The containment conditions or stipulation requirements for such experiments must be recommended by the RAC and set by NIH at the time of approval.

PHYSICAL AND BIOLOGICAL CONTAINMENT STRATEGIES FOR NIH-FUNDED RDNA RESEARCH ACTIVITIES

Regulated experiments must be carried out in accordance with physical and biological containment levels; the degree of containment is based upon the degree of potential hazard. Physical containment requires practices, equipment, and facility safeguards that lessen the chances that a recombinant organism might escape. As discussed above, the NIH first published safety guidelines in 1976, followed by the publication in 1984 of *Biosafety in Microbiological and Biomedical Laboratories* (BMBL). The BMBL guidelines address laboratory safety procedures for working with and handling infectious disease agents—they do not address laboratory security issues. The BMBL categorizes infectious agents and laboratory activities into four classes or levels (BL-1 to BL-4) and establishes safety requirements for each level based upon risk. Factors considered in determining the level of containment include agent factors such as: virulence, pathogenicity, infectious dose, environmental stability, route of spread, communicability, operations, quantity, availability of vaccine or treatment, and gene product effects such as toxicity, physiological activity, and allergenicity.

Experiments involving levels 2 through 4 and restricted risk group host organisms require IBC approval before recombinant experiments can be conducted. At the highest level (BL-4), nothing that is created should have any possibility of escape or of coming in direct contact with any laboratory workers. The containment conditions or stipulation requirements for such experiments must be recommended by the RAC and set by NIH at the time of approval. Containment conditions for experiments involving the introduction of rDNA into restricted agents are set on a case-by-case basis following NIH OBA review. The recommended practices, safety equipment, and facility safeguards in these guidelines establish a code of practice that is complied with voluntarily, one that all members of a laboratory community can together embrace to safeguard their colleagues and to protect the public. A permit is also required for all facilities working with such agents, although clinical laboratories used for research, diagnostic, reference, and/or verification purposes need only be certified (but do not require a license).

Some organisms, including smallpox (*Variola major*) may not be studied in the United States except at specified facilities. Smallpox is an acute contagious disease caused by *Variola* virus, a member of the orthopox virus family. It was one of the world's most feared diseases until it was eradicated by a collaborative global vaccination program led by the World Health Organization (WHO). The last known natural case was in Somalia in 1977. Smallpox was officially declared eradicated in 1980. All research activities, including storage of *Variola major* are restricted to two international collaborating centers for smallpox research. The WHO Collaborating Center for Smallpox Research in the United States is located at the CDC in Atlanta, Georgia, the other is located at the VECTOR Laboratory in Koltsovo, Russia. Since their initial appearance, the physical biocontainment levels for rDNA experiments have been progressively lowered over time. As experience provided confidence that rDNA technology could be applied without creating dangerous organisms that could not be contained, the prohibitions were replaced with a series of risk-based mechanisms for oversight and approval.

COMPLIANCE WITH AND ENFORCEMENT OF THE NIH GUIDELINES

The Principal Investigator (PI) is responsible for full compliance with the Guidelines in the conduct of rDNA research and for ensuring that the reporting requirements are fulfilled; the PI is held accountable for any reporting lapses. For experiments that require NIH approval prior to IBC approval, it is the responsibility of the PI to petition NIH OBA with the concurrence of the IBC.

Compliance with the Guidelines is accomplished by a combination of local self-regulation and limited federal oversight, with the ultimate enforcement resting in the federal funding power. Even if noncompliance were found, no penalties can be imposed other than restriction or termination of NIH funding. The primary mechanism in the Guidelines for enforcing compliance is local self-regulation. Noncompliance may result in: suspension, limitation, or termination of financial assistance for the noncompliant NIH-funded research project and of NIH funds for other rDNA research at the institution, or a requirement for prior NIH approval of any or all future rDNA projects at the institution. The Guidelines are designed to encourage industry's voluntary compliance by creating a parallel system of project review and IBC approval analogous to that required for NIH-funded projects, modified to alleviate industry's concerns about protection of proprietary information. A company's IBC determines whether the facilities meet the standards for the large-scale containment level but only for information-gathering purposes rather than to enforce these guidelines assigned by the RAC. A working group of the RAC may visit the companies and their IBCs from time to time. An important provision here is a process whereby a corporation may request presubmission review of the records needed to register its projects with NIH. The HHS Freedom of Information Officer informally determines whether the records have to be released; if so, they are returned to the submitting company.

REGULATION OF MICROBIAL AGENTS (LISTED AGENTS AND TOXINS)

The Antiterrorism and Effective Death Penalty Act of 1996 required the Secretary of HHS to establish and enforce safety procedures for the transfer of listed biological agents (select agents), including measures to ensure proper training and appropriate skills to handle such agents, and proper laboratory facilities to contain and dispose of such agents. These regulations provide:

- "safeguards to prevent access to listed biological agents for use in domestic or international terrorism or for any other criminal purpose • procedures to protect public safety in the event of a transfer or potential transfer of a listed biological agent in violation of the established safety procedures and safeguards
- the appropriate availability of biological agents for research, education, and other legitimate purposes."

The select agent list, which is subject to revision, includes those agents considered to be the greatest threats to human health. An expanded list of pathogens and toxins went into effect on February 11, 2003. Agricultural plant and animal pathogens are now also included; the other changes reflect taxonomic changes and a few reassessments of what constitutes the most dangerous biothreat agents.

The PATRIOT Act makes it a criminal offense for any person to knowingly possess any biological agent, toxin, or delivery system of a type or in a quantity that, under the circumstances, is not reasonably justified by prophylactic, protective, bona fide research, or other peaceful purpose. In addition, the new law prohibits transfer or possession of a listed biological agent or toxin by a "restricted person."

Title II, Enhanced Controls of Dangerous Biological Agents and Toxins, of the Bioterrorism Response Act substantially broadens the regulatory obligations for laboratories working with select agents. The Secretary of HHS has the authority to establish and enforce safety procedures, including: (1) proper training and appropriate skills to handle such agents and toxins; (2) proper laboratory facilities to contain and dispose of such agents and toxins; (3) measures to prevent access to such agents and tox- ins for use in domestic or international terrorism or for any criminal purpose; (4) procedures to protect the public safety in the event of a violation of the safety or security measures; and (5) appropriate availability of biological agents and toxins for research, education, and other legitimate purposes.

On February 7, 2003 the CDC's final interim rule, Possession, Use and Transfer of Select Agents, went into effect. On February 11, 2003 similar rules from the Animal and Plant Health Inspection Service (APHIS) of the USDA also went into effect. A USDA permit is required for work with plant or animal pathogens. In accordance with accepted scientific and regulatory practices of the discipline of plant pathology, an exotic plant pathogen (e.g., virus, bacteria, or fungus) is one that is not known to occur within the United States. Determination of whether a pathogen has a potential for serious detrimental impact on managed (agricultural, forest, grassland) or natural ecosystems is made by the PI and the IBC, in consultation with scientists knowledgeable about plant diseases, crops, and ecosystems in the geographic area of the research.

These regulations impose additional shipping and handling requirements on laboratory facilities that transfer or receive select agents capable of causing substantial harm to human health. They are designed to ensure that select agents are not shipped to parties who are not equipped to handle them properly or who lack proper authorization for their requests.

The major shift in the new regulations establishes who may possess select agents as well as who may send and receive those agents, adds biosecurity requirements to the biosafety requirements, incorporates the personnel restrictions of the PATRIOT Act, involves the FBI in performing background checks on individuals who may have access to or conduct research on select agents, and proscribes certain types of experiments.

POSSESSION OF SELECT AGENTS

The Antiterrorism and Effective Death Penalty Act of 1996 required the Secretary of HHS to issue regulations governing the transfer of biological agents that have the potential to pose a severe threat to public health and safety. The CDC was authorized to regulate transfers of pathogens of unique interest in terms of their capacity to be used as weapons (the select agents list). Accordingly, the CDC required that laboratories transferring select agents be registered.

The Bioterrorism Response Act adds new requirements for the Secretary of HHS to consider in listing agents and in preventing unlawful access to agents during transfers. Facilities that register their posses- sion and use of listed agents and toxins must provide "information regarding the characterization of listed agents and toxins to facilitate their identification, including their source; and safeguard and security requirements for registered persons."

Regulations specified under this law must "include appropriate safeguard and security requirements for persons possessing, using, or transferring a listed agent or toxin commensurate with the risk such agent or toxin poses to public health and safety (including the risk of use in domestic or international terrorism)." Registered facilities must limit access to listed biological agents and toxins only to those determined by the registered facility to have a legitimate need to handle or use select agents, and the secretary must be notified if a listed agent is lost, stolen, or released outside a biocontainment area of a facility.

IMPORTATION AND INTERSTATE SHIPMENT OF ETIOLOGIC AGENTS

The importation or subsequent receipt of human pathogens and vectors of human disease is controlled by the Public Health Service Foreign Quarantine Regulations (42 CFR Part 71. 56). Packages containing human pathogens or vectors originating in foreign locations must have an importation permit issued by the CDC. The importer is legally responsible for ensuring that the foreign personnel package, label, and ship the infectious materials according to the Interstate Shipment of Etiological Agents regulations (42 CFR Part 72), regulations of the Department of Transportation on Transportation of Etiologic Agents (49 CFR Part 173), and the Dangerous Goods Regulations of the International Air Transport Association. An applicant for a permit must be knowledgeable of safe practices and proficient in the handling of infectious materials, be directly responsible for work with the infectious materials, and reside at the receipt address for the facility where work with the material will occur. The permit application requires the importer to provide characterization information for the material, a description of the objectives of the intended use, and a designation of the biosafety level of the laboratory where the work will occur.

The CDC is also responsible for regulating the interstate shipment of indigenous human pathogens, diagnostic specimens, and biologic products. The shipment of these materials must be in compliance with the provisions of the Interstate Shipment of Etiological Agents regulations (42 CFR Part 72), which specify packaging and labeling requirements and procedures for notification of successful delivery or failure of delivery.

OVERSIGHT OF FOREIGN NATIONALS

This section briefly describes the current and emerging system of granting permission, to non-U.S. citizens through the visa system, for both short-term and extended stays, as well as two of the tracking systems. Issues related to sharing information with non-U.S. citizens are addressed in Chapter 3. The system is still evolving, so any description of current practice runs the risk of becoming rapidly out-of-date. At present, however, September 11th and its aftermath have significantly increased the level of scrutiny, the time involved, and the opacity of the process. It should also be noted that, beyond the requirements to designate responsible individuals in affected institutions, to date laws and regulations related to individuals have been almost entirely aimed at rejection and prevention. That is, they have been aimed to limit access rather than to create a process of licensing or certification that would convey some more general, authoritative approval for working in life sciences research comparable, for example, to the licenses doctors must obtain to practice medicine. The September 11th terrorist attacks greatly increased the concern and accelerated the plans for improving efforts to provide adequate scrutiny of visa applications and to track foreign nationals once they entered the United States. Foreign scholars planning shorter visits are also affected by increased concern for security, with impacts on the ability of researchers to take part in international meetings, conferences, or international research collaborations. Over time, these various restrictions could potentially alter the way research is conducted and have the potential to impede scientific progress in the United States. The Department of Homeland Security (DHS) has been given responsibility for the policy guidance and regulation governing the issuance of visas, with the Secretary for Homeland Security given ultimate authority to determine who may and who may not enter the United States. Where there are foreign policy considerations the Department of State will continue to exercise authority. Consular officers, who have responsibility for guiding the review and processing of visa applications, will also remain under the auspices of the Department of State. In testimony before the House Select Committee on Homeland Security on July 11, 2002, Secretary of State Colin L. Powell reported that the State Department adjudicated over 10 million nonimmigrant visa applications in 2001. Around 7. million visas, or about 70 percent of the total, were issued.

Additional Security Checks on Visa Applications

The Visas Condor program, initiated in January 2002, seeks to identify terrorists by checking a visa applicant's name against various U.S. government databases. Applicants are also required to fill out additional forms and be interviewed, fingerprinted, and subjected to additional identifying measures and background checks. Those affected by the Visas Condor program are predominantly Muslim men between the ages of 16 and 45 who come from any of approximately 26 (mostly Islamic) countries, but the system also applies to countries such as Russia and China. The State Department's goal is eventually to have the Visas Condor process take less than ten business days.

In response to earlier concerns the State Department, in consultation with other federal agencies, had created a Technology Alert List to provide guidance about which areas of science and technology were of particular concern. Applications from individuals with expertise in one of these areas would be sent to Washington for further review, usually by an agency with expertise in that field and perhaps by the FBI or intelligence services. The 16 categories on the list include "chemical and biotechnology engineering," which covers "technologies associated with the development or production of biological and toxin agents, pathogenics, biological weapons research." In practice, "technologies" tended to be defined broadly enough to affect life scientists doing a variety of research. Since

January 2002 the Visas Condor security checks and the Technology Alert List reviews have required explicit approval from Washington for each applicant. In the past, at least the Alert List review process permitted consular officers to issue visas if they had not received a negative report from Washington within a certain number of days, but that is no longer the case.

The agencies that need to provide clearance are determined by the State Department's Bureau of Consular Affairs and include the CIA and the FBI, as well as any other agency with a potential interest in the applicant. All applicants must be positively cleared by all the agencies involved in the review. This led to the backlogs and time delays reported in recent months. Consular Affairs officers have reported that in 2002, they conducted 35,000 Visas Condor and about 14,000 other checks. While this represents about a threefold increase in the number of cases referred to Washington, D.C., it is nonetheless a very small percentage of the total number of cases.

In May 2003, Secretary of State Powell announced additional requirements for those seeking nonimmigrant visas. Except for certain visa categories or for countries where a visa waiver is in effect, as of August 1, 2003 all individuals between the ages of 16 and 60 are required to undergo a personal interview as part of the visa application process. Substantial delays and increasing backlogs are anticipated in the visa process, since no additional resources are being allocated to consular officers and no overtime is to be used to handle the additional interviews. Furthermore, a new legislative mandate also requires that, as of January 1, 2004, all visitors entering the United States on a visa will be photographed and fingerprinted as part of U.S.-VISIT, the enhanced security screening process.

Tracking Systems

In addition to increased scrutiny of visa applications, the U.S. government is initiating a number of systems for tracking foreign students and visitors to the United States.

Student and Exchange Visitor Information System (SEVIS)

The new Student and Exchange Visitor Information System (SEVIS) is an electronic System aimed at keeping better track of foreign students once they have received visas to study in the United States. The Bureau of Citizenship and Immigration Services (formerly the Immigration and Naturalization Service, which was incorporated into the Department of Homeland Security) is responsible for SEVIS, although the program was developed in cooperation with the Departments of State and Education. SEVIS is designed to collect and report data on international student or exchange visitor status and changes, such as a change in one's program of study. It also provides system alerts, event notifications, and basic reports to the end-user schools, programs, and INS field offices. The timetable for its implementation and for colleges and universities to come into compliance with its regulations was accelerated after September 11th. Schools wishing to accept foreign students were required to register with SEVIS by January 30, 2003.

Interagency Panel for Advanced Science and Security (IPASS)

IPASS is a response to an October 2001 Presidential Decision Directive, "Combating Terrorism Through Immigration Policies," which directed federal agencies to develop student immigration policies through which the country "prohibits certain students from receiving education and training in sensitive areas." The White House's Office of Science and Technology Policy (OSTP) has been working with the White House's Homeland Security Council and others to develop and implement IPASS, although at the time of this report the Executive Order to create IPASS had not yet been signed.

PROFESSIONAL EDUCATION AND RESPONSIBILITIES OF LIFE SCIENTISTS

The Center for the Study of Ethics in the Professions lists over 850 "codes of ethics" on its website. A code of ethics is that profession's contract with the society it serves establishing in often very general terms acceptable moral behavior for practitioners of that profession. Some differ widely in their content, because of their origins and their specific purposes. Others are similar in the topics they cover and the general ethical standards they articulate, but differ in language and in the specific ethical problems or abuses they address. The Annex at the end of this chapter presents a representative cross-section of medical and scientific codes of ethics, from the Hippocratic Oath to the American Society for Microbiology's code of ethics and ethical standards for society members. There is a considerable literature on the formulation of professional oaths and codes of conduct. Some have called for the initiation of a pledge to be taken by scientists—perhaps at graduation—much as modernized versions of the Hippocratic Oath are taken by some medical students upon graduation.

Others focus less on the development of codes and more on the inclusion of an emphasis on the moral and social responsibilities of life scientists in the training of students and postdoctoral fellows. Particularly if efforts to address the social responsibilities of scientists are led by leaders in the field and senior investigators, it is argued, young scientists will come to value "the ethics of individual behavior within the scientific enterprise and the societal impact of scientific research." Whether mandatory or voluntary, the adoption of codes of conduct by professional organizations or national academies of science, and the integration of ethics education into the training of students should serve to sensitize "young scientists to reflect on the wider consequences of their intended field of work."

Arguably, to be effective, any policy or set of procedures intended to address concerns about the offensive application of life sciences research data will require "ownership" by the scientific community. To the extent that responsibilities to guard against intentional misuse are recognized in professional codes of conduct and explicated and examined in the context of the training of the next generation of practitioners in the life sciences, opportunities to develop and maintain ownership by the community will only be increased.

At the November 2001 Review Conference for the BWC, the United States formally proposed new ways to strengthen the regime against biological weapons. Among the recommendations put forward was one that called upon the countries that are parties to the BWC to support the development and adoption of a code of conduct for scientists working with pathogenic organisms.

Among the guiding principles of such a code of conduct would be a statement that "scientists will use their knowledge and skills for the advancement of human welfare and will not conduct any activities directed toward the use of microorganisms or toxins for hostile purposes or in armed conflict." This proposal will be taken up by an intersessional meeting of the parties to the BWC in 2005 in Geneva. Proposals for the creation of such professional codes of conduct for practitioners in the life sciences have also come from the International Committee of the Red Cross, the U.K. Foreign and Commonwealth Office, the European Union, The Royal Society, and others.

THE INTERNATIONAL SITUATION

There is a deep and long-standing foundation of scientific self-regulation, voluntary standards, and associational accreditation. Given the fundamentally international character of research in the life sciences, any serious attempt to prevent the misuse of research must include efforts at improving and harmonizing standards and practices internationally. Recently, this has been supplemented by some mandatory requirements on specific aspects of laboratory safety.

This section provides a brief overview of some of the major international programs. It also offers examples from the regulatory systems of two other countries with advanced biotechnology research capabilities: the United Kingdom and Japan. The Committee's charge did not extend to a comprehensive review of the international regulatory environment, but the Committee did examine some of the existing systems for possible positive or negative examples that might be relevant to the evolving U.S. situation.

Laboratory Safety

The Organization for Economic Cooperation and Development (OECD) has drafted quality management requirements called the Good Laboratory Practice (GLP) guidelines. Many national governments re- quire laboratories that carry out safety and toxicological testing for the approval of new products to meet the GLP guidelines.

Controls Over Access to and Transfers of Dangerous Pathogens

As discussed above, smallpox was declared to be eradicated by the WHO at the annual meeting of the World Health Assembly in May 1980. This led to the greatest international control over access to dangerous pathogens—an international agreement implemented by the WHO to restrict the repository of smallpox virus cultures to two designated facilities, one in the United States and one in Russia.

All countries other than the United States and Russia were to destroy their remaining stocks. The WHO, however, had no enforcement authority or means of verification and relied entirely on the voluntary cooperation of member states, leaving uncertainties about compliance.

There are several other nonlegally binding access control agreements. The Australia Group is an informal arrangement of 33 member countries plus the European Union that harmonizes national controls on the export of dual use materials and production equipment that, in the wrong hands, could increase the risk of assisting chemical and biological weapons (CBW) proliferation. The Group meets annually to discuss ways in which national-level export licensing measures can more effectively ensure that would-be "proliferators" are unable to obtain necessary inputs for CBW programs. Participants in the Australia Group do not undertake any legally binding obligations.

By enhancing the effectiveness of national export licensing measures, the Australia Group's activities serve to support the objectives and purposes of the BWC.

The participants in the Australia Group encourage all countries to take the necessary steps to ensure that they and their industries are not contributing to the spread of biological and chemical weapons. Export licensing measures demonstrate the determination of Australia Group countries to avoid involvement in the proliferation of these weapons in violation of international law and norms.

The effectiveness of the cooperation among the participating countries depends solely on their commitment to CBW nonproliferation goals and the effectiveness of the measures they each take on a national basis.

The European Union also imposes export controls on dual use biotechnology equipment and pathogenic microorganisms and toxins, including agents that could be used for biological warfare. To date, it is the only regional organization to undertake such an effort. International regulations apply far more comprehensively to transnational shipment of human, plant, and animal pathogens. Among the international organizations that set regulations controlling the international transfer of such material is the International Air Transport Association (IATA).

IATA Dangerous Goods Regulations require that packaging used for the transport of materials in specified hazard groups meet defined standards. Shippers of microorganisms within the more serious hazard groups must be trained by IATA certified and approved instructors. They also require shippers' declaration forms, which should accompany the package in duplicate, and specified labels are used for organisms in transit by air (IATA, 1998).

The Universal Postal Union (UPU) has established strict regulations on the shipment of pathogens through the mail. Other organizations regulate specific modes of transport. These regulations are primarily directed to the prevention of accidental release, but they also operate to track (but not to limit) who is supplying and receiving pathogens. The European Union is the only regional organization to regulate the shipment of pathogens.

The Situation in the United Kingdom

In light of the September 11th terrorist attacks in the United States, the focus has shifted from safety requirements in the laboratory toward greater scrutiny of dangerous substances and increasing the difficulty in gaining access to areas where such agents are stored and used.

The Antiterrorism, Crime and Security Act 2001 (ATCSA) part VII, is instrumental in this approach and attempts to tighten controls on access to dangerous pathogens and toxins used in research establishments and laboratories in the U.K. The pathogens and toxins affected are specified in Schedule 5 of the Act classified with their ACDP hazard group.

"Dangerous substance" means: (a) anything that consists of or includes a substance for the time being mentioned in Schedule 5; or (b) anything that is infected with or otherwise carries any such substance. Further substances may be added to the list by order of the Secretary of State. In addition, the ATCSA establishes the power to vet personnel working in such establishments and to mandate security provisions.

The owner of any premises that possess or use a dangerous substance must notify the Secretary of State. The occupier of the premises must ensure that only appropriate individuals are given access to the premises. A police officer may require provision of information about each person who has access to any dangerous substance kept or used there or who has access to specified premises and identify the access that the person has, or is proposed to have.

Moreover, a constable may require provision of information about what dangerous substances are kept or used at the premises, the measures taken to ensure the security of any such substance, and measures taken to ensure that access to the substance is given only to those whose activities require access and only in circumstances that ensure the security of the substance. A constable may require that measures be taken to ensure the security of any dangerous substance.

To assess compliance with those measures, a constable may, after giving at least 2 days notice, enter any relevant premises at a reasonable time. A constable who has entered any premises may search the premises, building, or site; require any person who appears to the constable to be in charge of the premises, building, or site to facilitate any such inspection; and require any such person to answer any question.

If research establishments do not meet personnel or security requirements, access to dangerous pathogens and toxins could be withdrawn. Where the Secretary of State reasonably believes that adequate measures to ensure the security of any dangerous substance kept or used in any relevant premises are not being taken and are unlikely to be taken, he may give a direction to the occupier of the premises requiring him to dispose of the substance.

Moreover, the Secretary of State may give directions to the occupier of any relevant premises requiring him to secure that the person identified in the directions is not to have access to any dangerous substance kept or used there nor to specified premises. The Secretary of State may not give the directions unless he believes that they are necessary in the interests of national security. Failure to comply with the relevant duties is punishable by imprisonment, a fine, or both.

RESEARCH OVERSIGHT

The United Kingdom

For research involving DNA, the U.K. has set up the Health and Safety Executive (HSE) under the Health and Safety at Work

Act of 1974 (HWSA). It is primarily concerned with the protection of human health from possible ill effects of any workplace activity. Genetic modification and any activities in which genetically modified cells or organisms are cultured, stored, used, transported, destroyed or disposed of, under conditions of containment, are subject to the control of HSE under the Genetically Modified Organisms (Contained Use) Regulations of 1992, which are made pursuant to the HSWA.

The following bodies were established specifically to provide policy guidance on issues arising from developments in modern biotechnology. The Advisory Committee on Genetic Modification (ACGM) is a nonstatutory body that advises the Health and Safety Commission/Executive and Ministers on human and environmental safety of the contained use of genetically modified organisms under the GMO (Contained Use) Regulations 1992 (based on EC Directive 90/219), as amended.

ACGM focuses on safety questions in the laboratory and industrial installations. It is not involved in policy approval. The Advisory Group on Scientific Advances in Genetics (AGSAG) is a nonstatutory advisory body that advises the Chief Medical Officer and the Director of Research and Development (DH) on potential implications for public health and for the National Health Service (NHS) of scientific advances in genetics. It also advises the NHS executive board on innovative genetic services and their evaluation.

Japan

Guidelines for rDNA experimentation define basic conditions required to promote and ensure safety for rDNA and related experiments. The experiments must be conducted under proper safety measures generally employed in microbiological laboratories, incorporating combinations of physical and biological containment measures as required by the safety evaluation of the experiment. Large-scale experiments with genetically engineered organisms must be conducted in a facility that has appropriate containment measures. Laboratory workers must be aware of the necessity of safety measures in the experiments, actually take those measures, and must have been thoroughly trained to ensure their expertise in standard methods and practices in microbiological experiments.

CONCLUSIONS

International regulation of biology is complicated by the lack of a multilateral consensus as to the basic security framework to which controls can be consistently applied. In contrast, the International Atomic Energy Agency (IAEA) oversees the Nuclear Nonproliferation Treaty (NPT) and nuclear safeguards agreements are negotiated with member states on a bilateral basis.

The Organization for the Prohibition of Chemical Weapons oversees implementation of the exceptionally detailed Chemical Weapons Convention. Nothing comparable exists with regard to the oversight of biotechnology.

The BWC articulates a widely shared global norm against the weaponization of pathogens and establishes statutory but not regulatory obligations on parties to the Convention. Nor is there any international oversight organization for biology. Efforts to strengthen the BWC by adding provisions for verification and compliance foundered in 2001 on fundamental diplomatic differences of principle and in particular cost-benefit analyses as to the effectiveness of the measures being proposed and whether multilateral versus bilateral approaches were the best way to prevent the development of biological weapons.

Multilateral discussions are continuing on ways to strengthen compliance with this treaty. At the BWC review conference in November 2002, member states agreed on a U.S. proposal to hold intersessional meetings in each of the next three years (2003–2005) before the 2006 Review Conference to discuss the five voluntary measures put forward by the U.S. to strengthen the BWC.

With regard to oversight of research, *no country* has developed guidelines and practices to address all aspects of biotechnology research. There are a range of norms, standards of conduct for research, regulations, and institutional practices, many of which have been developed to address questions about research involving human subjects or the treatment of laboratory animals. In addition, responsibility for regulation of various aspects of biotechnology research is frequently shared among different departments or agencies.

In the United States, the PATRIOT Act and the Bioterrorism Response Act already establish the statutory and regulatory basis for protecting biological materials from inadvertent misuse. Once fully implemented, the mandated registration for possession of select agents, designation of restricted individuals who may not possess select agents, and a regulatory system for the physical security of the most dangerous pathogens within the United States will provide a useful accounting of domestic laboratories engaged in legitimate research and some reduction in the risk of pathogens acquired from designated facilities falling into the hands of terrorists.

The Committee stresses that implementation of current legislation must not be overly restrictive given the critical role that the development of effective vaccines, diagnostics, therapeutics, and detection systems, along with a responsive public health system, will play in providing protection against bioterrorism—and other serious health threats. Otherwise these legislative solutions may unintentionally limit the research on dangerous pathogens by legitimate laboratories and investigators.

To be effective, a harmonized, international system for the regulatory oversight of the possession of dangerous pathogens and toxins, comparable to the one being put in place in the United States, is needed. Moreover, the different regulations now on the books do not add up to a systematic, generally applicable, means for the United States to respond to the challenges posed by research in the life sciences employing advanced biotechnology methods. Nor do they address the issues surrounding how to "manage" the knowledge and technologies produced through these research activities. At the moment, "control" over the results of these "dual use" research activities may be implemented at the point of information dissemination in the peer-reviewed literature.

A critical question is whether the various regulations and laws can be adapted, enhanced, supplemented, and linked to provide a system of oversight that will give confidence that the potential risks of misuse of dual use research are being adequately addressed. The Committee's answer to that question is contained in the following chapters.

3

ALPHAVIRUSES AND TERRORISM

OVERVIEW

Alphaviruses (formerly know as group A arboviruses) are a genera of arthropodborne viruses in the Togaviridae family that give rise to a spectrum of diseases in humans ranging from asymptomatic infections to fatal encephalitis. There are 28 types of alphaviruses classified by their antigenic properties. In the context of viral bioterrorism, several alphaviruses are particularly interesting due to their susceptibility to cultivation, their ability to cause fatal or serious illness, and a lack of measures available for their control. These viruses could be weaponized through their production and stabilization in either aerosolized wet or dried forms. The specific viruses likely to be used as a bioterrorist agent are Venezuelan equine encephalitis (VEE), Western equine encephalitis (WEE), and Eastern equine encephalitis (EEE).

HISTORICAL SIGNIFICANCE

During the 1930s, the viruses that cause WEE, EEE, and VEE were isolated from affected horses and were discovered to be antigenically related. In working with these viruses, it was discovered that they are highly contagious in aerosolized form, demonstrated by the many laboratory-acquired infections that resulted. In one incident in Moscow, 20 workers were infected within 24 hours after a vial containing the virus was dropped and broken. Although many other viruses could be used as biological weapons, WEE, EEE, and VEE possess several characteristics that make it attractive for weaponization:

- Ability to be produced in large quantities inexpensively
- Ability to remain stable and infectious as aerosols
- Ability to cause serious disease
- Existence of many subtypes making vaccine development difficult

ETIOLOGY

In nature, alphaviruses transmit their disease by vectors, mostly mosquitoes. However, it is aerosol transmission that leads to the concern of these viruses being manufactured as biological weapons since VEE, WEE, and EEE remain highly infectious in the aerosol state.

INCIDENCE AND PREVALENCE

During the past century, there have been occasional outbreaks of VEE in Latin America. The outbreaks involved tens to hundreds of thousands of equine and human cases. More recent outbreaks have occurred in Mexico.

In the United States there have been periodic outbreaks of EEE in the eastern states. As the name implies, WEE occurred in the western states as early as 1930. In addition to these natural outbreaks, there have been many cases of laboratory workers being infected from mishandling of these viruses.

RISK FACTORS

Human infections are acquired in areas endemic for vectors carrying the viruses. The infection pattern is seasonal. Alphaviruses have not been reported to be transmissible between humans through normal contact. Laboratory workers that handle and work with VEE, WEE, or EEE are at high risk.

PATHOGENESIS/LIFE CYCLE

Infection is transmitted by mosquitoes. When a vertebrate host is infected, a transient viremia occurs. Dissemination of the virus occurs as infected cells are lysed, releasing the virus. Ahost can be infected and seroconversion can occur in the absence of clinical disease. In humans, aerosol transmission is the main concern, as this would be the modality for biological warfare.

PRESENTATION

There are two forms of the disease. The first presents with fever, headache, malaise, and symptoms of encephalitis (e.g., eastern, western, or Venezuelan equine encephalitis viruses). The other form presents as fever, rash, and arthralgia (e.g., Chikungunya, Ross River, Mayaro, and Sindbis viruses). The clinical manifestations can start as relatively mild but quickly become fulminant encephalitis, followed by coma and death in 1 to 2 weeks. Children are more likely to die from an infection than adults. In pregnant women spontaneous abortions, stillbirths, and fetal abnormalities can often occur.

INCUBATION PERIOD/TIME OF ONSET

The incubation period is 1–6 days and the time of onset is acute.

SIGNS AND SYMPTOMS

VEE, Western, Eastern

- Acute onset of malaise
- High fever (101–105EF)
- Severe headache
- Rigors
- Photophobia
- Myalgias (predominantly in legs and lumbosacral region)
- Cough
- Sore Throat

- Vomiting
- Seizures

Chikungunya, Ross River, Mayaro, Sindbis

- Fever
- Severe arthralgia (polyarticular, migratory, affecting small joints of the hands, wrists, ankles, and feet)
- Rash (flush over face and trunk followed by maculopapular rash; face, palms, and soles may be affected as well)
- Generalized myalgias

DIAGNOSIS

Diagnosis is based on clinical presentation and history of exposure to the virus or suspected bioterrorist attack. Laboratory tests can confirm diagnosis through virus isolation.

LABORATORY

Certain alphaviruses, like Venezuelan equine encephalitis, can be isolated from the blood or throat swabs during the acute phase of the illness. Blood tests can detect a specific rise in IgG or IgM antibody. Cerebrospinal fluid should also be collected from patients with neurological symptoms. CSF analysis may reveal findings consistent with encephalitis (elevated white cells/mm3 that are predominantly mononuclear cells and elevated protein concentration). Other potential laboratory test findings include leukopenia, lymphopenia, and elevated serum glutamic oxaloacetic transaminase (SGOT).

DIFFERENTIAL DIAGNOSIS

- Influenza
- Flu-like illnesses from other potential bioterrorist agents (*Bacillus Anthracis*, *Yersinia pestis*, *Coxiella burnetii*)
- Brain abscess
- Lyme disease

- Rocky Mountain spotted fever
- Meningitis/encephalitis from fungal agents
- Lupus cerebritis
- Cerebral and granulomatous arteritis

TREATMENT

Supportive care is the mainstay therapy. Attention should be paid to fluid and electrolyte balance. Analgesics should be given for headaches and myalgias. Anticonvulsants may be given to patients with encephalitis. Nonsteroidal antiinflammatory drugs should be given for arthralgias. Currently, no antiviral drugs exist for the treatment of alphaviruses, though several compounds like interferon-alpha have been reported to mitigate the disease in animal models.

PROGNOSIS

The overall case fatality rate for Venezuelan equine encephalitis is less than 1%. It may reach 20–35% in children with encephalitis.

PREVENTION

There are two main controls for the disease. The first is disease surveillance of natural hosts. This will guide in determining whether measures to reduce the population of vector mosquitoes are needed. The second control is vaccination of hosts such as humans if at high risk, and other potential animal hosts, like horses. Formalin-inactivated vaccines for some types of WEE, EEE, and VEE exist for high-risk laboratory workers.

SPECIAL CONSIDERATIONS

Patients should be put in isolation with universal as well as droplet precautions. The virus is destroyed by heat (80EC for 30 minutes) and standard disinfectants.

RICIN

Ricin is on the Category B list of potential bioterrorism agents by the US Center for Disease Control and Prevention. It is of particular concern because it is available worldwide, is technically easy and inexpensive when preparing large quantities in liquid or crystal form, and the toxin is stable, as well as because ricin has received so much attention by the media.

Ricin is a potent toxin extracted from the bean of the castor plant, *Ricinis communis*. The entire castor plant contains ricin, but the greatest concentration is found in the seeds. The plant's most common use is for the production of castor oil, but it also grows uncultivated worldwide. Hexane or carbon tetrachloride is used to extract the oil from the plant, leaving a castor meal containing the toxin ricin.

Then, ricin is extracted from the castor meal by a salting-out procedure. Ingestion, injection, or inhalation could produce intoxication. There is no potential for spread by human-tohuman contact.

HISTORICAL SIGNIFICANCE

There have been several reports of ricin being used as a weapon both at home and abroad. A ricin-containing bomb, code-named "compound W," was developed and tested by the United States, in collaboration with Britain, before World War I. Ricin was used in injection form to assassinate Georgi Markov, a Bulgarian defector, in 1978. In 1994 and 1995, four men from a tax protest group were convicted of possessing ricin as a biological weapon. Plans linked to al Qaeda to produce ricin were found in Afghanistan in November 2001. In October 2003 a package containing ricin and a threatening note were sent to a South Carolina post office. In May and June of 2004, ground castor beans were found in jars of Gerber Banana Yogurt Dessert in California.

INCIDENCE AND PREVALENCE

Over 750 cases of ricin intoxication by ingestion have been reported. Ricin has been used as an injection in clinical trials, but reported cases of non-medicinal uses by injection are rare. In the

English-speaking world there are no reports of ricin intoxication by inhalation, but there is one incidence of workers being exposed to dust from castor beans around a processing plant.

PATHOGENESIS

Ricin toxin is a globular protein consisting of an alpha chain and a beta chain connected by a disulfide bond. The beta chain allows the toxin to bind to carbohydrates on the cell surface of eukaryotic cells. This triggers internalization of the protein by endocytosis. Once the protein is in the cytoplasm, the alpha chain enzymatically cleaves an adenine residue of the 28-S ribosomal subunit of RNA, inhibiting protein synthesis by the eukaryotic cell.

PRESENTATION

Incubation Period/Time of Onset

The initial signs and symptoms of ricin intoxication occur 6 hours after ingestion. Although there are no reported cases of inhalation, it is thought that signs and symptoms would occur within 8 hours. Death could take place 36 to 72 hours after exposure, and if death has not occurred within 5 days the victim usually recovers.

Signs and Symptoms

The infective dose is thought to be 3 to 5 :g/kg. Ricin is less toxic when ingested, probably due to the poorer absorption and enzymatic degradation by digestion. In general, ricin intoxication may lead to fever, fatigue, weakness, dehydration, leukocytosis, metabolic acidosis, hematuria, and elevated liver function tests. However, the clinical signs and symptoms of ricin toxicity vary with the route of exposure.

If ingested, ricin can lead to nausea, vomiting, abdominal pain, bloody diarrhea, mydriasis, fever, thirst, sore throat, anuria, hypovolemic shock, gastric and intestinal ulcerations, lymphoid necrosis of mesenteric lymph nodes and the spleen, liver necrosis, and diffuse nephritis. In reported cases, death occurred by day 3.

In cancer patients who have received ricin as an injection in clinical trials, flu-like symptoms, fatigue, muscular pain, and, rarely, seizures occurred.

In high doses (used in assassinations) there have been reports of severe local lymphoid necrosis, gastrointestinal hemorrhage, liver necrosis, diffuse nephritis, and diffuse splenitis.

One report of processing plant workers being exposed to castor bean dust led to an allergic syndrome of congestion, itchy eyes, urticaria, and chest tightness.

From animal studies, it is assumed that lethal ricin inhalational exposure in humans will lead to diffuse necrotizing pneumonia, hypoxemia, acidosis, and anorexia. Cough, fever, chest tightness, and pulmonary edema may also be seen as less severe signs and symptoms.

DIAGNOSIS

The diagnosis of ricin toxin would rely heavily on recognizing the signs and symptoms from many geographically clustered patients.

Laboratory

Radioimmunoassay and enzyme-linked immunosorbent assay (ELISA) are used to detect ricin in bodily fluids. Radioimmunoassay can monitor ricin toxin to concentrations as low as 50 to 100 pg/Ml. However, identification can be difficult because ricin binds quickly and is metabolized before it is excreted.

Pathology

Necrosis of respiratory epithelium may be seen within eight hours of inhalational exposure. Lymphoid necrosis in mesenteric lymph nodes and gut-associated lymphoid tissue, Kupffer cell necrosis, and evidence of diffuse nephritis may be seen if ingested.

Radiology

Although nonspecific, pulmonary edema may be seen on chest films.

DIFFERENTIAL DIAGNOSIS

Like the signs and symptoms of ricin poisoning, the differential diagnosis differs by route of intoxication. The differential diagnosis of inhalational ricin includes staphylococcal enterotoxin B, exposure to organofluorines, oxides of nitrogen, and phosgene. The differential diagnosis of ingestion of ricin includes enteric pathogens, mushrooms, caustics, iron, arsenic, and colchicine.

TREATMENT

Treatment for ricin intoxication is supportive. One of the most important things to do when exposed is for one to leave the area, remove clothing, and wash with soap and water. In general, it is important to monitor for hypotension, hepatotoxicity, and bone marrow suppression. For pulmonary intoxication, furosemide and respiratory support, including positive end-expiratory ventilatory therapy, may be needed. If ingestion of more than one castor bean per 10 kg of body weight occurs, activated charcoal followed by magnesium citrate should be used, along with fluid resuscitation. Patients who are asymptomatic 8 hours after exposure may be discharged.

PROGNOSIS

There have been relatively few deaths from ricin intoxication and only 2 since 1930. In one review looking at 751 cases, 1.9% of patients in one study died, and only about 6% who were symptomatic. Patients usually recover if death has not occurred in 3 to 5 days. Injection of ricin in clinical trials for cancer patients has led to two deaths.

PREVENTION

Avoiding exposure to ricin is the best prevention. A protective mask is the best protection against inhalation. If exposure to skin occurs, decontaminate with soap and water. Also, hypochlorite solutions can be used to inactivate ricin. Currently, there is no vaccine for ricin.

EPSILON TOXIN

Clostridium perfringens is an anaerobic, Gram-positive, spore-forming bacteria.

This ubiquitous organism is present in soil throughout the world and has been found in the stool of virtually every vertebrate organism ever tested. *Clostridium* species can produce a variety of toxins, and these are responsible for illness (Epsilon is 1 of 12 toxins). Epsilon toxin is a permease enzyme made by strains B and D of *C. perfringens.* This toxin is a CDC Category B Bioterrorism Agent since it has the potential to be aerosolized as a BT agent.

CLINICAL PRESENTATION

There are no human data for disease due to pure Epsilon toxin. If aerosolized Epsilon toxin occurs, then pulmonary edema, kidney failure, shock, and multi-organ failure may follow, based on animal studies.

DIAGNOSTIC TESTING

Growth of *C. perfringens* in culture and detection of toxin in research lab assay(s).

INFECTION CONTROL PRECAUTIONS

Universal precautions apply. Because this is a toxin-mediated syndrome, there is no potential for person-to-person spread.

TREATMENT AND PROPHYLAXIS

No antitoxin or vaccine is presently available. Treatment is supportive. ICU and ventilatory support may be necessary in an aerosolized Epsilon toxin exposure or when multi-organ failure and shock are present.

STAPHYLOCOCCUS ENTEROTOXIN B

Staphylococcus Enterotoxin B (SEB) is a heat-stable toxin that is a common cause of food poisoning. The toxin is secreted by the ubiquitous organism *Staphylococcus aureus* and is stable in aerosols. Although rarely fatal, it could render a high percentage of exposed individuals seriously ill within a few hours. SEB can be used as a weapon in aerosol form or by contaminating food or water supplies.

CLINICAL PRESENTATION

Symptoms begin after a brief latent period of 3 to 12 hours and will be different depending on the route of exposure. Typical symptoms include high fever, headache, myalgia, prostration, and dry cough. Vomiting and diarrhea may result from ingestion of toxin. In severe cases of inhalation, pulmonary edema, adult respiratory distress syndrome, and respiratory failure may also develop. In rare cases death may occur from dehydration.

DIAGNOSTIC TESTING

The diagnosis of SEB intoxication is primarily clinical and epidemiologic. The symptoms are generally nonspecific and overlap with many other clinical syndromes, including those of other BT agents. Because of the short incubation period, this agent is likely to lead to a sudden cluster of cases in a localized area. The toxin may be identified by ELISA of nasal swabs after aerosol exposure, or the antigen can be detected in the urine; however, neither of these tests is readily available.

PROPHYLAXIS AND TREATMENT

No vaccine against intoxication from SEB currently exists; however, a vaccine is under development and is being tested. Post-exposure treatment is supportive. Some patients may require IV hydration for fluid losses, and ventilatory support may be required in severe cases. The illness can last up to 2–4 weeks.

INFECTION CONTROL PRECAUTIONS

Because this is a toxin-mediated syndrome, there is no potential for person-to-person spread and no special containment equipment is required. Responders to contaminated areas should use an N95 respirator to prevent inhalation exposure to the toxin. Healthcare workers exposed to the toxin on skin or clothing require a simple change of clothes and shower with soap and water to provide adequate decontamination. Patient care requires the use of universal precautions but does not require any special equipment. Any food or disposable equipment contaminated with SEB should be discarded.

FOOD- AND WATER-BORNE AGENTS

Advances in sanitation and food sciences have given industrialized nations a safer food and water supply; however, the complicated systems involved in their processing offer multiple opportunities for human intervention and sources for contamination. In addition, disasters causing disruption of water and food delivery infrastructures may compromise their safety for human consumption. Contamination may occur with biologic, xenobiotic, or radiologic substances and may be intentional or inadvertent. Many of the major agents discussed elsewhere in this volume could potentially be spread via contaminated food or water. This chapter focuses on pathogens not discussed in other specific chapters.

HISTORICAL SIGNIFICANCE

In 1984 a religious cult contaminated salad bars in Oregon with *Salmonella typhimuriúm*. The intent was to disrupt voter turnout for a local election. More than 750 persons were afflicted by diarrhea, fevers, and dehydration. Epidemiologic investigation focused on a case-control study of restaurant patrons and found 751 clinical or cultureconfirmed cases. The restaurants, their banquet facilities, food products under preparation, employees, distributors and suppliers, the water supply, and restaurant equipment all were examined. A concurrent criminal investigation identified the cult's role in disseminating the pathogen. The *Salmonella* culture had been obtained from a commercial supplier and propagated in the cult's clandestine laboratory.

In January 2003 a disgruntled grocery worker tainted approximately 200 pounds of ground beef sold at a supermarket in Michigan. At least 92 patients had clinical presentations consistent with nicotine-containing pesticide intoxication. Epidemiology and lab studies confirmed that the food product had been contaminated at the level of the local grocery store, and not at a higher level in the food supply chain. Unintentional contamination with pesticides also has been reported.

In 1993 a malfunction at one of Milwaukee's water treatment plants caused an estimated 403,000 residents to be sickened with cryptosporidiosis. Investigators calculated that approximately 4400 were hospitalized and 69 died due to the disease during the outbreak. Economic losses due to healthcare costs and loss of productivity were estimated at greater than $96 million US.

PATHOGENESIS AND TRANSMISSION

Food-borne viral or bacterial disease typically causes a gastroenteritis-like syndrome. The onset of symptoms may be within hours if preformed toxins are present (e.g., *Staph* enterotoxin B and *Bacillus cereus*), hours to days if viral (e.g., Norwalk agent) or due to toxins formed within the alimentary tract by bacteria (e.g., enterotoxigenic *E. coli*), or days if caused by invasive bacteria (*Salmonella, Shigella, Campylobacter*, and *E. coli* spp.). Infection with *Salmonella typhi* may cause enteric fevers and generate a prolonged carrier state. Enteric bacteria and viruses also are spread silently among close contacts, food handlers, and caregivers, making their area of impact even broader.

CLINICAL PRESENTATION

Preformed bacterial toxins and viruses generally cause vomiting, crampy abdominal pain, and watery diarrhea that is self-limited. Care for these patients generally is supportive with maintenance of adequate hydration. Antiemetics offer symptomatic relief. Antiemetics with serotonin inhibition (e.g., ondansetron) may be used for persistent emesis in all age groups. Those antiemetics with dopamine antagonism (e.g., promethazine) should not be used in infants and young children due to the high incidence of side effects. Tetracycline, doxycycline, and fluoroquinolones also should not be used in children under age 18.

Some enteric bacteria invade the walls of the GI tract, causing bloody diarrhea and fevers. Systemic complications include dehydration, shock, hemorrhage, coagulopathy, sepsis, and renal failure (as in the case of HUS after *E. Coli* O157:H7 infection).

EVALUATION

Patients should be evaluated with standard laboratory evaluation, assessment of hydration status, and stool culture. Stool cultures often require special media and conditions for growth and identification. The local hospital, department of health, or reference lab should be consulted for specific transport and culture requirements. In addition, the local department of health should be contacted if a suspected food-borne incident has occurred so that epidemiologic investigations can be initiated if needed. Consider involvement of infectious disease consultants as well.

PREVENTION AND PRECAUTIONS FOR CAREGIVERS

Unless exposed to specific chemical agents, patients usually do not require decontamination prior to medical treatment. Strict hand-washing precautions should be adhered to in order to prevent spread of disease to others by rescuers, healthcare workers, or patients themselves. Security measures should be enforced surrounding watersheds, reservoirs, and water treatment plants to prevent intentional contamination of the water supply. Likewise, agricultural, auction, distribution, and food-processing facilities should be closely supervised. Quality control and environmental testing measures help to ensure safety of food and water for consumption.

TRICHOTHECENE MYCOTOXINS

Trichothecene mycotoxins are perhaps a more obscure cause of food-borne disease of some historical importance. Produced by fungus growing at low temperatures on grain, these toxins are extremely fastidious. Trichothecene mycotoxins may affect refugee populations or those involved in disasters that interrupt the normal harvesting and processing of cereal grains. They are thought to be responsible for the illness and death of thousands in Soviet Russia during and after World War II when wheat was unable to be harvested in a timely fashion. Their resistance to degradation makes them easy to weaponize. Refugees from Cambodia and Laos after the Vietnam War have reported "Yellow Rain," possibly dropped from low-flying aircraft, causing symptoms of trichothecene mycotoxin poisoning. It also has been suggested that these toxins have been used by both the Soviets in Afghanistan and by Iraq in its battles with Iran.

Trichothecene mycotoxins produce systemic toxicity and have irritant/vesicant properties. Research has found that trichothecenes inhibit DNA synthesis, protein synthesis, ribosome function, and mitochondrial protein synthesis. In addition, they produce single-strand DNA breaks and inhibit cellular thiol enzymes. The net result is multisystem toxicity, bone marrow suppression, and immune suppression, known as a "radiomimetic" syndrome. Trichothecenes are rapidly absorbed through abraded skin, inhalation, and the GI tract. The US Army has estimated the LD50 at 1.2 mg/kg by the oral route.

Dermal or ocular contact will cause irritation, blistering, and eye irritation, followed by systemic toxicity. Inhalation is accompanied by eye irritation, rhinorrhea, dysphagia, dyspnea, chest pain, and hemoptysis, followed by systemic symptoms that may lead to pulmonary edema and cardiovascular collapse. Oral ingestion causes mouth and throat irritation, vomiting and diarrhea, followed by GI bleeding and systemic toxicity. Chronic ingestion (e.g., in the case of contaminated grain) will cause alimentary toxic aleukia.

Poisoning with trichothecene mycotoxins is diagnosed based on environmental findings and the patient's clinical picture. It may be differentiated from mustard gas exposure by the presence of systemic symptoms and the absence of mustard gas agents on field testing. Exposure to ricin may be ruled out by the presence of skin irritation and blistering in the patient exposed to trichothecenes. Radiation levels will not be above background in environments contaminated with trichothecenes. Currently there is no field test for trichothecenes. Samples from grain or exposed surfaces may be sent to a reference lab for confirmatory testing (e.g., gas chromatography/ mass spectroscopy).

Trichothecenes and their metabolites may be detected in the serum and urine for up to 28 days after exposure. Clinical specimens should be sent to a reference lab for either antigen detection or GC/ MS techniques.

If the toxin has been ingested, activated charcoal should be administered. Treatment for those with trichothecene poisoning is supportive; there is no specific antidote.

Attention should be given to maintaining a patent airway, adequate respiratory effort and oxygenation, and hemodynamic status. Standard burn and wound care applies to skin wounds. Hematology/ oncology consultation should be obtained for those patients exhibiting signs of coagulopathy or bone marrow suppression. Antibiotic coverage should be considered for those patients with signs of sepsis or infection.

Rescuers should wear protective chemical suits as contact with contaminated skin or clothing leads to dermal irritation. Patients should be decontaminated with soap and water. Their clothing should be removed and confiscated. Surfaces and equipment need to be decontaminated in a solution of 1% sodium hypochlorite with 0.1 M sodium hydroxide for 1 hour of contact time. There are no special precautions for health care workers once decontamination is complete.

SUMMARY

Technology has provided us with both a safer, more nutritious food supply and purified water sources. Tampering or malfunction of these processes may alter their quality with the potential for widespread outbreak of food-borne or waterborne disease. Care of these patients should focus on hydration and antibiotic therapy in certain instances. Trichothecene mycotoxicoses may be of natural or artificial origin with a clinical presentation consistent with vesicant or radiation exposure. Treatment for these cases is supportive. Decontamination of equipment status post any food or waterborne outbreak requires special attention.

MELIOIDOSIS

Etiology

Melioidosis is on the Category B list of potential bioterrorism agents issued by the United States Centers for Disease Control and Prevention. It is a tropical disease caused by *Burkholderia pseudomallei*, a motile, aerobic, non-spore-forming Gram-negative bacterium found in soil and water. It is transmitted through direct contact of penetrating wounds or skin lesions with contaminated soil and water. Evidence for person- to-person transmission, inhalation of organisms, laboratory acquired infection, and vector transmission have also been documented. The clinical manifestations are widely varied, from asymptomatic to septicemia.

INCIDENCE AND PREVALENCE

Melioidosis is endemic in northern Australia and Southeast Asia. It is most common in Thailand, where the incidence is highest in rural areas and during the rainy season, and it is estimated that between two and five thousand cases of clinical melioidosis occur each year. However, the true incidence of the disease may be underestimated, as it is being more frequently recognized due to awareness and improvement in laboratory capabilities to isolate and identify the bacteria. In the United States confirmed cases are from travelers and immigrants and total 0–5 confirmed cases per year.

RISK FACTORS

Diabetes mellitus is the major risk factor for bacteremic melioidosis. Risk factors for non-bacteremic melioidosis include diabetes mellitus, occupational exposure, preexisting renal disease (most commonly renal calculi), alcoholism, and thalassemia. Diabetic rice farmers in endemic regions have a six to nine times higher risk for developing melioidosis than non-diabetics and non-rice farmers.

PATHOGENESIS/LIFE CYCLE

B. pseudomallei is not evenly distributed within the environment in endemic areas. Optimal environmental factors include: temperatures of 37–42EC, pH of 6.8, nitrite fertilizers, and absence of UV light. The organism is typically acquired by direct contact with soil or water, and the virulence of the strain, host immune status, and size of the inoculum play a role in whether exposure of the bacteria leads to disease.

The bacteria infect and survive inside several eukaryotic cell lines. After internalization, the bacteria escape from endocytotic vacuoles into the cytoplasm of the cell and induce actin polymerization at one pole, which forms membrane protrusions in order to spread from cell to cell. It also forms a capsule composed of hydrated glycocalyx polysaccharide, which facilitates formation of microcolonies, protecting the bacteria from antibiotics. *B. pseudomallei* is a difficult organism to kill because it is resistant to complement, lysosomal defensins, and cationic peptides, and it produces proteases, lipase, lecithinase, catalase, peroxidase, superoxide dismutase, and hemolysins.

The organism is found in the sputum, pus, urine, and feces of infected individuals, which contaminate their surroundings; however, the ability of *B. pseudomallei* to multiply once introduced into a new environment is unknown.

INCUBATION PERIOD/TIME OF ONSET

The incubation period for melioidosis can range from 2 days to many years. Infection often remains dormant in the immunocompetent individual, only to manifest itself when immunosuppression or a stressful physiological event occurs (burns/trauma).

PRESENTATION

Melioidosis has varied presentations: from no effect, asymptomatic seroconversions, and various clinically apparent infections. Acute localized infection occurs from inoculation through a break in the skin, is localized as a nodule, can produce fever and general muscle aches, and may rapidly progress to infect the bloodstream. Presentation of acute pulmonary infection may vary from mild bronchitis to severe pneumonia and is typically accompanied by a nonproductive cough or productive cough with normal sputum, high fever, headache, anorexia, and general malaise. It is not uncommon for the illness to be confused with tuberculosis. Acute bloodstream infection usually results in septic shock, is typically short in duration, abscesses are found throughout the body, and, depending on the original site of infection, can include respiratory distress, headache, fever, diarrhea, muscle tenderness, and disorientation. Chronic suppurative infection typically involves the joints, viscera, lymph nodes, skin, brain, liver, lung, bones, spleen, and parotid gland.

DIAGNOSIS/LABORATORY

Melioidosis should be suspected in any patient traveling from an endemic area who is severely ill and has a fever, especially patients with underlying predisposing conditions. The diagnosis is made by isolation of *B. pseudomallei* from blood, urine, sputum, throat, or skin cultures.

Cultures should be grown on routine blood agar or MacConkey's agar and Ashdown's selective medium for respiratory tract specimens. With Wright stain, *B. pseudomallei* demonstrates a bipolar safety pin appearance. Blood culture is the gold standard for diagnosis; however, this method of diagnosis comes with the disadvantage of being time consuming: the mean time to a result is 23.9 hours. Serological tests have the advantage of speed and can be helpful in areas where prevalence is low, but are not useful in endemic areas where the majority of the population is seropositive.

RADIOLOGY

Radiologic presentation is varied and nonspecific. With the acute form of the disease, multiple, small, irregular densities from 4 to 10 mm are the most common finding on chest radiograph. Segmental or lobar consolidation may be seen as the small nodules coalesce, and pleural effusions or empyemas may also be seen. In the subacute form of the disease, upper lobe infiltrates with cavitation are seen on chest radiograph and may be mistaken for tuberculosis. With the chronic form of melioidosis, infection is often extrapulmonary and osteomyelitis may be seen on plain films. Abdominal ultrasound should be done on all suspected cases as abscesses are often seen in the liver and spleen. Clinically hidden sites of infection may be found with radiolabeled white-cell scanning.

DIFFERENTIAL DIAGNOSIS

The differential diagnosis of melioidosis includes tuberculosis, malaria, typhoid fever, and leptospirosis.

TREATMENT

Treatment should begin with intravenous ceftazidime, imipenem, or the newer beta-lactam/beta-lactamase inhibitors. These treatments have a significantly better survival rate and less adverse effects compared with older conventional regimens of chloramphenicol, doxycycline, and cotrimoxazole. Parenteral treatment should be given for a minimum of ten days and should continue until the patient can take oral medication and has made a clear clinical improvement. Physicians who do not have much experience with treating this disease tend to switch antibiotic treatment prematurely because of the fear of resistance, although resistance occurs in less than 3% of patients. Intravenous therapy should be followed by a 20-week course of oral therapy. Conventional drugs used include a combination of chloramphenicol, doxycycline and trimethoprim-sulphamethoxazole. With this regimen, chloramphenicol is only given for the first 8 weeks. For pregnant women and children 8 years and younger amoxicillin- clavulanate is used.

PROGNOSIS

Prognosis depends on the manifestations of the disease and proper treatment. Mortality is high in the septicemic form of the disease, with a 40 to 90% mortality rate with disseminated septicemia and a 20% mortality rate with septicemia as well as single- organ involvement. Antibiotic treatment decreases mortality, but even after treatment relapse with high mortality rates is common.

PREVENTION

Prevention of melioidosis is difficult because in endemic areas contact with contaminated soil is common. People with skin lesions and risk factors such as diabetes should avoid contact with soil and standing water in endemic areas. Avoiding contact by wearing boots during agricultural work and by using blood and body fluid precautions in healthcare settings can help prevent transmission of the disease. There is no human vaccine for melioidosis.

NERVE AGENTS

Chemical weapons were first used on a large scale by Germany in World War I. The atrocities witnessed on the battlefield prompted a worldwide convention prohibiting the use of chemical weapons following World War I. Despite this sanction, dozens of countries have chosen to develop and deploy nerve agents, as they are relatively inexpensive to manufacture and raw materials are readily available. Nerve agents are derivatives of the organophosphate insecticides first synthesized in the 1930s. Although initially intended to be more potent insecticides, German scientists quickly recognized the compounds as potential weapons. Weaponized organophosphates are known by common chemical names and two letter designations. The German agents are given a designation of "G" followed by a letter, which denotes their order of discovery. During the Second World War, Nazi Germany manufactured and stockpiled thousands of tons of the agents Tabun (GA) and Sarin (GB). Although the weapons were never used, the Germans continued to develop more lethal agents such as Soman (GD), which was only made in small quantities. Seizing upon this work, British and American scientists continued to refine nerve agents as weapons through the 1950s, resulting in the Viper series of nerve agents, the most common of which is VX. Although little is known about their manufacture, it is thought that the former Soviet Union had produced large quantities of even newer agents.

The first documented use of nerve agents in combat was not until the Iran–Iraq war of the 1980s, when Iraq used combinations of nerve and blister agents against Iranian troops. It is also thought that the Soviets may have used nerve agents in a limited fashion in Afghanistan, while the Serbs allegedly employed them in Bosnia. Most recently, nerve agents have been considered a potential threat from terrorists and other extremist groups, as they are relatively inexpensive and require only rudimentary scientific expertise to produce.

More importantly, many of the precursors necessary for their production can be purchased from reputable sources such as chemical and agricultural companies. In 1994 and 1995 the Aum Shinrikyo cult in Japan exploited these circumstances, producing small quantities of liquid containing Sarin (GB). Members then released the liquid in an apartment complex and later into crowded subway terminals, killing 19 and injuring over 1300. Despite these relatively small events, the cult members were able to cause significant disruption and strike fear into hearts of millions of Japanese citizens.

PHARMACOLOGY OF CHOLINESTERASE INHIBITORS

Nerve agents exert their biological effects by inhibiting acetylcholinesterase. Acetylcholinesterase rapidly hydrolyzes the acetylcholine ester that acts at the postsynaptic neural junction to cause a nerve transmission. Inhibition of acetylcholinesterase leads to acetylcholine acting unopposed. The unopposed action of acetylcholine causes continual stimulation of skeletal muscles at the neuromuscular junction, which may result in a flaccid paralysis.

Excessive acetylcholine levels in the parasympathetic nervous system causes hyperactivity of gastrointestinal motility and glandular secretion. Acetylcholinesterase is also found on erythrocytes (erythrocyte or true acetylcholinesterase) and in the serum as butyrocholinesterase (pseudocholinesterase).

When a patient is exposed to nerve agents, the level of acetylcholinesterase is decreased and this can be used as an indicator of severity of exposure.

PRESENTATION

Exposure to nerve agents evokes myriad symptoms, which vary with dose and type of exposure. The agents are not gases, but liquids at room temperature, and can be inhaled as a vapor or absorbed through the skin and mucous membranes. Onset of symptoms varies from seconds, when large quantities of vapor are inhaled, to hours, when small amounts of liquid are absorbed through the skin. Absorption through the skin also varies with the ambient temperature and vascularity of the exposed surface. Following a vapor release, asymptomatic patients can be released from the emergency department immediately, while those with the potential for liquid contamination may require an observation period.

CLINICAL PRESENTATION

Low doses of nerve agent may cause nonfatal poisoning, which can present as increased production of saliva, rhinorrhea, and a feeling of pressure on the chest. The pupil becomes contracted (miosis), and accommodation is reduced so that short-range vision deteriorates. Higher doses cause the symptoms described above plus bronchoconstriction and secretion of mucus in the respiratory system with breathing difficulty. GI cramping and vomiting occur. Muscular weakness, twitching, and convulsions occur due to the effect on the neuromuscular junction by excess acetylcholine. If the dose is high, muscle paralysis occurs. Death is by suffocation due to paralysis of the muscles of respiration.

DIAGNOSIS

The diagnosis of nerve agent exposure is largely based on the history of exposure and clinical findings. It is most important that physicians obtain historical information regarding exposure to unknown substances, insecticides, or unusual odors (most nerve agents smell like fruity camphor). The history of the event also provides important information about the type of exposure. The ideal method for assessing nerve agent intoxication is to assay tissue cholinesterase levels. As this is not possible, plasma and erythrocyte cholinesterase levels can be used as surrogates. Erythrocyte cholinesterase (RBC-ChE) activity can be assessed in some hospital laboratories and is the best means for diagnosis. Inhibition of 50–90% of the enzyme activity is indicative of significant intoxication. This test is limited, however, by its availability, turnaround time, and variations in individual levels of cholinesterase.

DIFFERENTIAL DIAGNOSIS

The symptoms associated with nerve agent intoxication may be the result of other organophosphate compounds such as the carbamate insecticides. Cholinergic crisis can be the result of a variety of medication overdoses, including neostigmine, physostigmine, pyridostigmine bromide, PCP, phenothiazines, clonidine, and muscarinic mushrooms. In addition, CNS symptoms may be mimicked by stroke, seizure, or other neuromuscular disorders. Such clinical findings as rhinorrhea, lacrimation, and bronchospasm may also be present with exposure to riot-control agents.

TREATMENT

Nerve agents have a rapid effect, so that treatment must be immediate. The action of excess acetylcholine at the muscarinic receptor level can be reversed by atropine, which occupies the muscarinic sites and blocks the action of acetylcholine. However, atropine will not have any action at the nicotinic receptors such as the neuromuscular junction. Atropine will improve the effects of excessive parasympathetic stimulation (GI hyperactivity, bronchospasm, excessive glandular secretion and rhinorrhea) but will not reverse the flaccid paralysis seen with toxic doses of nerve agent. Assisted ventilation will be required for patients having such severe muscular weakness that they cannot oxygenate themselves.

Pralidoxime chloride (2-PAM) is the mostly widely available drug that can reactivate the organophosphate inhibited cholinesterases by removing the organophosphoryl moiety. Although the nerve agent initially binds reversibly to acetylcholinesterase, the binding becomes irreversible within a few minutes to several hours depending on the agent.

Once "aging" has occurred, displacement of the nerve agent with drugs such as 2-PAM will not occur. Armed forces operating in potential chemical warfare environments carry Mark I autoinjectors (containing pralidoxime chloride (500 mg) and atropine (2 mg), which can be immediately used if a nerve agent is encountered). Medical treatment depends upon the severity of the nerve agent exposure. This is gauged by the patient's symptoms as outlined below and in Table 1.

Minimal Exposure

Symptoms. With mild exposure the patient may have miosis, headache, rhinorrhea, and salivation, and complain of tightness in the chest.

Treatment. These patients may be managed by removing them from the source of exposure and that may require removal of their clothes. During the subway Sarin attack in Tokyo, patients' clothing continued to "off gas," which resulted in continued exposure of patients plus exposure to medical personnel. Most patients with mild exposure will not require treatment. If eye pain is severe, topical atropine or homatropine can be administered in the eye.

Moderate Exposure

Symptoms. These patients will exhibit all of the signs and symptoms seen with mild exposure plus increased breathing difficulty, muscular fasciculations, and severe rhinorrhea. The rhinorrhea in these patients may be so severe as to fill their gas mask if they are wearing one.

Treatment. These patients usually require atropine and pralidoxime IV or IM. The atropine and pralidoxime are dosed to clinical effect with a maximum of 1500 mg of pralidoxime being used, and the atropine dosing is administered until the patient's secretions are controlled. This will usually require 2 to 6 mg of atropine. If they were exposed to vapor, decontamination can usually be accomplished by removal of clothes. If they were exposed to liquid agent, they will require full liquid decontamination.

Severe Exposure

Symptoms. These patients will exhibit all of the signs listed above plus profound rhinorrhea, severe respiratory difficulty/arrest, flaccid paralysis, and convulsions.

Treatment. Aggressive airway management, including intubation may be warranted. Immediate antidotal therapy should be initiated using 4–6 mg atropine, 1–2 g pralidoxime, and 10 mg diazepam. Supportive ventilatory therapy may need to be maintained for a period of hours after administration of antidotal therapy. This group of patients will require full liquid decontamination.

PROGNOSIS

The prognosis of untreated nerve agent casualties varies with the severity of their exposure. However, those with severe exposures will die from respiratory arrest secondary to airway obstruction and diaphragmatic paralysis within minutes. Conversely, even patients in cardiopulmonary arrest should be treated if resources permit, because they can survive with adequate antidotal and supportive therapy. Patients with less severe exposures may survive delayed treatment but many have noted enduring neurological sequelae.

PREVENTION

The most effective prevention for nerve agent casualties occurs before the event. Few emergency responders have the proper training and equipment to deal with such a crisis. As a result, the best way of preventing casualties is to enforce bans on their manufacture and use and provide adequate intelligence and surveillance to prevent their use by rogue organizations. Other means of prevention include personal protective equipment, patient decontamination, and chemoprophylaxis. Current means of personal protection revolve around the use of protective suits and respiratory equipment. Both are necessary because of the potential hazards associated with inhalation of the vapor and skin absorption of the liquid. The minimum level of protection is level "C" PPE; surgical masks and latex exam gloves are inadequate, as demonstrated in the 1995 Tokyo Subway attack.

Chemoprophylaxis against nerve agents consists of administering reversible cholinesterase inhibitors prior to exposure to prevent binding of the irreversible inhibitors (nerve agents). This is particularly useful if the nerve agent threat is Soman (GD) or another rapidly aging agent. Chemoprophylaxis is fraught with complications, as it must be administered over a period of several hours prior to the exposure with the nerve agent and is not useful against agents with long aging times such as VX and Tabun (GA).

Physostigmine and pyridostigmine bromide were both studied for their potential use as nerve agent chemoprophylaxis, but pyridostigmine is the agent of choice as it has fewer side effects. Chemoprophylaxis is of very limited utility given its side effects, its indication only for a limited number of agents, and the need to administer it prior to exposure.

SPECIAL CONSIDERATIONS

For any suspected nerve agent intoxication, an act of terrorism must be ruled out. It is imperative that precautions to prevent contamination of the facility and staff be undertaken as soon as possible. The appropriate emergency management and law enforcement officials should be alerted immediately. Once measures to protect the staff and treat the patient are undertaken, every effort should be made to facilitate public health personnel in the investigation and containment of the event. It is worth noting that the first patients are likely to present to the nearest emergency rooms within minutes, prior to any alert of the medical community. This quickly leads to the nearest facility being overwhelmed despite efforts to evenly distribute patients.

VESICANTS

Sulfur mustard, more commonly known as "Mustard Gas," and Lewisite are the two major vesicant gases of concern today. Sulfur mustard was used extensively during World War I, and was the chemical weapon that caused the greatest number of casualties in that conflict. Lewisite was synthesized by the United States for use in the European theater in World War I, but the war ended before it was deployed.

Physical Characteristics

Sulfur mustard (military chemical weapon designation: HD) and Lewisite (military chemical weapon designation: L) are formulated alone or in combination with other agents to be liquids over a large range of temperatures. Although they are liquids, they rapidly evaporate due to their high vapor pressure; the resultant gases are denser than air, and thus persist near the ground after release rather than dissipating into the atmosphere. This greatly increases the likelihood that they poison their intended targets.

Mechanism of Action

Vesicant agents appear to react with the DNA of epithelial cells to form chemical complexes that activate cellular repair machinery. The resultant biochemical activity and inflammatory process promotes an exudation of fluid into the subepidermal space; this fluid then forms the characteristic blisters seen with these agents. In addition to acting as a vesicant, Lewisite may also release large amounts of arsenic when it reacts with epithelial cells, leading to systemic arsenic toxicity as well.

Presentation

Patients who have been exposed to vesicant gases may present with complaints referable to multiple symptoms, depending on which part(s) of the epithelium is involved:

Dermal toxicity. This is the hallmark of vesicant agent poisoning. Skin blisters tend to be large and painful. Patients exposed to Lewisite tend to develop blisters quickly (on the order of minutes), whereas those exposed to sulfur mustard tend to develop symptoms more slowly (over several hours). Patients exposed to massive doses of sulfur mustard, however, may develop symptoms much more quickly.

Pulmonary toxicity. Coughing, hypoxia, and airway obstruction may all be seen in vesicant gas poisoning due to the sloughing of respiratory epithelial cells.

Ocular toxicity. Ocular irritation of both the conjunctiva and cornea may occur, leading to temporary or permanent visual impairment.

DIAGNOSIS

There are no laboratory tests to assist in the diagnosis of vesicant gas poisoning. In general, a chemical weapons attack should be considered when several, several hundred, or several thousand previously healthy people, who have nothing in common but geographic proximity at a given time, present with similar symptoms. When these symptoms are dominated by dermal, pulmonary, and/or ocular complaints, special consideration should be given to vesicant gas poisoning. Other scene clues may assist in the diagnosis of vesicant gas poisoning. The presence of a yellow gas suggests sulfur mustard. Sulfur mustard is reported to have an odor of mushroom or onions, and Lewisite an odor of geraniums; a report of either of these smells may also help make the diagnosis.

DIFFERENTIAL DIAGNOSIS

Although the classic presentation of dermal, pulmonary and

ocular toxicity strongly suggests vesicant gas poisoning, several other diagnoses should be entertained when patients present with these complaints:

Irritant gases. Irritant gases such as phosgene, diphosgene, and chlorine may produce both ocular and pulmonary toxicity. These agents do not produce dermal toxicity, however.

Nerve agents. Nerve agents may produce pulmonary symptoms and airway obstruction due to increased secretions. Ocular toxicity and dermal toxicity are not expected with this poisoning, however.

Burns. Thermal injury may produce blisters that appear similar to those produced by vesicant gases. The location of the blisters differs, however; thermal burns generally occur on unprotected areas, whereas vesicant gas-induced blisters tend to occur on moist areas of the body (e.g., under the arms), even when these areas are protected by clothing.

TREATMENT

Treatment of a patient who is the victim of vesicant gas poisoning begins with removal of the patient to a safe area. Then next step consists of securing the airway, breathing, and circulation. If the patient is demonstrating apnea, or respiratory failure is imminent, or the patient cannot protect the airway, endotracheal intubation is warranted. Oxygen should be administered to all critically ill patients, especially when there is a suspected or documented hypoxia. Intravenous crystalloid should be administered to patients with hypotension or clinical evidence of hypovolemia. Decontamination should be performed by trained personnel as soon as possible.

Dilute household bleach may be used to decontaminate the skin and hair, but not the eyes. Tap water is appropriate for ocular decontamination, but may be used for skin and hair decontamination if household bleach is not available.

After aggressive skin and hair decontamination, povidone-iodine should be applied to the skin, as this agent has been shown to reduce dermal damage when applied soon after a vesicant agent poisoning. Pulmonary toxicity is treated with standard supportive measures, including treatment for acute lung injury (ALI) or the acute respiratory distress syndrome (ARDS) should they occur.

Treatment of such patients may challenge even the most competent of physicians. Assistance in the diagnosis and management of patients poisoned by vesicant agents, as well as any other toxins, may be obtained by dialing the local Poison Control Center. In the United States, the closest Poison Control Center can be reached by dialing 1-800-222-1222 from any phone.

PROGNOSIS

The prognosis for patients with vesicant gas poisoning is variable, and depends in large part on the dose absorbed and the availability of prompt, effective medical care. Minor exposures may cause irritation but no lasting effects; severe exposures, especially in circumstances in which access to medical care is limited, may easily result in death.

PREVENTION

Prevention of vesicant gas poisoning lies first and foremost with prevention of a vesicant gas attack. Federal, state, and local government agencies, and in particular the US Department of Homeland Security, are actively working to assure that such attacks do not happen on United States soil. Pretreatment with topical agents known as highly reactive nanoparticles may limit the toxicity of sulfur mustard. Such agents are currently experimental. Although initial results are encouraging on a scientific level, it is unlikely that pretreatment would be effective in a practical sense, as one would need to know that an attack was going to occur for pretreatment to be effective.

SPECIAL CONSIDERATIONS

Chemical weapons attacks, such as vesicant gas attacks, may generate thousands of patients in a short period of time, rapidly overwhelming even the most prepared of emergency response systems. When such an attack is suspected, the hospital disaster plan should be activated, and local, state, and federal authorities should be immediately notified. One way to be certain that these disparate groups are notified in a timely fashion is to involve the local Poison Control Center early in the event; the center can then help with issues of diagnosis and management, as well as passing information along to the relevant agencies.

Vesicant agents were commonly used during World War I, and produced hundreds of thousands of casualties. Although used infrequently since that time, vesicant agents are established Weapons of Mass Destruction (WMDs), and therefore a potential tool for terrorists everywhere. Clinicians should understand the chemistry, presentation, diagnosis, differential diagnosis, and treatment in the event of vesicant gas attacks in order to be adequately prepared.

PULMONARY AGENTS

Pulmonary agents were originally developed for use as chemical warfare agents in World War I. They currently are employed primarily in industrial applications either as substrates, products, or byproducts. Due to their ease of synthesis, however, their diversion to use as weapons of mass destruction (WMDs) is a very real possibility. This chapter discusses chlorine, phosgene, and nitrogen dioxide (NO2). Generally, highly soluble gases (i.e., ammonia) produce upper respiratory tract (e.g., eyes, nose, and throat) disease since they are readily absorbed, while less-soluble gases (phosgene and nitrogen dioxide) penetrate deeper with subsequent lower respiratory tract pathology. The reader should refer to specific chapters regarding other gases.

CHLORINE (CL2)

Pathogenesis

This irritant gas is heavier than air and intermediately soluble in water, explaining its action as both an upper- and lower-airway irritant with delayed onset of lowerairway symptoms after exposure. Chlorine gas is readily available from several occupational sources, including building maintenance workers as well as public swimming and water purification plants. Chlorine may be formed from inadvertent mixing of an acid with household bleach (sodium hypochlorite). When inhaled, chlorine reacts with pulmonary water to form hydrochloric acid (HCl) and hypochlorous acid (HOCl) plus nascent oxygen (O–). This combination leads to diffuse pulmonary inflammation, necrosis, acute lung injury, and oxidant injury.

Clinical Presentation

Patients characteristically present with mild eye irritation initially, followed by the onset of respiratory symptoms several hours after exposure. Due to the delayed onset of pulmonary symptoms, patients may have had a prolonged period of breathing chlorine gas at moderate concentrations.

Irritation of the lower airways will cause cough, dyspnea, and a sensation of chest tightness. Acute lung injury results from inflammation and noncardiogenic pulmonary edema, and is characterized by dyspnea and hypoxia; wheezing or rales may be noted on physical exam. Cough, chest pain, and frothy sputum also can be present.

Diagnostics

Chest radiographs may demonstrate bilateral alveolar infiltrates with a normal cardiac silhouette, differentiating it from congestive heart failure. Tachycardia and hypoxia can be detected with pulse oximetry. Hypoxia and metabolic acidosis may be seen on blood gas analysis.

Differential Diagnosis

Considerations in the differential diagnosis of chlorine exposure include other pulmonary irritants such as phosgene, asthma/reactive airway disease (RAD), and other causes of acute lung injury (ALI)/ adult respiratory distress syndrome.

Treatment

Chlorine exposure is treated with supportive care with an emphasis on optimizing oxygen delivery. Care should be taken to ensure a patent airway, even if endotracheal intubation is required. Aerosolized bronchodilators may be required. There are insufficient data to support using parenteral steroids at this point. Treatment with aerosolized bicarbonate is controversial and has not been demonstrated to improve survival, but may provide symptomatic relief to those with mild symptoms. Skin burns are treated as thermal burns, with decontamination, wound care, and pain control. Eyes should be irrigated until a pH of 7.4 is reached and examined for signs of corneal abrasion as well as foreign particulate matter.

Prevention and Protection for Caregivers

A self-contained breathing apparatus (SCBA) may be required for rescuers at the scene.

Special Considerations

Pediatric patients are at greater risk for severe toxicity when compared to adults due to their higher minute volume per kilogram of weight as well as their short stature; these physical attributes expose them to higher concentrations of chlorine. Children more commonly develop stridor than adults due to their smaller airway size, and treatment with aerosolized racemic epinephrine should be provided if this is the case. Patients with signs of mild toxicity should be observed for up to 24 hours for the development of delayed-onset pulmonary edema. Pulmonary symptoms should resolve over the course of a month; however, a prolonged RADS-like syndrome may be present.

PHOSGENE (COCL2)

Phosgene is another of the original chemical agents used in WWI, used under the designation CG. Its use currently is limited to industrial applications where organic compounds such as isocyanates are produced; it is formed from the combustion of organochlorine compounds and may be present at fire scenes, particularly in the industrial setting. It is best known for its odor of "freshly mown hay" and such an agreeable fragrance may not prompt exposed individuals to evacuate. As it is heavier than air, phosgene can cause asphyxiation if victims are found in low-lying areas. Children are more vulnerable to its toxic effects for the reasons described above.

Pathogenesis

Phosgene undergoes slow hydrolysis in the distal portions of the lungs to produce hydrochloric acid, crosslinking of cellular structures, and reactive oxygen species.

Clinical Presentation

Delayed onset (up to 24 hours) of acute lung injury is the chief manifestation of toxicity, although battlefield exposures have been reported to have onset of symptoms within 2–6 hours. As in the case of chlorine, pulmonary edema is noncardiogenic. Systemic illness and death occur because of hypoxia. Long-term effects of phosgene exposure include pulmonary scarring, emphysema, and airway reactivity.

Treatment

Treatment again consists of airway support and oxygenation. Positive pressure may be warranted. Bronchodilators should be administered if the patients exhibit any signs of respiratory distress. Patients with known exposure should be observed for a prolonged period (i.e., up to 48 hours) due to the risk of delayed-onset ALI.

Prevention and Protection for Caregivers

Rescuers should use positive pressure demand SCBA. Phosgene may cause skin burns, so chemical suits are required (Responder, Tychem 10000, or Teflon brands). If liquid phosgene is involved, then the victims' clothing should be removed and double bagged to prevent off gassing.

NITROGEN DIOXIDE (NO_2)

Nitrogen dioxide is a pulmonary irritant that is primarily associated with lowlevel environmental exposures but of interest to disaster medical personnel because it is created by high-temperature combustion (as in an explosion) and decay of silage (causing silo-filler's disease).

At room temperature, NO_2 forms a clear to brown colored liquid. Above its boiling point (21EC), it is a reddish-brown, pungent gas. Heavier than air, nitrogen dioxide may act as a suffocant to those close to the ground and may cause more severe toxicity in children. It is likely that NO2 will be found in mixture with other oxides of nitrogen (e.g., NO and N_2O_4) and with products of combustion (e.g., sulfur oxides, carbon monoxide, carbon dioxide, and cyanide).

Pathogenesis

Nitrogen dioxide is poorly water soluble and creates nitrous and nitric acids after contact with pulmonary water. In addition to direct corrosive effects, lung damage occurs due to the formation of reactive oxygen species and impairment of normal immune responses.

Clinical Presentation

Those exposed initially complain of mild eye and upper-airway irritation, followed by shortness of breath, cough, and chest pain. Wheezing and noncardiogenic pulmonary edema are the result. Symptoms may be delayed in onset up to 48 hours. Late effects include bronchiolitis obliterans and reactive airways disease syndrome (RADS). Exposure to admixed gases will cause methemoglobinemia, carboxyhemoglobinemia, and metabolic acidosis.

Diagnosis and Evaluation

There are no specific tests necessary for those with nitrogen dioxide exposure; however, obtaining an accurate history is paramount and the clinician should rule out other causes of shortness of breath and/or hypoxia with chest x-ray, ABG, co-oximetry, a methemoglobin level, and routine labs.

Treatment

Treatment is supportive with emphasis on stabilizing an airway and oxygenation. Bronchodilators may be used for patients with wheezing. Oxygen should be administered to any hypoxic patient. Patients should be observed for 48 hours because of the potential for delayed onset of pulmonary edema. Corticosteroids may be of benefit in reducing inflammation and preventing bronchiolitis obliterans.

Skin or eye irritation is treated by having affected areas irrigated copiously with water for at least 20 minutes. Methylene blue may be required for methemoglobinemia. Hyperbaric oxygen therapy should be considered for those with carbon monoxide poisoning. After discharge, patients should be reexamined within 1 month and again at 3 months for progression to BO; pulmonary consultation may be required. Bronchiolitis obliterans is characterized by persistent cough, fever, malaise and shortness of breath after the initial insult has resolved.

Prevention and Protection for Caregivers

Rescuers should wear SCBA and chemical-protective suits. Those individuals exposed to liquid or gaseous nitrogen dioxide should be decontaminated in showers to remove any residue on skin and hair. Clothing should be double bagged and discarded in an appropriate manner, since off-gassing of any liquid NO2 present poses a risk to healthcare personnel. Exposed or irritated eyes should be irrigated with plain water for at least 20 minutes.

Exposure to irritant gases usually causes pulmonary symptoms and disease from generation of reactive species. Patients with known or suspected exposure should be observed for >24–48 hours for the development of noncardiogenic pulmonary edema. Treatment in general is supportive with emphasis on improving bronchial airflow and optimizing oxygenation. Corticosteroids may be beneficial for prevention of bronchiolitis obliterans in those exposed to nitrogen dioxide.

CYANIDES

Cyanide is often perceived as the archetypal poison, with accidental and intentional ingestions since ancient times. It is associated with the Jonestown mass-murder suicides and the Tylenol poisonings in Chicago in 1982. It was used as a military weapon in World War I and in the Nazi gas chambers during World War II. More recently cyanide-based weapons have been used during wars in the Middle East. In the last ten years, cyanide has been used by terrorists in Tokyo subways and by al Qaeda.

Sources of Exposure

Exogenous sources of cyanide include food exposures (bitter almonds, cassava, various fruit seeds/pits), medicines (Laetrile, nitroprusside), and industrial exposures (e.g., electroplating, mining, plastic manufacturing, fumigation). Smoke inhalation in building fires produces cyanide secondary to combustion of natural (e.g., wool, silk) and synthetic (e.g., polyurethane, plastic) materials. Tobacco smoke is also a source of cyanide. As military and terrorist weapons, the compounds of interest are volatile liquid hydrogen cyanide and cyanogen chloride.

Incidence and Prevalence

The incidence of cyanide toxicity is not well known. Only rarely are fatal exposures reported to the Poison Control Centers. Cyanide toxicity may be important in the approximately 10,000 deaths per year from smoke inhalation.

Pathophysiology

Liquid or gaseous hydrogen cyanide and alkali salts of cyanide are rapidly absorbed through inhalation, ingestion, or absorption through the eyes and skin. Toxicity results from prevention of oxygen uptake at the cellular level. By inhibiting cytochrome oxidase, aerobic metabolism cannot occur. Organs with high-energy requirement such as the brain and the heart are most affected. Increased anaerobic metabolism leads to rapid accumulation of lactic acid and a resultant metabolic acidosis.

PRESENTATION

Time of Onset

The onset of symptoms varies based on the chemical form, the concentration or dose, and the route of exposure. Symptoms develop within seconds of inhalation of high concentrations of hydrogen cyanide, and death can occur within minutes. Cyanide salts are potent poisons and symptoms occur within minutes, and death within hours.

Signs and Symptoms

The earliest symptoms of cyanide toxicity are related to central nervous system stimulation. Headache, confusion, dizziness, and anxiety are accompanied by tachypnea, secondary to primary stimulation of the respiratory center. The earliest cardiovascular effect is tachycardia. Nausea and vomiting may occur.

Significant exposures quickly progress to stridorous breathing and CNS-based respiratory depression with hypoventilation and apnea. Bradycardia, heart block, dysrhythmias, and hypotension are late cardiovascular findings that often precede complete cardiovascular collapse. Final CNS manifestations include seizure, opisthotonos, fixed and dilated pupils, stupor, coma, and death.

DIAGNOSIS

The diagnosis of cyanide toxicity is challenging because of a lack of pathognomonic signs. The clinical toxidrome of bright red venous blood, profound metabolic acidosis, and bitter almond breath is only rarely present. Blood cyanide levels are useful in confirming toxicity; however, acute management should begin before laboratory confirmation is available.

Laboratory

Cyanide levels can be measured directly. Normal plasma cyanide levels are <0.004 :g/ml, but may be higher in smokers. Whole blood levels are higher because cyanide concentrates in red blood cells. Levels correlate with degree of symptoms. Rapid tests have been developed, including a paper test that has been shown to detect levels over 0.5 mg/liter, and a rapid whole blood assay which may become more available in the future. Surrogate tests that may suggest cyanide toxicity in an appropriate clinical context include lactate levels >10 mmol/L and a refractory anion gap acidosis. Little difference may exist between simultaneous arterial and venous pO2 (arterialization of venous blood) secondary to decreased peripheral oxygen extraction.

Pathology

There are no specific pathologic changes that characterize cyanide toxicity. Evidence of tissue hypoxia may be seen, most notably CNS changes including necrosis and demyelination.

Radiological

There are no pathognomonic changes on radiography. Pulmonary edema may occur with significant exposures.

Other

ECG changes are nonspecific. Tachycardia and nonspecific ST-T changes reflect myocardial cellular hypoxia, and may be pronounced in those with underlying cardiovascular disease. AV block, bradycardia, and nodal or idioventricular rhythms occur with progressive cellular hypoxia.

DIFFERENTIAL DIAGNOSIS

Symptoms of cyanide toxicity are nonspecific so the differential diagnosis is broad and dependent on clinical context. With inhalation exposures, carbon monoxide and hydrogen sulfide gas impair oxygen delivery much like cyanide. The differential for anion gap acidosis is best known by the mnemonic MUDPILES (methanol, uremia, DKA, paraldehyde, INH, lactate, ethanol, salicylates).

TREATMENT

Rapid treatment of cyanide poisoning is essential for survival. Initial supportive measures should include 100% oxygen by face mask or endotracheal intubation, intravenous fluid resuscitation with addition of sodium bicarbonate for pH <7.15, and cardiac monitoring. Mouth-to-mouth resuscitation should be avoided. Hyperbaric oxygenation has been suggested but has not been proven to be effective. Gastric lavage and/or activated charcoal are indicated for ingestions within 1 hour of presentation. Hemodialysis and hemoperfusion are ineffective, except with high levels of thiocyanate, which is dialyzable. Cyanide antidote kits in the United States are composed of amyl nitrite, sodium nitrite and sodium thiosulfate. Additional agents are currently being used in parts of Europe.

PROGNOSIS

Early recognition and treatment of cyanide toxicity usually leads to a favorable outcome; however, cases are frequently not identified as cyanide toxicity until too late. There is limited data to suggest neurological morbidity—including hyperreflexia, dystonia, cognitive deficits, and parkinsonism—may occur in those surviving exposure.

PREVENTION

Removal from continued exposure is the key to preventing toxicity. Evacuation with gaseous exposures and topical decontamination for liquid exposures by removal of clothing and copious skin washing are paramount.

NUCLEAR DETONATION/IONIZING RADIATION EXPOSURE

Recent terrorist threats have placed the potential use of a "dirty bomb" on center stage. "Dirty bombs" disperse radioactive particles through the use of conventional explosives. The low-level radiation contained in the particles that are used to create such a bomb make the conventional explosives the primary danger. Success in treating the victims of a "dirty bomb" attack depend upon: proper planning, identification of potential exposure, prevention of further contamination, implementation of the basic resuscitation principle, and identification of Acute Radiation Syndrome (ARS), which is unlikely in the case of such an attack.

Many countries, some designated as terrorist states, have or are in the process of developing traditional nuclear weapons technology.

The four types of radiation that can cause injury include alpha, beta, gamma, and neutron. Alpha particles cause no significant threat by external exposure but if taken internally can cause local injury. Beta particles are known to cause skin and eye injury with external contamination and similar damage as alpha particles when internalized.

The radiation from gamma and neutron particles penetrates significantly and can cause severe whole-body exposure. High-dose exposure to radiation can lead to ARS, which causes injury to the following organ systems: hematopoietic, gastrointestinal, and central nervous system. Molecular changes within the cells that are exposed to long-term ionizing radiation can lead to the development of cancers over time.

PATHOGENESIS

Types of Radiation Injury

Irradiation. The patient is exposed to penetrating radiation from an external source that is not deposited on the body's surface. Exposure stops when the patient leaves the area of radioactive contamination. The patient is not contaminated and poses no risk to others.

External Contamination. The patient is exposed to radiation when radioactive material is deposited on the body's surface. The patient poses a risk to others and must be decontaminated.

Internal Contamination. The patient is exposed to radiation when radioactive material is incorporated into the body through ingestion, inhalation, or absorption through intact or wounded skin. The patient exposure continues until the material is expelled from the body.

The patient poses a risk to others and must be externally decontaminated. Definitive treatment is specific to each radioactive material.

Prevention of Further Contamination

- Determine the source of exposure to see if irradiation or contamination has occurred. Unless the sealed container of a radioactive source is intact, assume that contamination has occurred.
- Once notified that potentially exposed patients are en route to your facility, activate your hospital emergency response plan. This often includes contacting hospital resources such as: a Radiation Safety Officer, Nuclear Medicine, Radiation Oncology, or Radiology.
- Prepare a triage site outside of the hospital near an entrance.
- Designate areas of treatment for contaminated and non-contaminated patients, separated by a buffer zone.
- If possible use separate entrances for contaminated and non-contaminated patients.
- Remove all unnecessary equipment from the contaminated treatment area and cover necessary equipment and flooring with well-secured plastic.
- Obtain baseline radiation levels of the treatment area with a radiation detection device, such as a Geiger counter.
- Although radioactive exposure from patients in the hospital is minimal, healthcare workers should utilize personal protective devices including gowns, face masks, eye protection, shoe covers, and two layers of gloves. The inner glove should be taped securely at the wrist and the outer

glove should be changed between patients and frequently during the treatment of a patient to avoid recontamination.

- All staff should wear personal dosimeters.
- Patient clothing should be removed by EMS at the scene or staff prior to entering the treatment area.
- Patients should be wrapped in a clean sheet prior to all transports.
- If radioactive exposure is recognized during the treatment of a patient already in the emergency department, designate the area as the contaminated treatment area.

Presentation

ARS is caused by irradiation to all or most of the patient's body by a high dose of penetrating radiation in a short period of time (see Table 1, on acute radiation syndromes). Patients may present at any point of the syndrome. Cutaneous or local radiation syndrome presents like a thermal burn and should be treated as such. If an explosion has occurred, patients may present with blunt or penetrating trauma, thermal burns, or blindness from the flash. Significant psychological stress may be encountered, especially following a terrorist attack.

DIAGNOSIS

Obtain a history of symptoms, occupation, recent or past treatment with radiation or nuclear medicine, and if others have similar symptoms. Maintain a high index of suspicion in patients at risk who present with nausea, vomiting, and leukopenia. Contamination may be detected with a radiation detection device, such as a Geiger counter.

DIFFERENTIAL DIAGNOSIS

- Acute radiation syndrome
- Radiation Therapy-Induced Immunosuppression
- Chemotherapeutic-induced immunosuppression

TREATMENT

Initial triage and treatment is to address immediate life-threatening conditions using basic the resuscitation principle. Remember, in the case of a "dirty bomb" traumatic injuries from the blast are the most life-threatening and the radioactive contamination does not pose an immediate threat.

Once the patient is medically stable, decontamination can commence.

Decontamination

- Outer clothing and shoes should have been removed prior to arrival. This can reduce contamination by 90%. Anything removed from the patient (clothing, shoes, hair, blood, urine, stool, etc.) should be double-bagged in plastic and given to the Radiation Safety Officer.
- Irrigate open wounds first with saline or water, then cover with a waterproof dressing to avoid further contamination.
- A water pick or core biopsy technique can be used for puncture wounds.
- Proceed with decontamination of the remainder of the skin, starting with the most contaminated areas. Gently wash with soap and water so as not to break or damage the skin. Skin breakage could potentially lead to internal contamination.
- Rinse eyes with saline or water.
- Wash hair with any available shampoo not containing a conditioner, as conditioners are known to bind material to the hair.
- Consider cutting hair in cases of significant contamination.
- Foreign shrapnel should be handled with forceps and treated as radioactive until proven otherwise.
- Dispose of water appropriately. If you do not have a special containment system, notify the local sewage department immediately.

- Check urine, stool, and nasal swabs (from each nostril) to determine the presence of internal contamination.
- Obtain a baseline complete blood count (CBC) with differential on presentation and every 6–8 hours for 48 hours if total-body radiation is suspected.
- Most sources recommend appropriate broad-spectrum antibiotics if signs of infection occur. These include nausea, vomiting, and diarrhea.
- Prophylactic antifungal and antiviral agents can also be considered, especially if signs of immunosuppression or pancytopenia are present.

PROGNOSIS

Depends upon the following factors: proximity to source, amount of shielding from the source, and length of exposure; in general, the earlier the onset of nausea and vomiting, the worse the prognosis (especially if <4 hours).

SPECIAL CONSIDERATIONS

- Nuclear detonation is much more devastating. Explosions such as those in Japan during the second world war included a nuclear fission reaction. This is very different from the low-level radioactive particles that would be involved in a "dirty bomb".
- "Dirty bombs" are radioactive devices in which radioactive material is dispersed without nuclear detonation but rather through the energy imparted by conventional explosives.
- Trauma from the conventional explosives and the psychological impact on the public would be the most dangerous features of a terrorist attack using a "dirty bomb".
- Nuclear reactors and radioactive material from hospital treatment areas are additional sources of radioactive material that can serve as potential terrorist targets.

4

Other Hazardous Material Used by Terrorists

INTRODUCTION

Disasters involving exposures to hazardous materials are relatively rare events, but they still represent one of the most common disasters in the community setting. Experts agree there are over 100,000 hazardous materials in our society. Chemicals are also effective terrorist weapons. These materials can be solids, liquids, or gases. Exposures can result in significant morbidity. Acutely, these materials can produce acute trauma such as burns, pulmonary edema, respiratory arrest, explosion injuries, and neurological injuries. Chronic effects may include progressive organ dysfunction, infertility, birth defects, and cancer.

Victims of hazardous material (HazMat) incidents often seek medical assistance and care in the emergency department. The risk of personal injury due to secondary contamination to EMTs, other pre-hospital medical personnel, and staff mandates specific policies and personal protection equipment (PPE) to prevent exposure to offgassing chemicals and direct unprotected contact with the victim.

Ahazardous material is any substance that is potentially toxic to the environment or to animals and humans. However, accurate and reliable data on the public health consequences of hazardous materials releases are difficult to obtain. Few agencies worldwide mandate reporting human exposure to hazardous materials to governmental authorities. In the United States, the Agency for Toxic Substances and Disease Registry (ATSDR) has maintained active state-based HazMat emergency event system since 1990.

ATSDR data reveal that 79% of these hazardous material releases occur at fixed sites (i.e., industrial sites, schools, farms, and manufacturing facilities) and 21% are transportation related. A single substance is released in 90% of reported events. Volatile organic compounds, acids, ammonia, pesticides, and other organic substances are most commonly involved.

A patient is considered contaminated when direct physical contact with a hazardous material has occurred and the substance remains on the body or clothing. When hazardous materials are present at an emergency, incident, or disaster, patients must be decontaminated before or during medical treatment.

Many disasters are not actual chemical incidents, but involve a large number of chemically exposed patients. Examples include natural disasters, transportation accidents, and the potential of a BT attack. In these situations, victims are dispersed over a widespread area. Contamination is often discovered by EMS teams during triage. Affected patients must be removed from the source and decontaminated before they are moved to a treatment area to protect rescuers, medical personnel, and expedite patient care.

The proper personal protection equipment is essential when hazards are present, as well as appropriate reference sources including the regional poison center, or from the material safety data sheet (MSDS).

The basic principles of decontamination are summarized as follows:

- Move the patient away from further exposure
- Remove the patient's clothing and jewelry
- Wash the patient, or use dry wiping for water reactive materials.

REGULATIONS

For healthcare workers, HazMat preparedness is a matter of worker safety. Hospitals must support systems that protect ED personnel and other healthcare workers who are caring for contaminated patients. Because many contaminated patients receive initial care (i.e., decontamination) at the hospital, ED personnel, as well as the facility, are at risk of secondary contamination if victims are not treated appropriately. OSHA regulations require workplaces to be free from recognized hazards that may cause serious physical harm or death to employers. Employers are also required to provide appropriate PPE and training to employees who may have the potential of being exposed to hazardous materials.

OSHA, the National Institute for Occupational Safety and Health (NIOSH), and the Joint Commission on Accreditation of Hospitals (JCAHO) have developed regulations and standards specific to HazMat emergencies.

As a result, every ED must address certain regulatory issues specific to decontamination including the following: a written hospital emergency response plan; personal protection equipment including fitness to wear PPE; and a minimum of training to meet OSHA's First Responder Awareness Level, including an understanding of how to recognize a potential HazMat problem and respond accordingly. Specific PPE is discussed elsewhere in the text as it pertains to these standards.

In the event of a mass casualty incident (MCI) that results in HazMat contamination and poses a threat to life or health, performing emergency decontamination is necessary. Patients should be directed outside the ED near the entrance to await evaluation and decontamination. In addition, the hospital HazMat response plan should be activated. Fortunately, the vast number of exposures involve only one or two victims. However, terrorists have shown the willingness and capacity to use hazardous chemicals when attacking civilians. As such, hospitals need the assessment skills, decontamination equipment, and other appropriate resources to offer care for such patients.

MARITIME DISASTERS

Disasters at sea have plagued society since ancient times. Although travel by sea is no longer as common as it was before the advent of aviation, sea disasters still occur, both with passenger and cargo vessels. According to the US Coast Guard, almost 50% of deaths and over 75% of the injuries that occur at sea are due to incidents on board that are not related to operation of the vessel (e.g., falling overboard, crush injuries, and fires). The majority of injuries and deaths are associated with ships with a high intensity of industrial activity, such as fishing vessels.

The definition of disaster takes on a relatively new meaning when applied to the maritime situation. At sea the communities are very small and resources are minimal compared to shore-side catastrophes, so not much is required to turn a shipboard emergency into a disaster.

Maritime disasters can be roughly divided into the following four groups: collisions, weather-related events, fires, and infectious diseases. Collisions between seagoing vessels are relatively uncommon. Unfortunately, a far greater number of shipwrecks are caused by rocks and reefs. Collisions occur with sudden onset and often with little or no warning. The most common cause is a combination of navigational hazards and bad weather. Receiving facilities must be prepared to handle trauma, hypothermia, and immersion injuries. Weather problems usually have a gradual onset with some warning. While bad weather is usually no surprise, its effects of capsizing and foundering usually are. The latter, foundering, is often due to a breach of the structural integrity of the ship and almost always results in loss of the vessel. In contrast, a fire may become a disaster without threatening the viability of the ship itself because of its effects on the ship's systems and inhabitants. Almost half of vessel fires start in the engine room with no warning. Fortunately, most on-board fires are easily contained, but many individuals may suffer from its effects from burns, smoke inhalation, and carbon monoxide (CO) poisoning. Food- and waterborne disease outbreaks are common and typically have a gradual onset with some warning. According to the Centers for Disease Control and Prevention (CDC), approximately 1 in 400 cruises has an outbreak of a diarrheal illness that is significant enough (>2%–3% of the crew or passengers) to warrant epidemiologic investigation. Overall, the Norwalk Virus is the most common cause, and facilities should be prepared to handle dehydration and electrolyte disturbance.

MARITIME DISASTER PLANNING

All ships are required to have a safety plan that includes a disaster plan in accordance with the International Maritime Organization. This includes standard procedures and drills. The medical department on cruise ships is part of this plan and is included in the drills. Lifeboat(s), stretcher team, fire and basic life support drills should be part of the safety plan. Large cruise ships also usually have their own disaster plan for which they are responsible with regard to maintenance and implementation. Such vessels also have a secondary medical space for both the storage of additional medical supplies and equipment, as well as area where medical care can be rendered if the main infirmary is overcrowded or inaccessible.

The sequence of events in a maritime disaster response is somewhat different than that in shore-side disasters. This is primarily related to location and the fact that external resources are distant. Unless the vessel happens to be in coastal waters within a few hundred miles of a Coast Guard airbase, no chance for rapid air evacuation exists and no hospital will be in close proximity.

Incidents usually involve specialized response teams, and not the standard municipal police, fire, and emergency medical service (EMS) personnel. Due to environmental factors, most deaths usually result from hypothermia, shock, or drowning. Injuries may also occur from blunt or penetrating trauma, thermal burns, or from exposure to hazardous materials that may be carried as cargo, such as heavy fuel oil. Any resultant oil spill can also complicate rescue and recovery operations.

Sometimes in maritime disasters evacuation may be necessary. Radio contact with the Coast Guard is initiated, and the usual method of mass evacuation is by a military or command ship. If no outside help is available, lifeboats serve as the ambulance of last resort. According to international law, all ships must have an adequate number of lifeboats that are provisioned with food, water, and medical supplies. As a result, shore-side emergency departments and EMS systems usually have adequate time to prepare for the reception of victims from a maritime disaster.

AVIATION DISASTERS

Crashes involving aircraft have occurred since the beginning of flight. With both the capacity and number of commercial airliners increasing, the risk of a catastrophic event involving an aircraft has multiplied. By 1997 the number of commercial air passengers had increased to 630 million, and it is expected to exceed 985 million by the year 2009. Aviation accidents have the potential for significant loss of life and for generation of a high number of casualties.

There are many causes of aviation disasters. They may result from acts of terrorism but much more frequently are related to human error (pilot or control tower), mechanical failure, or limiting factors including weather (dense fog, icing, and wind shear). Most accidents are usually the result of a combination of these factors. The majority of aviation accidents involve private aircraft (including helicopters) or smaller commercial planes. Although crashes involving large commercial aircraft represent the minority of accidents, they tend to garner more media and public attention. Since the 1980s, aviation safety has improved dramatically, reducing the number of fatalities by 34%. The aviation community has used past experiences to improve safety aspects of modern aircraft. The US National Transportation and Safety Board (NTSB) develops regulatory and safety policies and investigates aviation incidents (an occurrence with no injury or death) and accidents (bodily harm or death). According to the NTSB, most preventable passenger deaths can be attributed to lack of familiarity with safety procedures, despite preflight instructions. In addition to aircraft crashes, other accidents include turbulence, rapid decompression, and explosions aboard the aircraft.

PRE-HOSPITAL CONSIDERATIONS

From a pre-hospital perspective, the unique considerations that involve aircraft accidents must be addressed. The first consideration is access to the scene. In aviation crashes over open sea, response efforts are centered at the nearest land areas. Such crashes present unique challenges to emergency medical services (EMS), search and rescue, and primarily recovery efforts since there are unfortunately few survivors. Air crashes occurring in and around an airport will often occur within the confines of the flight line. Larger and busier airports may either suspend or continue active flight operations near the crash site. EMS units should receive prior training on responding to these situations and have established communication links with the airport control tower and fire/rescue units. A triage area should be established, and all victims should be directed to the triage area. This is important, as it improves the process of identifying and assessing all survivors. Responders need to be aware of the particular hazards associated with downed aircraft: leaking aviation fuel, potential fire hazards, toxic fumes, and scattered debris, which may be hot. Security issues and evidence preservation (terrorist events) are also concerns.

MECHANISM OF INJURY

Injuries from air crash disasters may result from: rapid deceleration, blunt trauma, penetrating trauma, burns, smoke inhalation, hazardous materials exposure, and dysbarisms due to rapid decompression and altitude changes. Rotary wing accidents due to helicopter crashes typically result in vertebral injuries and fractures. This occurs because of the intense vertical deceleration forces. Thermal injuries are infrequently seen due to the success of the crashworthy fuel systems used in helicopters. Fixedwing aircraft fly at much greater altitudes and therefore need to have compressed cabins. Sudden changes in cabin pressure can lead to hypoxia and rapid decompression problems. The latter include clinical problems such as pneumothoraxes, hypothermia, and decompression sickness. Complications from aircraft fires are common and range from thermal injury and burns to smoke inhalation and inhalation of toxic gases including carbon monoxide and hydrogen cyanide. Additionally, the mental health impact and environmental factors associated with particular crashes, such as neardrowning, need to be considered.

PREVENTION OF INJURIES

More people are using airplanes today as a mode of transportation. For this reason, aircraft crashes require pre-hospital care providers, emergency personnel and public health agencies to make special preparations, adequate plans, and drills in order to appropriately respond to an air crash disaster. The unique hazards associated with these types of disasters should also be understood to help reduce further risk to both responders and survivors.

RESUSCITATION ALGORITHMS FOR CARDIOPULMONARY ARREST

The healthcare provider responding to a disaster needs to be prepared to recognize and treat cardiac arrest. Several factors may play a role in deciding on resuscitative efforts in a disaster: cause of the arrest (if known), time down, size and scope of the disaster, triage protocol, and available resources.

This chapter has been presented in algorithmic format for simplification

A. Airway

1. Open airway with chin lift or jaw thrust maneuver if c-spine compromise is suspected
2. Remove any foreign debris

B. Breathing

1. Assess breathing by the "look, listen, and feel" method
   — look at the chest rise

— listen for breath sounds

— feel breath (exhalation) from mouth/nose against your cheek

2. Consider supplemental oxygenation via bag-valve mask ventilation or intubation

C. Circulation

1. Check pulses (carotid/radial/femoral)
2. Check skin color and cap refill (<2 seconds)
3. Start CPR if no palpable pulse

D. Disability

1. Perform a quick neurologic assessment using the AVPU scale (alert, responds to verbal stimuli, responds to painful stimuli, or unresponsive)

E. Exposure

1. The patient should be completely disrobed to assess for other visible injuries (i.e., open fractures or stab wounds)

Primary Survey: the primary survey is used to quickly assess and effectively manage most immediate life-threatening issues.

PULSELESS VENTRICULAR TACHYCARDIA/ FIBRILLATION

— Shock 200 J, shock 300 j, shock 360 j

— Oxygen, monitor, IV access, intubate

— Epinephrine

* 1 mg IV
* Alternative: vasopressin 40 Units IV x1
* Shock 360 J
* Continue every 3–5 minutes
* Shock 360 J

— Amiodarone

* 300 mg IV push (may repeat 150 mg; max 2.2 g over 24 hours)

    * Maintenance: 1.0 mg/min or 360 mg over first 6 hours, then 0.5 mg/min or 540 mg IV over 18 hours; precautions: low BP/HR
    * Shock 360 J
- — Lidocaine
    * 100 mg IV (1–1.5 mg/kg) (may repeat to max of 3 mg/kg)
    * Maintenance: 1–4 mg/min
- — Magnesium
    * 2 g IV (if hypomagnesemia/prolonged QT or torsades)
- — Procainamide
    * Use if VF/VT breaks and recurs
    * 50 mg/min IV (max 17 mg/kg, so approx 20 min)
    * Maintenance: 1–4 mg/min
    * Precautions: low BP, double QRS, or max dose discontinue

ASYSTOLE

- CPR
- Epinephrine 1 mg IV q 3–5 min
- Atropine 1 mg IV q 3–5 min (max 0.04 mg/kg or approx 3 doses)
- Transcutaneous pacing

PULSELESS ELECTRICAL ACTIVITY (PEA)

- CPR
- Epinephrine 1 mg IV q 3–5 min
- Atropine 1 mg IV q 3–5 min (max 0.04 mg/kg or approx 3 doses)
- Correct underlying etiology

The Five "T's"

- o Tamponade
- o Tension pneumothorax
- o Thrombosis, cardiac
- o Thrombosis, pulmonary emboli
- o Tablets (overdose)

The Five "H's"

- o Hypovolemia
- o Hypoxia
- o Hydrogen ions (acidosis)
- o Hypothermia
- o Hyper/hypo K+, Mg2+, and Ca2+

BRADYCARDIA

Atropine 1 mg IV

Transcutaneous Pacing

Dopamine 5–20 ¼g/kg/min

Epinephrine 2–10 ¼g/min

TACHYCARDIA

Unstable

- Shock non-sinus rhythms

Stable:Wide

- Stable VT load with amiodarone 150 mg IV over 10 minutes and magnesium 2 grams IV if polymorphic
- Supraventricular Tachycardia (SVT) with aberrancy: treat like VT (no reliable criteria to distinguish the difference!)

Stable: Narrow

- Atrial Fibrillation/Flutter: these should be thought of as the same problem

  * Less than 48 hours: cardiovert with electricity or amiodarone
  * Greater than 48 hours: rate control (beta blockers, calcium channel blocker, digoxin) and anticoagulate
- SVT: vagal maneuvers, adenosine 6 mg IV push (may repeat with 12 mg), verapamil
- Multifocal Atrial Tachycardia (MAT): rate control (calcium channel blocker preferred over beta blocker if COPD/ asthma) and treat underlying disorder (usually COPD)

CLINICAL PEARLS

- Unstable may be defined as: hypotension, chest pain, dyspnea, altered mental status, and acute congestive heart failure
- Verapamil and adenosine are contraindicated for wide complex tachycardia
- Drugs that can be given through the endotracheal tube (NAVEL): naloxone, atropine, valium or vasopressin, epinephrine, lidocaine (remember to use 2–3 times the dose)
- Guidelines for Amount of Joules for Cardioversion/ Defibrillation
  * Aflutter: start 50 J
  * VT/VF: start 200 J
  * All other rhythms: start 100 J
- Do not cardiovert in normal sinus tachycardia! Treat underlying disorder.
- Wolf-Parkinson-White Syndrome: avoid ABCD (adenosine, beta-blockers, calcium channel blockers, digoxin) because AV nodal blockade will cause paradoxical increase in heart rate.

The ability to diagnose and manage shock (defined as widespread inadequate tissue perfusion) is central to the practice of disaster medicine. It behooves everyone involved (EMTs, paramedics, nurses, physicians, etc.) to be able to identify the different types of shock, as it is truly a life-threatening condition. If it is not emergently reversed, systemic inflammation, organ dysfunction and death may ensue.

ETIOLOGY

Trauma and infection are the most likely etiologies of shock in the disaster setting. Trauma most commonly will cause hypovolemic shock from blood loss, but it can also result in neurogenic shock from a cervical spine injury and obstructive shock from a traumatic tension pneumothorax or cardiac tamponade. All Category A biological agents (defined by the Centers for Disease Control as those with the greatest impact on public health) can cause septic shock.

TYPES OF SHOCK

- Hypovolemic: decreased intravascular blood volume, e.g., hemorrhage
- Neurogenic: vasodilatation from loss of central sympathetic tone resulting in a relative hypovolemia, e.g., cervical spine injury impinging on the spinal cord
- Obstructive: a physical obstruction to blood flow, e.g., cardiac tamponade
- Septic: severe infection causes vessel dilatation and leakage, e.g., pneumonic plague infection
- Cardiogenic: loss of forward blood flow because of inability of heart to adequately pump, e.g., massive myocardial infarction
- Anaphylactic: histamine release in response to allergen causes severe inflammation and loss of vascular tone and capacitance, e.g., peanut allergy

PRESENTATION

In the majority of cases, especially in disaster medicine settings, the history will identify the most likely type of shock. Severe burns and physical injuries are most likely to result in hypovolemic shock due to fluid or blood loss. Consider septic shock if there is exposure to biological agents. Neck injuries resulting in neurogenic shock are not usually subtle, but the diagnosis can be overlooked when there are multiple simultaneous injuries. Consider obstructive shock (tension pneumothorax or cardiac tamponade) with penetrating injuries.

Signs and Symptoms

The presentation of shock varies with the type and etiology. Hypotension after trauma is usually due to hemorrhage. The ensuing hypovolemic shock results in peripheral vasoconstriction to divert the reduced blood volume to the critical organs; therefore, the skin is cool and moist and the neck veins are flat. A reflex tachycardia is common. Patients usually complain of lightheadedness, especially with standing (orthostasis).

Warm skin in a trauma patient is suspicious for neurogenic shock. The body is unable to peripherally vasoconstrict due to loss of sympathetic tone.

Warm skin is expected, on the other hand, in cases of septic shock. Bacterial endotoxins cause peripheral vasodilatation and leakage. Fever (rarely hypothermia) and diaphoresis are also common. The heart initially becomes hyperdynamic to increase the circulation of a relatively reduced blood volume, resulting in tachycardia and a strong pulse. In the latter stages of septic shock, the pulse weakens and the extremities become cool.

A puncture wound to the chest should prompt inspection of the neck veins and auscultation of the heart and lungs to diagnose obstructive shock.

Unilateral decreased breath sounds, low oxygen saturation, jugular venous distention, and possible tracheal deviation are signs of a tension pneumothorax; patients usually complain of shortness of breath and chest pain. In the setting of hypotension, jugular venous distention and muffled heart sounds (Beck's Triad), one should consider cardiac tamponade.

DIAGNOSIS

Empiric criteria for the diagnosis of circulatory shock requires 4 of the following: (1) ill appearing or altered mental status, (2) heart rate >100, (3) respiratory rate >22 or PaCO2 <32 mm Hg, (4) arterial base deficit <–5 mEq/L or lactate >4 mM, (5) urine output <0.5 ml/kg/hr, (6) arterial hypotension >20 minutes duration.

Once the diagnosis of shock is determined, the critical task is to identify the type of shock in order to treat appropriately.

Hypovolemic Shock

Consider in cases of suspected hemorrhage or severe burns. Tachycardia, low blood pressure, and cool, moist skin are characteristic.

Neurogenic Shock

Consider in cases of spinal cord trauma. Low blood pressure, bradycardia, and warm skin are characteristic.

Obstructive Shock

Consider in chest trauma cases. Chest pain, shortness of breath, unilateral decreased breath sounds, jugular venous distention, hypotension, tachycardia, and tracheal deviation are characteristic of tension pneumothorax. Hypotension, jugular venous distention, and muffled heart sounds (Beck's Triad) are characteristic of cardiac tamponade.

Septic Syndrome

Two or more Systemic Inflammatory Response Syndrome (SIRS) criteria (see below) in addition to hypotension or organ dysfunction (can include lactic acidosis, oliguria, or altered mental status) is considered sepsis.

Hypotension despite adequate fluid resuscitation is considered septic shock. SIRS Criteria: (1) temperature >38°C or <36°C, (2) heart rate >90, (3) respiratory rate >20 or $PaCO_2$ <32 mm Hg, (4) WBC count >12,000 or <4,000 or Band neutrophilia >10%

TREATMENT

Always start with the ABCs.

Hemorrhagic Shock

1. Control hemorrhage, if possible
2. Infuse intravenous fluids (20 ml/kg) and, if available, packed red blood cells (5–10 ml/kg)

Neurogenic Shock

1. Ensure c-spine immobilization
2. Infuse intravenous fluids (20 ml/kg)
3. Treat hypotension (systolic BP < 90) and bradycardia with atropine 1 mg (may repeat to a maximum of 0.04 mg/kg)
4. Consider dopamine starting at 5-20 ¼g/kg/min

Obstructive Shock

1. Tension pneumothorax
   a. Needle thoracostomy of chest with 14–16 gauge needle in the second intercostal space on the mid-clavicular line provides immediate decompression
   b. Chest tube should be placed for more definitive decompression
2. Cardiac tamponade
   a. Infuse intravenous fluids (20 ml/kg) as temporizing measure
   b. Pericardiocentesis, if not stable enough for transport to the operating room
   c. Thoracotomy to open the pericardial sac and relieve the tamponade, if patient loses vital signs

Septic Shock

1. Ensure adequate ventilation and oxygenation

2. Infuse intravenous fluids (20 ml/kg initially but an adult patient may require 5–6 liters before adequate urine output is restored)
3. Antimicrobial therapy tailored to suspected source
4. If crystalloid resuscitation fails, start a vasopressor
    a. Dopamine 5–20 ¼g/kg/min
    b. Norepinephrine 0.1–1.0 ¼g/kg/min

INTRAVENOUS FLUID REQUIREMENTS AND BLOOD PRODUCTS

Numerous bioterrorism agents can cause alterations in fluid homeostasis. Similarly, all trauma patients are at significant risk for fluid disturbances. There are numerous agents available to correct fluid disturbances. A basic understanding of physiology as well as knowledge of the various fluids available will enable the clinician to choose an appropriate fluid replacement and successfully manage these challenging patients.

FLUID COMPARTMENTS

The total body water (TBW) comprises 60% of the body's total weight in males and 50–55% in females. These values vary, however, according to age, lean body mass, and weight. The TBW is lower in young lean individuals, and is higher in older obese individuals. The TBW resides in two compartments: the intracellular fluid (ICF) and the extracellular fluid (ECF). The ICF accounts for two-thirds of the TBW (approximately 28 liters), while the ECF accounts for a third (approximately 14 L). The ECF can be further subdivided into intravascular and interstitial compartments. The intravascular and interstitial compartments account for 25% (approximately 3.5 L), and 75% (approximately 3.5 L), respectively, of the ECF.

Movement of fluid between compartments occurs via passive diffusion. Normally, the capillary membrane separating the intravascular and interstitial compartments is permeable to water, small solutes, and electrolytes. The net flow of water occurs as a result of the osmotic pressure gradient between compartments. Sodium and chloride constitute more than 90% of the effective solutes in the ECF.

The serum sodium concentration determines the relative amount of water and sodium in the plasma. The size of the ECF and ICF compartments are dependent on the amount of water within each compartment, while the distribution of water is dependent upon the osmolality.

FLUID REQUIREMENTS

Fluid administration should equal fluid losses. An average individual must consume enough fluid to equal the losses in urine (12–15 cc/kg/d), stool (3 cc/kg/d), and sweat (0–1.5 cc/kg/d). An additional 1 L of fluid is lost due to insensible losses from the respiratory tract (500–700 cc/d) and skin (250–350 cc/d).

With rigorous energy expenditure, however, these losses can be much greater. The presence of a fever results in an additional loss of 10% fluid per °C. Thus, under normal circumstances, to maintain homeostasis, the average adult needs to consume 2–3 L of fluids per day. In addition, losses from the gastrointestinal tract due to vomiting or diarrhea, major body stressors, or hyperventilation can result in substantially larger losses.

Fluid losses can occur in several common situations. Perhaps the most obvious scenarios include hemorrhage, vomiting, or diarrhea. Other less common, but equally important, sources include nasogastric suctioning and external drainage from biliary, enteric, or pancreatic fistulas.

In general, the fluid loss in these settings is isotonic with the fluid depletion initially occurring from the ECF. Fluid sequestration into the extracellular or interstitial spaces is commonly referred to as "third-spacing" and also results in isotonic loss. Common etiologies of "third spacing" include peritonitis, pancreatitis, intestinal obstructions, burns, and crush injuries. Areview of hypertonic and hypotonic fluid losses is beyond the scope of this chapter.

INTRAVENOUS SOLUTIONS

If free water were infused, it would distribute proportionally throughout all fluid compartments. In clinical practice, an infusion of D5W is considered to be the most similar to free water. Ringer's lactate and 0.9% normal saline are isotonic fluids and are considered crystalloids. Crystalloids are composed of sodium, chloride, and often other small molecule solutes. Infusions of crystalloids are confined to the ECF, and distribute proportionately between the interstitial and intravascular compartments. Table 1 summarizes the composition of commonly used intravenous fluids. Colloids are solutions containing high-molecular-weight substances such as proteins and polysaccharide polymers. Because of their large size, colloids stay in the intravascular space and exert an osmotic force. Common colloids in use include albumin, hydroxyethyl starch (HES, or Hetastarch), and dextran. For patients in hypovolemic shock, some authors argue that colloids should be used in addition to crystalloids. In theory, the high oncotic pressure of the colloids promotes fluid retention in the intravascular space. Despite the fact that colloids remain in the intravascular space for 3–6 hours, compared to 30 minutes with crystalloids, large trials have failed to demonstrate any clinical benefit with the use of colloids. Because colloids are much more expensive than crystalloids and the use of hespan can result in a coagulopathy, the routine use of colloids is minimal, if at all.

FLUID REPLACEMENT

Acid–base and electrolyte disturbances frequently accompany fluid loss. Without an adequate circulating volume, renal function may be altered, which impairs the kidney's ability to correct acid–base and electrolyte abnormalities. Healthy individuals can compensate for dehydration and elevated osmolality by becoming thirsty and subsequently drinking water. Seriously ill or confused patients, however, have inadequate compensatory mechanisms. If a patient has a water deficit (as evidenced by hypernatremia), and a salt deficit (as evidenced by orthostasis), 10–20 cc/kg of isotonic crystalloids should be administered. If the patient is hemodynamically unstable, these fluids should be infused as quickly as possible, and can be repeated as necessary. In hemodynamically stable individuals, the fluids should be given over an hour.

Once orthostasis is corrected, if volume depletion persists, the total water deficit should be calculated. Half the total deficit should be given within the first 8 hours, with the remainder given over the subsequent 16 hours.

Measuring urine output is an excellent method of ensuring adequate fluid resuscitation. The minimal acceptable urine output is 0.5 cc/kg/hr for adults and 1 cc/kg/hr for children. In addition to correcting a fluid deficit, patients who are not able to consume oral liquids need intravenous maintenance fluids. As a general rule, maintenance fluids are based on the following formula:

1st 10 kg of body weight ® 4 cc/kg/hr

2nd 10 kg of body weight ® 2 cc/kg/hr

Each additional kg (beyond 20 kg) ® 1 cc/kg/hr

Thus, a 60-kg individual needs (10)(4) + (10)(2) + (40)(1), or 100 cc/hr. It is important to note that this formula is a generalization and does not take into account ongoing losses. Any ongoing loss should be replaced in addition to maintenance fluids.

BLOOD

Once blood is collected from a donor, it is separated into various parts. Blood components that are available for transfusion include packed red blood cells (PRBCs), fresh frozen plasma (FFP), cryoprecipitate, platelets, and white cell preparations. (See Table 2 for a list of blood products.)

There are four main ABO groups and over 400 RBC antigens that are currently identified. Ensuring ABO compatibility is the most important step in the crossmatching procedure. Antibody screening and Rh typing are performed with a routine type and crossmatch.

The ideal transfusion involves a self-donor, where the patient donates his own blood prior to elective surgery. Patients with chest trauma may be candidates for autotransfusion. In the absence of these scenarios, however, a complete type and crossmatch should be done, if permissible. In acute hemorrhage, waiting for a full type and crossmatch may not always be feasible. In such circumstances, incomplete crossmatch, type-specific, or type O blood can be used. Type-specific blood, which can be obtained faster than a full crossmatch, involves matching the ABO and Rh group. An incomplete crossmatch involves matching the ABO and Rh groups, plus an antibody screen. Rh positive blood can safely be given to all patients except women of childbearing age.

CRITERIA FOR TRANSFUSIONS

A hemodynamically unstable patient with acute blood loss requires immediate fluid resuscitation with a 20 cc/kg bolus of crystalloids, which can be repeated as needed. If, however, a patient remains unstable after 2–3 L or 40–50 mg/kg of crystalloid, blood should also be given. As a general rule, every 1 cc of blood lost will necessitate 2–3 cc of crystalloid replacement.

For patients with acute hemorrhage, the need to transfuse blood depends on the amount of blood lost as well as the patient's comorbid conditions. Any patient with an acute blood loss of more than 15% total blood volume should be considered for blood transfusion. In general, the decision to transfuse blood should not be based solely on the hemoglobin.

For example, a hemoglobin of 8 g/dl in an asymptomatic individual with no comorbid risk factors and no ongoing blood loss may not necessitate a transfusion. However, in the presence of active bleeding, cardiac or pulmonary disease, evidence of cardiac ischemia (chest pain, shortness of breath) dizziness with mild exertion, sepsis, or hemoglobinopathies, PRBCs should be transfused to achieve a hemoglobin of 10 g/dl. In general, each unit of PRBCs will raise the hemoglobin 1 g/dl, and raise the hematocrit 3%.

Patients who have thrombocytopenia may need platelet transfusion. As a general rule, in the absence of bleeding, platelet transfusion should occur once the platelet count is <20,000. In the presence of bleeding or coagulation disorder, or if a major procedure is anticipated, platelet transfusions should occur once the count is <50,000. On average, each unit of platelets will raise the platelet count by 5,000–10,000/mm3. Adults, on average, require 6–10 units of platelets, while children require 1 U/10 kg body weight. Crossmatching is not necessary for platelet transfusion, but Rh-negative patients should receive Rh negative platelets.

Each unit of FFP contains prothrombin, fibrinogen, clotting factors V, VII, VIII, IX, and XIII, antithrombin III, and proteins C and S. Each milliliter of FFP contains 1 unit of activity of any clotting factor. The decision to use FFP for factor deficiency should be calculated to provide at least 30% plasma factor concentrations. Thus, usually 10–15 cc/kg of FFP is needed. For reversal of coumadin, 5–8 cc/kg of FFP is usually required, as one unit of FFP reduces the prothrombin time by 2 seconds. Acrossmatch is necessary for FFP. Cryoprecipiate contains factors VIII and XIII, von Willebrand's factor, fibrinogen, and fibronectin. Cryoprecipitate can be used to promote hemostasis in any bleeding patients, although usually FFP is preferred, as FFP contains more clotting factors. Cryoprecipiate can be given for patients with von Willebrand's disease, hypofibrinogenemia (fibrinogen <100 mg/dl), hemophilia A, and bleeding due to thrombolytic therapy.

TRANSFUSION RISKS

Transfusing blood is not without risks. While blood is screened for numerous viruses including HBV, HCV, and HIV, transmission of these viruses can still occur. Other adverse reactions to transfusions include acute hemolytic transfusion reactions, febrile transfusion reactions, allergic reactions, transfusion-related acute lung injury (TRALI), graft-versus-host disease, circulatory overload, and hemosiderosis.

MASSIVE TRANSFUSIONS

A massive transfusion is defined as replacement of more than 10 units of blood during several hours, or transfusing the entire blood volume over 24 hours. Beyond all the risks of standard transfusions, recipients of massive transfusions are also at risk to develop hypothermia, hypocalcemia, dilutional thrombocytopenia, DIC, and ventricular arrhythmias.

DECONTAMINATION

Decontamination is defined as the reduction or removal of chemical, biological, or nuclear agents so they are no longer hazards. Agents may be removed by physical means or be neutralized chemically (detoxification). Decontamination of the skin is the primary concern, but decontamination of other systems must also be done when necessary. To ensure appropriate and timely patient care as well as optimal response, emergency personnel must understand decontamination procedures and the proper use of personal protective equipment.

ASSESSMENT, DECONTAMINATION,AND INITIAL TREATMENT OF PATIENTS

The primary goals for emergency personnel in a hazardous materials incident include:

- Establishment of decontamination zones (see below)
- Cessation of patient exposure
- Patient stabilization
- Containment of the hazard to prevent further contamination
- Patient treatment without jeopardizing emergency personnel safety

While not all chemicals pose a hazard for secondary contamination, until the risk is known, termination of exposure is best accomplished by removing the patient from the incident area and then decontaminating the patient.

The essential requirements for any decontamination task are:

- Safe area to keep a patient while undergoing decontamination
- Method for washing contaminants off a patient
- Means of containing the rinsate
- Personal protection equipment (PPE) (see Table 1) for personnel treating the patient
- Disposable or cleanable medical equipment to treat the patient

5

Establishment of Decontamination Zones

HOT ZONE

The Hot Zone is immediately dangerous to life or health. Accordingly, Level A personal protective equipment with self-contained breathing apparatus or suppliedair respirator is required for first responders or other personnel working inside the Hot Zone, where contact with hazardous materials is likely, including chemical gas or vapors, biological aerosols, or chemical and/or biological liquid or powder residue.

WARM ZONE

The Warm Zone is an uncontaminated environment into which contaminated victims, first responders, and equipment are brought. In classic HazMat (hazardous materials) response, the Warm Zone is adjacent to and upwind from the Hot Zone. However, experience with previous disasters indicates that contaminated victims capable of fleeing the Hot Zone are likely to bypass emergency medical services and go directly to the nearest hospital, in which case the Warm Zone may occur outside the emergency department or even inside the hospital.

The protective equipment required depends on whether victims were exposed to a biological, chemical, radiological agent, or unknown agent or agents. The route of exposure may be inferred from the presence of contaminant on the clothing and skin of victims.

Vapor or aerosol exposure leaves no or minimal contaminant on victims, and material breathed into the lungs is not exhaled to contaminate others. Liquid or powder exposures may leave visible residue. In a similar manner, handling victims exposed to biological aerosols poses little risk to emergency care personnel outside the Hot Zone.

KNOWN BIOLOGICAL WARFARE AGENT HAZARDS

Personnel handling victims contaminated with bioterror (BT) agents require respiratory protection. Skin protection is largely unnecessary, because these are not active through unbroken skin (with the single exception of the mycotoxins). Personnel handling victims who have been exposed to a known BT agent aerosol are not required to wear protective equipment because secondary aerosolization of residual agent from clothing, skin, or hair is insignificant. When victims are contaminated with a known liquid or powder, Level D (universal precautions) and PAPR (powered air purifying respirator) with an HEPA (high-efficiency particulate air) filter are required until decontamination is complete. Level C personal protective equipment and PAPR HEPA filter may be considered if the residue on victims is suspected of containing mycotoxins.

Known Chemical Warfare Agent Hazards

Personnel handling victims contaminated with chemical warfare agents require respiratory and skin protection. When victims are exposed to a known gas at standard temperature and pressure (such as chlorine, phosgene, oxides of nitrogen, cyanide), no personal protective equipment is required, because victims cannot breathe out hazardous gas and harm others. When victims are exposed to a known vapor from volatile liquid (such as a nerve agent or blistering vapor), PPE (personal protection equipment) is required, because responders may be exposed to low levels coming from the victims. When victims are contaminated with a known volatile liquid, Level

C PPE with PAPR and chemical cartridge is required until decontamination is complete. In general, Level C PPE is used when the inhalation risk is known to be below levels expected to harm personnel and when eye, mucous membrane, and skin exposures are unlikely.

Known Radiation Hazards

When victims are exposed to external radiation but not contaminated with a radiation- emitting source, no PPE is required. If any doubt exists whether victims or their clothing are contaminated, they should be surveyed with a Geiger-Müller counter.

When victims are contaminated externally with radioactive material (on their skin, hair, wounds, clothes), use Level D PPE (for example, waterproof barrier materials, such as surgical gown, mask, gloves, leg, and/or shoe coverings; universal precautions) until decontamination is complete. Double layers of gloves and frequent changes of the outer layer help reduce the spread of radioactive material.

Handle radioactive materials with tongs whenever possible. Lead aprons are cumbersome and do not protect against gamma or neutron radiation. For this reason, experts currently recommend against their use when caring for a radiation-contaminated victim. However, healthcare workers should wear radiological dosimeters while working in a contaminated environment. When victims are contaminated internally with radioactive material, wear latex gloves when handling body fluids (urine, feces, wound drainage).

Unknown Hazards (Biological, Chemical or Both)

According to current US government (OSHA) regulations, Level APPE is required for personnel responding to an unknown hazard. Some experts maintain that Level C PPE with PAPR (with organic vapor cartridge and HEPA filter) provides adequate protection until decontamination is complete. Unfortunately, no single ensemble of PPE can protect emergency care personnel against all hazards.

Cold Zone

The Cold Zone should be completely uncontaminated. Nevertheless, victims exposed to certain biological warfare agents may develop disease that can be transmitted to others. This situation then poses a risk of secondary spread to medical personnel. The type of protective equipment required depends on the route of transmission of these infectious diseases.

Respiratory Droplet/Airborne Particles

PAPR with HEPA filter provides the greatest degree of respiratory protection against biological-associated disease spread by respiratory droplet (such as smallpox or pneumonic plague) or airborne particles (possibly smallpox) when treating victims with obvious disease. Disposable HEPA filter masks also work.

Evidence exists that smallpox may be transmitted by airborne particles under certain circumstances. Some people develop a very dense rash and severe cough when infected with smallpox. These victims are also likely to have many lesions involving the mouth and throat. During bouts of severe cough, they may shed virus into the air. Medical personnel should wear latex gloves while handling the skin of people with smallpox, because smallpox may potentially be transmitted by contact with pox lesions that have not yet crusted over.

Blood or Body Fluid

While in contact with victims who have contracted biological-associated disease spread by blood or body fluid contact (hemorrhagic fever from Ebola, for example), Level D PPE (standard precautions) is generally protective. Higher levels of protection may be necessary, however, if such victims have coughing or extensive bleeding.

PERSONAL PROTECTIVE EQUIPMENT

Respirators

Level C protection is the recommended minimum level of

protection. Based on specific knowledge of the released agent, or if there is no information at all, then Level B protection is recommended. Powered air-purifying respirators (PAPRs) are recommended over simple air-purifying respirators. Canisters should provide HEPA filtration and protection against organic vapor and acid gases at a minimum. FR57 canisters provide NIOSH-approved protection against organic vapors, acid

gases, ammonia, methylamine, chlorine dioxide, HF, and formaldehyde; they are also effective in military testing against nerve agents, mustard, riot control agents, cyanide, and acidgas related agents.

Suits

The difference between Levels C and B has to do with the durability of the suit and the impermeability of the suit to various chemicals. If the threat is unknown, it is best to use Level B protection. An average person will take an XL suit at the smallest since flexibility of garments are minimal, and tearing is a concern if too small a suit is worn. Duct tape (or chemically resistant tape) can be used to reinforce the zipper front and crotch of the suit as additional protection. Tyvek SL offers moderate general protection against a majority of chemical agents, including nerve agents and mustard, but resistance to many organic agents is limited. This is probably a reasonable minimum level of protection for the healthcare decontamination setting. Tychem F offers improved protection against chemical and other BT agents. Tychem BR offers even a higher level of protection.

Booties

The decontamination team may need abrasion resistance, depending on the surfaces where the decontamination area is located. In general, butyl rubber booties that can be pulled over shoes will suffice. Providers should never rely on the suit-incorporated booties for adequate protection of the feet. The junctions between the suit and boot should be taped with duct tape.

Gloves

Heavy butyl over gloves and thinner nitrile inner gloves offer protection against a broad range of agents, and are inexpensive. Cuffs should be long enough to reach at least 2 inches above the sleeve cuff. Silvershield inner gloves may also be used and provide additional protection against prolonged contact with halogenated hydrocarbons. The junction between gloves and suit should be sealed with duct tape.

Radiologic

Standard suits block alpha and beta particles. Neither the suits nor radiology lead aprons are effective against gamma radiation. Inhaled radioactive dusts are generally well-controlled by a HEPA level filter. Decontamination personnel should have radiation badges or radiation pagers immediately available to their personnel as well as having G-M counters.

Prioritizing Casualties for Decontamination

Responders must prioritize victims for receiving decontamination, treatment, and medical evacuation, while providing the greatest benefit for the greatest number. Although many emergency response services prepare for such incidents, few are currently capable of treating victims inside the Hot Zone. Therefore, whenever large numbers of victims are involved, it is recommended that they be sorted into ambulatory and non-ambulatory triage categories using the START categories.

FACTORS THAT DETERMINE HIGHEST PRIORITY FOR AMBULATORY

Victim Decontamination

- Casualties closest to the point of release
- Casualties reporting exposure to vapor or aerosol
- Casualties with evidence of liquid deposition on clothing or skin

- Casualties with serious medical symptoms
- Casualties with conventional injuries

Non-Ambulatory Casualties

These are victims who are unconscious, unresponsive, or unable to move unassisted. They may be more seriously injured than ambulatory victims and will remain in place while further prioritization for decontamination occurs. It is recommended that prioritization of non-ambulatory victims for decontamination should be done using medical triage systems, such as START.

Gross Patient Decontamination

Primary assessment can be undertaken while simultaneously performing gross decontamination in the outer edge of the Hot Zone or in the Warm Zone. Once lifethreatening matters have been addressed, rescue personnel can direct their attention to more thorough decontamination and secondary patient assessment. Appropriate personal protective equipment and clothing must be worn until the threat of secondary exposure no longer exists. If there is a risk of secondary contamination, gross decontamination should be performed simultaneously with initial patient stabilization. The sooner the patient is decontaminated, the sooner he or she can be transferred to the Cold Zone for further evaluation and treatment.

All potentially contaminated clothing, jewelry, and watches should be removed and doubled-bagged, sealed, and labeled. Any obvious contamination should be brushed or wiped off, followed by a 1-minute-long rinsing from head to toe with tepid water. If the suspected chemical is water-reactive, a longer rinsing period and a greater volume of water is required.

Care should be taken to protect any open wounds from contamination by covering them with a water-repellent dressing (e.g., Chux). Throughout these procedures, every effort should be made by emergency personnel to avoid contact with any potentially hazardous substance(s).

Secondary or Definitive Decontamination

If conditions permit, a more deliberate decontamination process—known as secondary or definitive decontamination—should be initiated on each patient before transfer into the Cold Zone. This process includes washing the individual, usually with soap and water, in an organized and thorough manner. Determining the adequacy of decontamination can be very difficult, however, and is often based on a best clinical judgment rather than objective data. Detection monitors have limited value and are not generally available to most agencies. When a patient cannot be definitively decontaminated, they should be loosely wrapped in a cocoon-like fashion with a blanket or sheet prior to transfer to the Cold Zone.

The minimum equipment required for patient decontami-nation by emergency response personnel are listed above. These lists are **not** comprehensive, and are provided to guide departments in developing their own equipment lists based on community needs and requirements.

With few exceptions, intact skin is more resistant to hazardous materials than injured flesh, mucous membranes, or eyes. Therefore, secondary decontamination should begin at the head and proceed downward, with initial attention paid to contaminated eyes and open wounds. Washing should be done using warm water, soft bristle brushes or sponges, and a mild soap, such as dishwashing liquid. Decontamination of non-ambulatory patients is more difficult and labor-intensive. Invasive procedures (e.g., intubation) should not be initiated in the Contamination Reduction Zone unless absolutely necessary. All potentially contaminated patient clothing and belongings that have been removed and bagged should remain in the decontamination area.

Pediatric Decontamination Considerations

The complexity of managing a hazardous materials incident is increased when children are involved. While protective to the wearer, PPE may be frightening to a young child, resulting in less cooperation and greater psychological trauma. Whenever possible, children and parents should remain together while undergoing decontamination and medical treatment. Increased susceptibility to hypothermia is an important consideration in determining to what degree a child is decontaminated in the field as opposed to being grossly decontaminated, wrapped in a blanket for transport, and then given definitive decontamination at the hospital or other heated location.

Mass Population Decontamination

Certain HazMat incidents result in large numbers of patients being exposed (or potentially exposed) to a chemical agent. In this situation, it will be necessary to implement proper triage to prioritize patients entry through the decontamination process, or to quickly expand the decontamination system to clean more patients simultaneously. Large volumes of water from charged hose lines and specially mounted nozzles or deluge guns on fire engines can be used to quickly rinse large numbers of individuals. Once through the decontamination process, patients should be given towels and temporary clothing.

Patient Treatment

Some contaminated patients may require treatment with antidotes, though most cases can be handled with symptomatic care.

PATIENT MANAGEMENT UNDER MASS CASUALTY CONDITIONS INVOLVING HAZARDOUS CHEMICALS

There are several important differences in disasters involving hazardous materials. A HazMat disaster may require setting up mass screening and decontamination centers. It may also be necessary to establish casualty collection points to provide stabilizing care in the field prior to transport. A major WMD/NBC incident may overwhelm any one hospital. Training in the appropriate procedures to be followed is essential for potential responders to a hazardous materials incident involving mass casualties. Triage may also be complicated for NBC exposures associated with the delayed onset of signs and symptoms of certain biological or chemical agents. If possible the patient, should be decontaminated before being transported to the emergency department to protect EMS and emergency department staff.

CRITICAL INCIDENT STRESS MANAGEMENT

Situations involving large numbers of ill or injured individuals, and which risk harm to the responder(s), are sources of critical incident stress. To minimize the occurrence of acute or long-term psychological consequences in response personnel, stress debriefing sessions should be held shortly after the incident. Acute stress reactions recognized during and after the incident should be immediately addressed by qualified peer debriefers or other mental health professionals.

ACUTE INHALATION INJURY

Industrial societies regularly produce large amounts of potentially toxic irritant gases. Although recent events have made us all too aware that toxic gases may be used as weapons of mass destruction, accidental exposures remain the greatest threat. For example, over half a million workers are annually exposed to anhydrous ammonia.

Smaller numbers are exposed to a variety of other irritant gases that are used in a multitude of industrial processes. In addition, thousands are smoke inhalation victims, exposed to toxic gases from the burning of a variety of materials. This most commonly occurs in commercial or home fires, where large amounts of carbon monoxide, hydrogen cyanide, hydrogen chloride, acrolein, sulfur dioxide, phosgene, and other irritant gases are produced.

The magnitude of these exposures is quite significant. The leading cause of death from acute inhalation injury is due to carbon monoxide and hydrogen cyanide in residential exposures, and hydrogen sulfide and hydrofluoric acid in occupational exposures. Approximately 5% of workplace deaths are due to asphyxiation or poisoning. This brief review of acute inhalation injury will focus on classification, diagnosis, and treatment for asphyxiants and irritants.

ASPHYXIANT GASES

Pathology

Asphyxiant gases cause death either as simple asphyxiants, as occurs with methane gas accumulation (in a coal mine), or by causing cellular asphyxia by a chemical means, as occurs with carbon monoxide. Carbon monoxide is the second most common atmospheric pollutant after carbon dioxide. It is produced by incomplete combustion from fires, faulty heating systems, volcanic eruptions, and internal combustion engines, as well as a variety of industrial processes. Carbon monoxide is an odorless, tasteless gas. Early symptoms (headache, sore throat, shortness of breath, and fatigue) can mimic the flu, especially when an entire family is affected from an exposure related to a faulty home heating system. Serious clinical effects such as tachycardia, arrhythmias, angina, and mental status changes can occur when carboxyhemoglobin concentrations exceed 20% (especially in nonsmokers) and effects are nearly always fatal when carboxyhemoglobin concentrations exceed 60%. Clinical effects may occur at lower concentrations in subjects already suffering from cardiopulmonary diseases. Carbon monoxide toxicity is related to decreased oxygen transport due to its preferential binding to hemoglobin and the resulting leftward shift of the hemoglobin oxygen dissociation curve and decreased oxygen utilization due to direct cytotoxicity by inactivating intracellular respiratory enzymes. Hydrogen cyanide is also produced by fires and manufacturing processes. Hydrogen cyanide toxicity does not affect oxygen transport but does decrease oxygen utilization due to direct cytotoxicity by inactivating intracellular respiratory enzymes.

Hydrogen sulfide (H2S) is a gaseous asphyxiant that decreases oxygen transport by the formation of methemoglobinemia and inhibits oxygen utilization by inhibition of cellular enzymes. H2S gas exposure is encountered in various industries, including: farming, oil and petroleum refining, rayon manufacturing, food processing, and other manufacturing processes. Exposures to very low concentrations (0.003–0.02 ppm) produce a noxious odor smelling like rotten eggs. In addition to being an asphyxiant, H2S is also an irritant, with respiratory and eye irritation beginning around 50 ppm. Because olfactory function is lost at around 100–200 ppm, if the victim can still smell the gas the concentration is usually not high enough to cause severe injury. However, the clinical diagnosis can be aided if the healthcare provider detects the smell of rotten eggs on the victim's clothing or breath. H2S produces intense irritation of mucous membranes and can cause pulmonary edema. Concentrations above 750–1000 ppm can cause respiratory paralysis, syncope, and sudden death. Death is due to direct central nervous system toxicity, pulmonary edema, or asphyxiation.

Diagnosis and Treatment

Although the diagnosis can be suspected by careful history, the physical examination is nearly useless as "cherry red mucous membranes" and cyanosis are only found at very high levels of carbon monoxide poisoning. High levels of carbon monoxide cause hypoxia by affecting oxygen transport and utilization. However, a carbon monoxide partial pressure of only 1 mm Hg can saturate over 50% of hemoglobin without affecting respiration and gas exchange. For this reason, measuring oxygen partial pressure is not useful in diagnosing carbon monoxide intoxication. Moreover, the spectra of oxyhemoglobin and abnormal hemoglobins such as carboxyhemoglobin are so similar that noninvasive oxygen saturation measurements are also useless in diagnosing carbon monoxide intoxication. Only direct measurements of the percent content of carboxyhemoglobin and methemoglobin (oximetry panel) can definitively make the diagnosis of carbon monoxide intoxication and H2S intoxication, respectively. An oximetry panel should be routinely performed for patients with smoke inhalation, suspected carbon monoxide, or H2S intoxication, and inhalation injuries of unknown type.

Carbon monoxide toxicity should be immediately treated with 100% oxygen, which reduces the half-life of carboxyhemoglobin from approximately 250 to 40 minutes. This half-life can be reduced to less than 20 minutes if treatment with hyperbaric oxygen is available. Hyperbaric oxygen therapy is recommended for patients with carbon monoxide levels exceeding 20 to 25%, or at lower levels if carbon monoxide induced cardiac or neurologic dysfunction is suspected. Hydrogen cyanide toxicity also requires confirmation with blood levels. Treatment is with a "cyanide treatment kit," containing sodium nitrite and thiosulfate solutions. H2S toxicity if promptly diagnosed can be treated with methylene blue (1–2 mg/kg intravenously) and sodium nitrite solution, but not thiosulfate solution. Hyperbaric oxygen therapy has been suggested as an additional form of therapy for these asphyxiants.

IRRITANT GASES

Pathophysiology

The health effects of an acute exposure to an irritant gas or vapor are dependent on the physiochemical properties of that particular gas or vapor, as well as specific host factors. The extent of exposure varies considerably and is most pronounced in subjects with preexisting airway diseases. Acid and alkaline gases such as chlorine and ammonia produce extreme alterations in pH that cause tissue damage by direct contact. Other gases produce chemical reactions that cause free radical release, inflammation, and membrane damage.

The site of pulmonary injury is most dependent on the water solubility of the gas. High-solubility gases (e.g., ammonia, sulfur dioxide, formaldehyde, or methyl isocyanate) can affect all exposed mucous membranes, including: ocular (irritation, erythema, and conjunctivitis, and with heavy exposure delayed-onset of cataracts), nasal (irritation, congestion, rhinorrhea, and erythema), facial burns (skin and lip), pharyngeal (throat and tongue irritation, burns and edema), and laryngeal (burns, edema, and obstruction) injuries.

Intermediate-solubility gases such as chlorine may produce upper-airway irritation, but the mucous membrane irritation is not as intense as for highly soluble gases.

Because of its intermediate solubility, chlorine's effect extends more distal, producing both upper- and lower-airway injury, and pulmonary edema. Low-solubility gases, like phosgene or oxides of nitrogen, produce little in the way of upper-airway irritation, but produce intense damage to the lower airways and pulmonary edema. The low-solubility gases are more likely to produce delayed-onset symptoms and delayed-onset pulmonary edema, usually within the first 24 hours. Several factors may influence the severity of lung injury.

For the most part, pulmonary injury severity is determined by (1) gas solubility and (2) exposure duration multiplied by gas concentration. Problems in escaping the exposure due to orthopedic problems or to falling or mouth breathing due to nasal obstruction may also play important roles in determining exposure and injury severity. For example, if gas density is high (e.g., chlorine or phosgene), the gas cloud may hug the floor, thereby increasing exposure to a victim who has fallen.

Oxides of nitrogen, like nitrogen dioxide, commonly produce a triphasic illness pattern. Initial presentation may be that of cough, wheeze, dyspnea, central chest pain, fever, sweating, and weakness. Physical examination may reveal wheezes and crackles, and the patient may be hypotensive and cyanotic. The patient's x-ray may be normal or may show pulmonary edema. This phase of the illness will resolve and the patient may be relatively asymptomatic and then 2 to 8 weeks later develop symptoms of bronchiolitis obliterans. Presentation includes the late development of fevers, chills, wheeze, cough, dyspnea, and chest pain associated with wheezes and crackles on physical exam. The chest films may be normal or may show diffuse, small nodules. Chest CT scans with expiratory imaging may show air trapping, bronchial wall thickening and nodules suggestive of bronchiolitis obliterans.

Diagnosis and Treatment

The early management and treatment of acute inhalation injury from an irritant gas is summarized below and is primarily supportive, including immediately removing any contaminated clothing that might further increase the absorption of a substance through the skin.

1. Start high-flow 100% oxygen and consider arterial blood gas and cooximetry panel.
2. Obtain history of any odors or knowledge of specific toxic agent.
3. Examine patient for eye injuries, flush eyes, and treat if inflammation is noted.
4. Examine patient for burns to face, nose, mouth, or throat.
5. If victim is hoarse, has difficulty phonating, facial burns or carbonaceous sputum, evaluate the airway with laryngoscopy or bronchoscopy and if edema is present, consider early intubation.
6. Examine chest and consider early use of bronchodilators, mucomyst, and or inhaled corticosteroids.
7. Peak flow rates and/or bedside spirometry may be helpful in diagnosing or documenting reversible bronchospasm. Full pulmonary function tests (volumes, diffusion, and/or provokability) should be reversed for a later timepoint.
8. Chest x-rays may be useful as a baseline but are generally not helpful in the acute setting unless the patient has significant hypoxemia or asymmetric breath sounds.
9. Observe patient for delayed pulmonary edema for 24 hours if the patient is hypoxemic or has been exposed to a low-solubility gas, such as phosgene.

Careful attention to the eyes is important since there may be late development of cataracts with heavy exposures. If the gas has already been identified, then knowing its solubility can help in the triage of exposed victims.

For example, high-solubility gases (sulfur dioxide or ammonia) affect the upper airways and only cause lower-airway injuries when the dose effect is large. Thus, if a potential victim, exposed to ammonia, has no upper-airway signs or symptoms (watery, teary eyes, red face, rhinitis, red sore nose, erythema of the posterior pharynx or hoarseness), it is unlikely that the patient has inhaled a dose high enough to cause lower-airway injury.

The patient who presents with tachypnea and stridor, particularly with some hoarseness, is at a high risk of developing progressive laryngeal edema and complete obstruction of the airway, and therefore should be considered for emergency intubation. Certainly if symptoms of upper-airway damage are present, a prompt inspection of the larynx by a laryngoscope or fiberoptic laryngoscope would be imperative, since once sufficient edema develops these patients are extremely difficult to intubate and one may have to do an emergency tracheostomy. If upper-airway edema is present, pharmacologic treatment includes nebulized racemic epinephrine and systemic corticosteroids. If edema is minimal and early intubation is not required, conservative care to maintain airflow consists of positive pressure breathing (BIPAP or CPAP) or a mixture of helium/ oxygen gas that due to its lower density can improve upper-airway flow dynamics by reducing turbulence.

However, in the presence of edema not immediately requiring intubation, conservative care should only be done if frequent monitoring to assess edema progression and emergent intubation is possible.

When the patient is exposed to a low-soluble gas, like phosgene, upper-airway signs and symptoms are not expected and observation is required because it may take as long as 24 hours for reactive airways dysfunction syndrome or pulmonary edema to develop. The development of reactive airways dysfunction syndrome (RADS) or asthma after exposure to irritant gases is the most common long-term complication. Early treatment with inhaled bronchodilators and inhaled corticosteroids is a wellproven treatment approach for those with symptoms and reversible bronchospasm. Reversible bronchospasm can be confirmed by documenting improvement in flow rates after treatment with either a peak flow meter or spirometry. Currently, no studies exist to determine whether early use of inhaled corticosteroids is a viable prophylactic strategy. However, the side effects of inhaled corticosteroids are minimal. Sinusitis may accompany lower-airway inflammation, and treatment with nasal corticosteroids, decongestants, nasal anticholinergic agents, and antihistamines are typical interventions.

Observation is critical if the patient complains of dyspnea or if tachypnea is noted, as these may be the earliest signs of impending pulmonary edema after acute inhalation exposure. While chest imaging is not useful in the early detection of pulmonary injury if the patient is asymptomatic, it is valuable if the patient is in respiratory distress or if pulmonary auscultation is abnormal or asymmetrical, in which case, oximetry (remember, not useful with chemical asphyxiants such as carbon monoxide and H2S), arterial blood gases, and chest radiographs should be immediately obtained. Treatment is supportive. Abnormal gas exchange if severe should be treated with positive pressure ventilation aiming for the lowest mean airway pressure possible while still supporting gas exchange. Intubation may also be necessary if bronchial secretions are excessive and require frequent pulmonary toilet by catheter or bronchoscopic suctioning. Systemic corticosteroids are controversial for the treatment of noncardiogenic pulmonary edema and there is probably no role in the acute treatment of inhalation lung injury.

In the weeks following irritant gas exposures, the patient may continue to suffer from sinusitis, RADS, and asthma. Chronic cough syndrome may also result from irritant gas exposures. When chest radiographs and/or chest CT scans are normal, chronic cough is usually due to asthma or RADS, sinusitis, and/or gastroesophageal reflux. When chest imaging is abnormal, cough may be due to pneumonia or bronchiolitis obliterans. Prophylactic antibiotics have been suggested because sloughing of the tracheal mucosa offers a good culture media for bacteria. However, there is no evidence that prophylactic antibiotics reduce the incidence of pneumonia. Instead, antibiotics should be used only if pneumonia occurs and when possible targeted to the organisms responsible.

Chest physiotherapy, high-frequency percussive ventilation, bronchodilators, and frequent suctioning may be helpful in those patients with mucus plugs and thick secretions. Bronchiolitis obliterans is a serious complication that usually responds to oral steroids, but may be progressive or even fatal if not treated promptly. It is unlikely that early treatment with only antibiotics or inhaled steroids is preventive. Some might argue that, given the possibility of bronchiolitis obliterans, early treatment with oral steroids (prednisone at 40–60 mg/daily) for 8 weeks might be a reasonable prophylaxis strategy after exposure to those gases known to cause this problem, particularly in those patients with silo-filler's disease or those exposed to high doses of NO_2 or SO_2. Others believe that the occurrence of severe or life-threatening bronchiolitis obliterans after inhalation injury is too rare to warrant the routine use of oral steroids. Experimental anecdotal therapy for acute inhalation injury includes nebulized sodium bicarbonate or nebulized mucomyst (N-acetylcysteine) to break up secretion and to reduce free radical damage. The long-term consequences of irritant inhalation injury are summarized below in order of most common first:

- Complete resolution of symptoms
- Reactive airways dysfunction syndrome (RADS) or asthma
- Chronic bronchitis
- Bronchiectasis, i.e., ammonia, SO_2
- Bronchiolitis obliterans, i.e., NO_2, SO_2
- Bronchostenosis, i.e., mustard gas
- Restrictive interstitial fibrosis

SMOKE INHALATION

Pathophysiology

Inhalation injury associated with burns from fires comprises approximately a quarter of those patients admitted to a burn unit.

Smoke contains toxic gases (asphyxiants and irritants) along with particulate matter that is coated with the chemicals of combustion and pyrolysis. Smoke particles cause airway damage due to direct irritation and via the toxic effects of the chemicals adsorbed to the surface of these particles. Particles greater than 10 microns in diameter cause upper-airway injury, as they typically do not penetrate into the lower airways.

The subglottic or supraglottic edema following smoke inhalation (due to thermal, irritant gas, or large particles) may lead to upper-airway obstruction. Upper-airway obstruction may develop slowly over the first 12–24 hours due to initial hypovolemia and other inflammatory factors. Particles less than 3 microns in diameter cause lower-airway injury and, in fact, particles greater than 3 microns in diameter may also penetrate into the lower airways when (a) aerosolized and respired in high concentrations, (b) if the subject is a mouth breather, thereby bypassing nasal defense mechanisms, or (c) if the subject has high minute ventilation, as may be seen in firefighters. Suspicion of a smoke inhalation injury is warranted whenever there has been exposure to a fire in an enclosed space, especially if the patient displays signs of altered mental status, facial burns, stridor, carbonaceous sputum, respiratory distress, or an admission carboxyhemoglobin greater than 10%.

Diagnosis and Treatment

The most common clinical problems associated with smoke inhalation are (1) upper and/or lower-airway inflammation and (2) carbon monoxide toxicity, although hydrogen cyanide toxicity has gained recent attention. Fiberoptic bronchoscopy is very useful in evaluation of burn patients for airway injury by demonstrating carbonaceous material, airway edema, erythema, ulcerations, hemorrhage, blisters, or ischemia. During bronchoscopy, intubation should be considered, preferably over the bronchoscope, if there is evidence of upper- or lower-airway edema or if carbonaceous material has penetrated past the vocal cords. Because edema is an ongoing process in burn injuries and intubation may become increasingly difficult, it is nearly always better to intubate too soon rather than too late. Xenon-133 ventilation scanning has been used in burn patients to detect airway injury missed by fiberoptic bronchoscopy. It has a high sensitivity, but there are false positives in patients with obstructive airway disease. All patients with a history of smoke inhalation and any of the above-noted physical signs should have direct measurement of carboxyhemoglobin and arterial blood gases, as noninvasive measures of oxygen saturation are incorrect in this setting. Chest x-rays are valuable only in those patients who have respiratory symptoms, such as tachypnea, dyspnea, and hypoxemia. Pulmonary edema is an extremely rare complication unless a specific irritant gas is a byproduct of combustion, and infiltrates usually will not be apparent without ventilation/perfusion mismatching and the consequent development of hypoxemia. In the presence of significant burn injuries, treatment with systemic corticosteroids is contraindicated, as their use has been shown to increase mortality due to sepsis. Other than the above-noted specific issues, the management and treatment of smoke inhalation and its long-term clinical consequences are no different than for other irritant gas exposures.

PULMONARY FUNCTION TESTS

Pulmonary function tests should be obtained as soon as the patient is stable. It is our practice to obtain complete pulmonary function tests (PFTs) as soon as the patient is ambulatory and no longer requiring supplemental oxygen. We obtain complete PFTs again at 3, 6, 12, and 24 months after exposure in the symptomatic patient. Spirometry frequently is normal in the presence of mild obstructive or restrictive disease from inhalation injury. Also pseudo-restriction (symmetrical reductions in forced vital capacity and forced expiratory volume at 1 s) may occur in obstructive airways disease due to air trapping. Therefore, measurement of a bronchodilator response and/or lung volumes is necessary, especially when spirometry is abnormal or at the lower limits of normal. Airflow obstruction may be due to RADS, asthma, or anatomic airway narrowing.

Bronchodilator response or methacholine challenge testing can be performed to confirm obstructive airways disease and airway hyperreactivity. However, no conclusions about chronicity should occur until treatment and proven persistence are documented after at least 3 to 6 months have elapsed. Because early transient bronchial hyperreactivity may occur in the weeks following irritant gas exposures, detection of early bronchial hyperreactivity may not always predictive of long-term airway injury and irritability. However, in firefighters with heavy exposure to dust and irritant gases in the first days of the World Trade Center collapse, bronchial hyperreactivity demonstrated by methacholine challenge testing after 1 or 3 months post-exposure was predictive of persistent airway hyperreactivity and RADS.

Restrictive changes in lung function progress very slowly and may not be detected until 2 or more years after the toxic exposure. The most common abnormality is an isolated reduction in residual volume. Isolated reduction in lung diffusion may occur but is usually accompanied by reduction in lung volumes. Although most patients exposed to irritant gases and/or smoke inhalation will recover completely, others may develop chronic airway hyperreactivity, obstructive lung disease (asthma, RADS, chronic bronchitis), bronchiectasis, bronchostenosis, bronchiolitis obliterans, or restrictive interstitial fibrosis.

ELECTRICAL INJURIES

Electrical injuries may be commonly seen in a disaster. They often occur due to damaged caused to buildings and infrastructure. Flooding also places individuals at risk, as electrical currents can readily travel through water. Individuals are at particular risk for injury during disaster recovery and cleanup. In the United States electrical injuries are the fifth leading cause of fatal occupational injury and contribute 3–6% of admissions to burn units.

Alternating current (AC) is commonly found in households and is defined as current that changes direction on a cyclic basis. Standard household current is 60 cycles/s. Direct current (DC) travels in a constant direction and may be found in batteries, railways, and automobile electrical systems. High-voltage systems are considered those greater than a thousand volts. Ohm's law deals with the relationship between voltage and current in an ideal conductor. This relationship states that the potential difference (voltage) across an ideal conductor is proportional to the current through it. The constant of proportionality is called the resistance, R. The current flowing through the resistance is I. So Ohm's law may be stated as I = V/R. In the human body, resistance increases from lowest to highest as follows: nerves, vessels, muscles, skin (variable depending on moisture), tendon, fat, and bone.

INITIAL ASSESSMENT

Treat as any critically ill patient and follow general resuscitative measures: ABCs, cardiac monitor, IV fluids, and oxygen. Initial responders need to make sure that they do not become part of the circuit. Several types of electrical injuries may occur: true electrical injuries (victim becomes part of the circuit), arc burns (current strikes skin but does not enter the body), flame injuries (typical thermal injury), and blunt injuries (being thrown from the source).

FURTHER ASSESSMENT

Important parts of the history include: type of electrical source, duration of contact, any associated blunt trauma, factors at scene, and resuscitative measures provided. A detailed physical exam should be performed paying particular attention to the following systems:

Neurological

- Multiple presentations
    - Acute CNS symptoms (maintain your standard differential diagnosis for these entities)
    - Coma
- Altered mental status
- Paralysis

- Seizures
- Respiratory arrest (paralyzed respiratory center in medulla)
    * Delayed neurological symptoms
- Mimics ascending paralysis, transverse myelitis, and incomplete cord transection
- A few days to years

Skin

- Surface burns do not predict the extent of the underlying injury.
- Entrance burns (contact of source)
    * Small, well circumscribed, full thickness
    * Depressed center
    * Dry, charred appearance
    * Most commonly on the hands
- Exit burns (ground)
    * Exploded or blown out appearance
    * Frequently found on the feet
- Oral commissure burns
    * Pediatric
    * Significant cosmetic problem
    * Delayed labial artery hemorrhage (2 days to 2 weeks)
    * Skin findings may be absent with current source over wide area (lowresistance/ low-voltage electrical injury)
- Vascular
    * Extensive and variable lesions
    * Progressive necrosis
    * High amputation rate with high-voltage injuries

Musculoskeletal

- Observe for compartment syndromes

- Fractures/dislocations (10–15%)
- Osteoschisis (longitudinal fracture from passing current)

DIAGNOSTIC STUDIES

Except for the most minor of injuries, diagnostic studies are indicated and should include: EKG, electrolytes, renal function, CPK (peak levels predict amount of muscle injury and risk of amputation), myoglobin (serum and urine), urinalysis, and radiographic studies (indicated by associated trauma).

MANAGEMENT

- ABCs (reassess)
- Cardiac monitoring
  - Risk of arrhythmia is pathway dependent
  - Ventricular fibrillation — AC
  - Asystole — DC and high-voltage AC
  - Any abnormal rhythm is possible
  - The major cause of death is cardiac dysrhythmias.
- IV Fluids
  - Maintain urine output at 1–1.5 ml/kg/hr
  - Various burn formulas do not apply to electrical burns
  - Goal is to prevent renal complications of rhabdomyolysis
- Burn care
  - Mafenide acetate for full-thickness burns
  - Sulfadiazine silver for extensive burns (>15% BSA)
- Extremities with burns splinted in position of function
  - Reassess frequently
  - Early surgical management
- Other manifestations as per standard of care for that entity.

PROGNOSIS

Only 5% in high-voltage group were able to return to their previous job.

DISPOSITION

Asymptomatic patients with a normal physical exam after low-voltage exposure may be discharged. Admission criteria include: all high-voltage injuries, intermediatevoltage injuries (>600 V), suspicion of conductive injury, dysrhythmia in pre-hospital setting or in the ED, abnormal EKG findings, documented loss of consciousness, and associated injuries that requires admission. All significant electrical injuries should be transferred to a burn center.

SPECIAL CONSIDERATIONS

- Electrical injuries are more similar to crush injuries than to typical thermal burns.
- Surface burns underestimate extent of underlying injury.
- Surface burns may be absent in the wet patient.
- Low-voltage injuries account for half of deaths due to electrical injuries.
- Massive fluid replacement is key.
- AC is more dangerous than DC.
- The current threshold of tetanic contraction is 10–15 mA.

6

Toxicology and Terrorism

Toxicology is the study of how toxins (street drugs, prescribed medications, occupational toxins, or chemical weapons) interact with living organisms. Fundamentally, toxicology is the discipline that concerns itself with the care of the poisoned patient. Not only are entire textbooks written about toxicology, but they are written about specific subdivisions of toxicology: medical toxicology, environmental toxicology, regulatory toxicology, and others. A detailed discussion of the entire discipline, obviously, is beyond the scope of this introductory chapter.

Disaster medicine must concern itself with toxicology because many weapons of mass destruction and terror are toxins. A working knowledge of the principles of toxicology, therefore, is crucial for anyone who might deal with mass casualty incidents or terrorist attacks. This chapter will focus on those areas of medical toxicology that are pertinent to disaster medicine and the response to chemical or biological terrorism: identifying an incident as a toxin-mediated event, initial assessment and stabilization, post-stabilization assessment, and treatment.

IS A TOXIN INVOLVED IN THE ATTACK?

The initial key to identifying a mass toxic exposure is to have a high index of suspicion. Unless a clinician is willing to consider a poisonous gas attack as a possible etiology of unexpected pulmonary symptoms in a large number of patients, or cyanide poisoning in patients with coma and unexplained metabolic acidosis, the diagnosis will be missed.

The characteristic scenario of a mass toxic exposure is that of otherwise healthy multiple victims—several or several hundred—who develop a similar set of symptoms over a short period of time. In the case of immediately acting poisons (such as hydrogen cyanide gas), there will be little question that a toxin is involved. In cases of poisons that produce a delayed symptom complex (such as oral ricin poisoning), the diagnosis may only be made after a coordinated effort by federal, state, and local agencies.

Clues on the scene may suggest a toxic exposure, and even the agent involved. The presence of an unexplained gas or mist immediately before symptoms occur suggests a toxic exposure, as does a history suggesting that symptoms are worse in those persons closest to the area from which the gas or mist emanated. Some gases have characteristic appearances and odors; a yellow gas that smells like bleach suggests chlorine gas, an odor of freshly mown hay suggests phosgene, and an odor of onions or garlic suggests a vesicant gas.

Patients' symptoms may not only help determine that a toxin is involved, but also which toxin is involved. As a general rule, toxins produce similar symptoms in all patients. Some toxins, particularly those that alter autonomic function, produce characteristic "toxidromes" (see below) that may help establish the diagnosis. In addition to the physical examination, laboratory analysis may help establish a diagnosis; cyanide, for instance, leads to a marked increase in the mixed venous oxygen saturation due to a failure to utilize oxygen on a molecular level.

INITIAL ASSESSMENT AND STABILIZATION

Assessing the patient with a potential toxic exposure follows the basic tenets of Emergency Medicine: secure the airway, breathing, and circulation. Patient decontamination may also be necessary in cases of toxin-induced disasters or chemical terrorism.

Airway

Loss of consciousness (as may be seen with cyanide), loss of muscle tone (as may be seen with botulism), or the presence of copious secretions (as may be seen with organophosphorus nerve agents) may all lead to primary airway failure. In all such patients, the airway should be secured. The preferred method of securing the airway in poisoned patients is via endotracheal intubation; as a general rule, poisons due not alter airway anatomy, although as noted above the patient may have copious secretions.

Breathing

Hypoxia may complicate any one of several toxic exposures. Vesicant gases and pulmonary agents may produce acute lung injury and hypoxia. Organophosphorus nerve agents may produce suffocating pulmonary secretions that interfere with gas exchange. Organophosphorus nerve agents or botulism may lead to diaphragmatic insufficiency and a failure of appropriate air movement into the lungs. In any case, the appropriate treatment is supplemental oxygen; a reasonable target is an oxygen saturation of greater than or equal to 95%

Circulation

Hypotension should initially be treated with intravenous crystalloid; if this fails, vasopressors should be used. Because the hypotension seen with poisoned patients is frequently the result of peripheral vascular collapse, direct acting alpha-adrenergic agonists (such as neosynephrine or norepinephrine) are usually the first-line recommendation.

Decontamination

Decontamination is a crucial intervention in the initial assessment and stabilization of a patient who is poisoned as part of a terrorist attack. In such cases, dermal decontamination is usually the focus as agents of biological and chemical terror are likely to be aerosolized. Gastrointestinal decontamination (gastric emptying and/or administration of activated charcoal), while an important intervention in the hospitalbased treatment of poisoned patients, is unlikely to be helpful in the treatment of disaster- related toxic exposures, as mass exposures are unlikely to occur during the oral route. Incidents such as staphylococcal enterotoxin B poisoning, where gastrointestinal decontamination may actually be indicated, are the exception rather than the rule.

POST-STABILIZATION PATIENT ASSESSMENT

Physical Examination

A portion of the physical examination will, by necessity, be performed as part of the assessment of airway, breathing and circulation. After initial stabilization and decontamination, a more detailed examination may reveal injuries not initially suspected, such as a concussion effect from a blast that may accompany the detonation of a chemical weapon.

Amore detailed physical examination may also reveal the presence of a toxic syndrome, or toxidrome, which provides a diagnosis in the absence of historical information or laboratory data. The toxidrome examination consists of assessing vital signs, mental status, pupil size, oral mucous membranes, lung sounds, bowel sounds, and the skin. Several agents that may be employed in terrorist-related disasters might be expected to produce classic toxidromes. Frequent reexamination is a key component of the successful care of the poisoned patient. Patients who initially appear to be stable, such as the patient who has a mild cough and normal transcutaneous oxygen saturation after mustard gas exposure, may go on to develop acute lung injury and the acute respiratory distress syndrome several hours later. Such patients, despite their benign initial examination, may quickly deteriorate and require endotracheal intubation.

Laboratory Evaluation

The laboratory evaluation of a potentially poisoned patient is driven by the patient's symptoms and the possible agents involved.

Patients who present with a mild cough after a respiratory agent attack may need no more than a chest x-ray; patients with oral ricin poisoning may need an extensive laboratory evaluation to assess for the sequelae of this disease.

One test that is unlikely to be of benefit in evaluating potential victims of toxinrelated disasters is the "toxicology screen." Such screens typically test for drugs of abuse (cocaine, amphetamines, LSD, PCP, marijuana), which are unlikely to be used in terrorist attacks. Even a positive result would be unhelpful, as it would likely be an incidental finding. The "toxicology screen," therefore, really has no role in the routine management of poisoned patients in the disaster setting.

TREATMENT

Contrary to popular opinion, the treatment of the poisoned patient rarely consists of finding the correct antidote. Most of the life-saving treatment of a poisoned patient consists of securing the airway, breathing, and circulation; performing adequate decontamination; and providing ongoing supportive treatment. Occasionally, however, patients are poisoned with an agent that may be reversed with the appropriate antidote. A partial list of these poisons, with their antidotes, is provided.

Toxicology is discipline that concerns itself with patients who have been poisoned. In the field of disaster medicine, the important principles of toxicology include identifying an incident as a toxin-mediated event, initial assessment and stabilization, post-stabilization assessment, and treatment.

MEASLES

Measles is caused by an RNA virus of the genus *Morbillivirus* in the family Paramyxoviridae. It remains a major killer of children under 5 years in the developing world, where mortality rates may approach 5–40%. Humans are the only natural hosts of the disease. Transmission is via direct contact with respiratory droplets, and airborne spread is less common. Unfortunately, 5% of vaccine recipients will not form an antibody response. Risk factors for acquiring the disease include: overcrowding, disaster or refugee camp situations, malnutrition, immunocompromised children, and unvaccinated children under 18 months of age.

PRESENTATION

The incubation period is 7 to 14 days from exposure to first signs/symptoms of disease.

Patients are contagious 1 to 2 days prior to onset of illness and until around 4 days after the rash appears.

Signs and Symptoms

The prodromal phase of the illness begins with fever and coryza (rhinorrhea) over the first 24 hours; then cough and severe conjunctivitis develop 1–2 days later. Also seen 24–48 hours after respiratory symptoms develop are Koplik spots. These are bright red spots with a gray/white center seen on the buccal mucosa (inside of the mouth). These Koplik spots, seen with any of the other symptoms, assure the diagnosis of measles. 24 to 48 hours after Koplik spots develop, a maculopapular rash develops.

Complications and Physical Findings

- Otitis Media
- Pneumonia (measles pneumonia and superimposed bacterial pneumonia) with respiratory distress
- Croup
- Diarrhea and dehydration
- Encephalitis
- Cervical adenitis
- Splenomegaly
- Corneal ulcers; keratomalacia; blindness (worsened by Vitamin A deficiency)

- Hemorrhagic measles
- Encephalitis in children older than 2 years of age (10–20% fatality; neurologic sequelae common in survivors)
- Subacute Sclerosing Panencephalitis (SSPE): very rare late complication patients 5–15 years old; slow progressive degenerative disease
- Death
- Complications are especially severe in children younger than 5 years, with no history of being immunized, who are immunocompromised (cancer, HIV), and/or malnourished.

DIAGNOSIS

Measles IgM antibody levels in serum are seen in the acute phase. Measles IgM is detectable for 1 month after onset of rash.

Measles virus can be isolated from urine, blood, and nasopharyngeal secretions. In regions where no laboratory facilities are available, the clinical diagnosis, especially if Koplik spots present, is adequate and should warrant treatment.

DIFFERENTIAL DIAGNOSIS

Viral Illnesses Such as Roseola

TREATMENT

- Vitamin A200,000 IU PO immediately (preserves eyesight and lowers disease severity)
- Active immunization (MMR) best if given within 3 days of exposure. MMR not to be given to children younger than 6 months of age (see "Prevention" below)
- Ophthalmic antibiotic drops or ointment
- Systemic Antibiotics for respiratory disease
- Hydration (IV or PO)
- Nutrition

- Passive immunization (immune globulin) if given less than 6 days after exposure and available.
- Criteria for immune globulin
  * Children younger than 12 months of age and pregnant women should receive immune globulin IM (0.25 ml/kg; maximum: 15 ml) as soon as possible after exposure
  * Immunocompromised children of any age should receive immune globulin as soon as possible after exposure (0.5 ml/kg IM; maximum: 15 ml)
  * Infants younger than 6 months of age should receive immune globulin soon after exposure, but not the vaccine
  * Children older than 12 months of age should receive vaccine alone within 72 hr of exposure, and not immune globulin
  * Pregnant women and immunocompromised persons should receive immune globulin but not vaccine

PROGNOSIS

General mortality rate of 5%, which may increase to 40% during epidemics.

PREVENTION

MMR Vaccine is routinely recommended for all children worldwide by 12 to 15 months of age. It should be given as young as 6 months if there is an outbreak and exposure, but the immune response is felt to be suboptimal when given under 1 year. A second MMR vaccine is recommended routinely at 4–6 years of age but may be given at any time provided that an interval of at least 4 weeks has elapsed since the first vaccine dose. If a child receives an MMR vaccine under 1 year of age, two more doses, separated by at least 1 month, should be given after the first birthday. Contraindications to the MMR vaccine include: pregnancy, children under 6 months of age, immunodeficiency, HIV infection, cancer, and untreated active TB.

7

Terrorism Causing Deadly Diseases

DIARROHEA AND DYSENTERY PATHOGENESIS

Hippocrates said, "the influence of water upon health is very great. Such as are marshy, standing, or stagnant, must in summer be hot, thick and stinking, because there is no outflow ... In the summer there are epidemics of dysentery, diarrhea, and long quartan fever." Outbreaks of diarrhea have historically occurred whenever there were crowded living conditions, and particularly whenever the normal patterns of trade, food supply, and social structure or governmental authority were disrupted.

Etiology

The clinical definition of diarrhea is three or more episodes of loose stool or any loose stool with blood during a 24-hour period. Chronic diarrhea is when symptoms last more than 2–4 weeks.

Incidence and Prevalence

An estimated 744 million to 1 billion episodes and nearly 5 million deaths from diarrhea occur per year worldwide.

Risk Factors

Natural and manmade disasters that produce overcrowding, a scarcity of safe drinking water, improper elimination of human waste, and the contamination of food during or after its preparation are risk factors for the spread of infectious diarrhea Acute diarrhea is acquired thorough the fecal–oral route. Infectious diarrhea can be classified as noninflammatory or inflammatory. Noninflammatory diarrhea results from disturbance of absorption of fluid and electrolytes and does not involve invasion of the intestinal mucosa. The most common pathogens of noninflammatory diarrhea include viruses and protozoans. Inflammatory diarrhea results from invasion of intestinal mucosa, inducing an inflammatory response that results in colonic malabsorption and the presence of fecal leukocytes and blood. The most common pathogens include bacteria.

PRESENTATION

Incubation

Incubation varies with each implicated pathogen. Rapid onset of symptoms usually within 6 hours of ingestion suggests a preformed toxin. This includes *Staphylococcus* and *Bacillus cereus*. Onset of symptoms, more than 8 hours, suggests *Clostridium perfringens*.

Signs and Symptoms

Noninflammatory diarrhea is described as watery and voluminous. There is absence of fever and abdominal pain. Inflammatory diarrhea is described as a small volume of loose stool that may contain blood or pus. Fever as well as abdominal pain is typical.

CLINICAL PEARLS

Cholera (*Vibrio cholerae*)

It has a short incubation: usually less than 1 to 5 days. It is a dose-dependent enterotoxin-mediated infection with copious, watery, painless diarrhea also know as "rice water stools." Vomiting may occur.

If not treated promptly it may quickly lead to severe dehydration and death. Monitoring of intake and outtake of fluids and electrolyte balance is important to prevent death. The treatment should involve aggressive oral rehydration; if this is not possible, then intravenous hydration.

Shigella (*Shigella dysenteriae*)

Shigella is made up of four serogroups; type one is the most virulent and the cause of epidemic dysentery. Classic symptoms include bloody diarrhea, abdominal cramps, fever, and rectal pain. Complications include seizures, renal failure, and hemolytic uremic syndrome. Fatality ranges from 5 to 15%.

Salmonella (*Salmonella species*)

The species of *Salmonella* include typhi, paratyphi, typhimurium, and choleraesuis.

The incubation period ranges from 8 to 48 hours after ingestion and usually lasts 3–5 days. The symptoms include watery diarrhea, which may lead to blood dysentery, fever, crampy abdominal pain, and vomiting.

DIAGNOSIS

Laboratory

Microscopic examination is the traditional tool of investigation. Stool culture has been the mainstay in obtaining the causative agent of diarrhea. If stool is preserved for more than 24 hours, fecal leukocyte examination is unreliable. Examination of stool for ova and parasites in acute diarrhea is not cost-effective. Most parasitic infections cause a persistent or chronic clinical course.

Other

Dehydration is the main cause of morbidity and mortality in the patient with diarrhea. Postural changes in blood pressure (decrease of 10 mm Hg) and pulse rate (increase of 10 beats/min) indicate volume depletion. Measurement of urine output, body temperature, and observation for abdominal distention and rebound tenderness are necessary for appropriate treatment. Rectal examination for occult blood is a cheap and inexpensive way to diagnose inflammatory diarrhea.

DIFFERENTIAL DIAGNOSIS

The differential diagnosis of diarrhea includes colonic neoplasm, inflammatory bowel disease, malabsorption syndromes including tropical sprue, bacterial overgrowth or celiac sprue, HIV, and lactose intolerance.

TREATMENT

Most acute diarrheal illness is self-limited, and no therapy is necessary. The goal of therapy is to restore fluid loss and prevent dehydration. In large-volume diarrhea (noninflammatory) carbonated drinks and juices should be avoided; instead, glucosecontaining electrolyte repletion is recommended.

In the case of inflammatory diarrhea, antibiotics may be warranted. If suspected or culture proven *E. coli*, *Shigella*, *Salmonella*, or *Campylobacter*, the use of ciprofloxacin 500 mg orally twice daily for 3–7 days is recommended. If *E. coli* O157:H7 is suspected, no antibiotic is advised, as studies suggest it may be harmful. If *Vibrio cholerae* is suspected or culture proven, doxycycline 300 mg orally in a single dose or a fluoroquinolone in a single dose is recommended. In cases of giardiasis, treatment with metronidazole 250–750 mg orally every 8 hours is recommended for a duration of 7–10 days. If *Entamoeba histolytica* is the cause of diarrhea, then treatment with metronidazole is warranted. A common occurrence after the illness includes lactose intolerance; patients should be advised to temporarily avoid dairy products.

PROGNOSIS

The primary cause of mortality in infectious diarrhea is dehydration. Approximately 5 million deaths worldwide occur each year, and are attributable to dehydration. Through thoughtful strategies aimed at prevention and access to health care including cost-effective evaluation and treatment, there is a chance at preventing death.

PREVENTION

Prevention is achieved by protecting the water and sewage systems, avoiding overcrowding, advocating hand hygiene, and boiling contaminated water. The traditional vaccine against cholera (based on whole, killed cells) is characterized by low levels of efficacy. It is not recommended for the control of epidemics. The new vaccines might be considered, but with these there is a rapid loss of protection, giving a false sense of security

MALARIA

Malaria has a global distribution throughout the tropics. At least 300–500 million new cases of malaria occur annually, resulting in 5 million deaths. These statistics are probably not an accurate reflection of the impact malaria has, since many of the afflicted countries do not have the proper public health surveillance systems to report and record this disease. It is important to understand the concept of stable versus unstable malaria. Stable malaria occurs in regions where the population is constantly being exposed. Therefore, much of the population will develop partial immunity by 5 years of age. In these regions mortality rates are not as high, except in the pediatric and pregnant women population. Unstable malaria occurs in regions where the disease is seasonal or sporadic; here the population is afforded no partial immunity. In these regions, malaria contributes much more significantly to morbidity and mortality. Obviously, travelers and individuals who have been away from a stable malarious for several years have no immunity. Several traits are felt to afford partial protection against malaria: sickle cell trait, SS individuals as well (usually early death), G6PD deficiency, the thalassemias, hemoglobin C, and a negative Duffy blood type (*P. vivax*: West Africa).

PATHOGENESIS

Malaria is transmitted from the bite of the female anopheles mosquito, which usually feeds from late afternoon through dawn. Other means of transmission include: blood transfusions, shared needles, airport malaria (where one is infected with a mosquito who has traveled on a plane), and (rarely) congenitally. There are four different species involved: *Plasmodium falciparum* (causes complicated malaria), *P. vivax*, *P. ovale*, and *P. malariae*. A detailed life cycle is beyond the scope of this handbook; however, several key features will be highlighted. During a blood meal the mosquito injects the sporozoite, which makes its way to the cells of the liver, where it can replicate into a schizont or remain dormant as a hypnozoite (seen in *P. vivax* and *ovale* infection). Infected liver cells release the schizont into the bloodstream, where it attacks erythrocytes. Inside the newly infected erythrocyte an immature trophozoite develops and one of two pathways can occur. The trophozoite can mature, producing further schizonts, which eventually causes rupture of the cell and allows for other erythrocytes to become infected or the trophozoite can develop into a gametocyte that is released into the bloodstream and taken up by the mosquito during a blood meal. The gametocyte is essential for continuation of the life cycle of the parasite in the mosquito.

PRESENTATION

Depending on the species of malaria, the incubation period can be quite varied. With *P. falciparum* the incubation period is around a week; however, it sometimes can be several weeks to months. With *P. vivax* and *ovale* secondary infection with activation of the hypnozoite can occur many years later. Although all four species clinically cause malaria, it is *P. falciparum* that causes complicated malaria and contributes significantly to the morbidity and mortality seen. Malaria always presents with cyclical fevers; other symptoms may include: fatigue, malaise, arthralgias, headache, upper respiratory complaints, nausea, vomiting, and diarrhea. On physical examination, manifestations of anemia may be noted (pale conjunctiva and tongue, increased respiratory rate, tachycardia, a new heart murmur), mild hepatomegaly, jaundice in severe cases, and splenomegaly (particularly with prolonged or repeated infections). Complications of severe malaria include: cerebral malaria (seizures, coma), anemia, congestive heart failure (secondary to anemia), pulmonary edema, jaundice, acute renal failure, metabolic acidosis, disseminated intravascular coagulation, and hypoglycemia (particularly in children).

DIAGNOSIS

There should be a high index of suspicion for malaria in all individuals presenting with a fever from the tropics. A thick and thin blood film should be obtained. The thick film is useful to screen for evidence of malaria, and if negative a thin film is not necessary. If the thick film is positive, a thin film should be performed to identify the species and the percentage of infected red blood cells. It is important to remember that a negative blood film does not exclude the diagnosis of malaria. Rapid diagnostic dipsticks have been developed for *P. falciparum*, based upon plasmodial histidine rich protein and parasite-specific LDH. Other means to diagnosis include: fluorescence microscopy (quantitative buffy coat), DNA probes, PCR, and antibody detection (useless in acute infection). On a complete blood count, anemia and thrombocytopenia may be appreciated.

DIFFERENTIAL DIAGNOSIS

* Typhoid fever
* Upper respiratory infection
* Viral hepatitis
* Dengue fever
* Acute HIV
* Schistosomiasis
* Brucellosis
* Trypanosomiasis
* Visceral leishmaniasis
* Rickettsial infections
* Relapsing fever

TREATMENT

Several principles determine treatment for malaria. One needs to define a case as either being complicated or uncomplicated. Complicated cases would be those with evidence of significant systemic involvement (cerebral malaria, acute renal failure, pulmonary edema, metabolic acidosis, DIC), severe anemia, significant other comorbid problems, and those unable to tolerate oral medication. As soon as a patient shows signs of improvement and is able to tolerate oral medication, they should be switched over from intravenous therapy. If an individual has been infected from a chloroquinesensitive region (Central America, Haiti, Dominican Republic, and pockets of the Middle East), chloroquine should still be mainstay treatment. Ideally, patients receiving intravenous quinine/ quinidine should be place on a cardiac monitor. Rapid administration of either agent may cause hypoglycemia. Supportive treatment is also important: blood transfusions, hydration, nutrition, treating other underlying infections, correcting hypoglycemia, and dialysis. Some of the more common treatment regimens are listed below, availability of agents will vary depending upon country.

Uncomplicated Chloroquine Sensitive

Chloroquine 500 mg PO BID x 2-3 days

Uncomplicated Chloroquine Resistant

Quinine 650 mg PO TID and Doxycycline 100 mg PO BID both for 7 days

Atovaquone/Proguanil 1 g/400 mg PO QD x 3 days

Mefloquine 750 mg PO then 500 mg PO 12 hr later

Halofantrine 500 mg PO x 3 doses

Complicated Malaria

Intravenous quinine 20 mg/kg in dextrose loading dose given over 4 hours, then 10 mg/kg TID given over 2 hours, switch to oral quinine when able to tolerate, for a total treatment length of seven days Intramuscular quinine (same dose as above)

Quinidine is used as first line treatment in the United States, instead of quinine. Intravenously it is administered as a loading dose of 10 mg/kg salt over 1–2 hours and then as a continuous infusion of 20 ¼g/kg/min salt. Alternatively, a loading dose of 24 mg/kg salt over 4 hours followed by 12 mg/kg over 4 hours every 8 hours. Switch to oral quinine when able to tolerate, for a total treatment length of 7 days.

Artesunate 3.2 mg/kg IM on day 1, then 1.6 mg/kg IM QD. Switch to an oral agent when able to tolerate.

Artesunate 2.4 mg/kg IV on day 1, then 1.2 mg/kg IV QD. Switch to an oral agent when able to tolerate.

Eradication of the Hypnozoite form of P. vivax and ovale
Check glucose phosphate dehydrogenase status prior to treatment
Primaquine (15 mg base) PO QD x 14 days

PROGNOSIS

Early diagnosis and prompt treatment favor a good prognosis. Unfortunately, many times the diagnosis of malaria is not entertained or treatment is delayed, contributing significantly to the mortality seen. It should be remembered that once the onset of symptoms of *P. falciparum* develop death may occur within 12 hours.

PREVENTION

Four measures can significantly decrease the chance of acquiring malaria. Mosquito nets are imperative when sleeping in the tropics, unless excellent screening is in place. The use of an insect repellant containing between 25 and 50% DEET on exposed skin surfaces. Treating one's clothes and mosquito net with permethrin. Lastly, using an appropriate antimalarial for chemoprophylaxis.

Adetailed discussion on chemoprophylaxis is beyond the scope of this handbook; however, it is important to remember that failure of a properly prescribed antimalarial for chemoprophylaxis is rare, whereas noncompliance is very common. Options include:

Chloroquine (in sensitive regions) 500-mg tab, 1 week prior to travel, once a week while in a malarious endemic region, and once a week for 4 weeks afterwards.

Mefloquine (suitable everywhere, except along the Thailand/ Cambodia border) 250 mg tab, 1 week prior to travel, once a week while in a malarious endemic region and once a week for 4 weeks afterwards.

Atovaquone/proguanil 250/100 mg tab, 1 day prior to traveling, once a day while in a malarious endemic region and once a day for 7 days afterwards. Doxycycline 100 mg tab, 1 day prior to traveling, once a day while in a malarious endemic region and once a day for 4 weeks afterwards.

MALARIA

Meningitis is an inflammation of the membranes of the brain or spinal cord that may be caused by bacteria, viruses, mycoplasma, spirochetes, fungi, or parasites. Pathogens gain access to the CSF either by hematogenous spread or by direct extension from a purulent parameningeal focus.

BACTERIAL MENINGITIS

Epidemiology

The epidemiology of bacterial meningitis changed dramatically between 1985 and 1995. The total number of cases decreased by 55%, to about 5800 cases per year, and the median age increased to 25 years. This is due to routine childhood vaccination with a conjugate vaccine to *H. influenza* type B. Mortality varies by causative pathogen and is highest for meningitis due to *S. pneumoniae.* Likely bacterial pathogens depend on the patient's age and underlying health status:

- Age less than 3 months: group B strep, Gram-negative enteric bacilli, *L.* monocytogenes
- Age 3 months to 18 years: *N. meningitides*, *S. pneumoniae*, *H. influenzae*

- Age 18 to 50 years: *S. pneumoniae*, *N. meningitidis*
- Age greater than 50 years: *S. pneumoniae*, *L. monocytogenes*, Gram-negative bacilli
- Immunocompromised: *L. monocytogenes* or Gram-negative bacilli
- Head trauma, neurosurgery, or with CSF shunt: Staphylococci, Gram-negative bacilli, *S. pneumoniae*

Diagnosis

Clinical presentation varies by the patient's age. Older children and adults present with fever, headache, photophobia, and nuchal rigidity. Kernig and Brudzinski signs may be present. Patients may also have lethargy, malaise, vomiting, altered mental status, and seizures. Skin findings include petechiae and purpura. Shock and cardiovascular collapse may be present. Neonates and infants present with fever, irritability, altered sleep patterns, vomiting, and poor feeding. A bulging anterior fontanel may be present on exam. Elderly patients may present with only altered mental status.

Lumbar puncture is the mainstay of diagnosis and should be performed as promptly as possible in patients with suspected CNS infection unless there is concern for increased intracranial pressure. Cerebrospinal fluid should be sent for cell count with differential, protein, glucose, Gram stain, and bacterial culture. Other tests such as India ink stain, VDRL, Lyme titer, stain for acid-fast bacteria, PCR for herpes, cryptococcal antigen, or cultures for anaerobic bacteria, viruses, mycoplasma, and fungi should be performed as indicated. Cell counts in acute bacterial meningitis are usually markedly elevated (greater than 500 cells/mm3), with a predominance of neutrophils. Gram stain may show bacteria. Protein is elevated and glucose is decreased. Bacterial antigen detection may be useful for patients who received antibiotics prior to LP.

Computerized tomography (CT) scanning should be performed before lumbar puncture in patients with focal neurologic deficits, papilledema, seizures, evidence of head trauma, or altered mental status, which preclude careful neurologic examination to avoid the risk of cerebral herniation. When head CT is indicated, it should be performed after blood cultures have been drawn and empiric antibiotic therapy started.

Management

Antibiotics should be instituted as soon as possible. Empiric choice of antibiotics is directed toward the most likely pathogens based on the patient's age and underlying health status:

- Age less than 3 months: ampicillin plus gentamicin or cefotaxime
- Age 3 months to 18 years: cefotaxime or ceftriaxone
- Age 18 to 50 years: cefotaxime or ceftriaxone
- Age greater then 50 years: ampicillin plus cefotaxime or ceftriaxone
- Immunocompromised: ampicillin plus ceftazidime
- Post–head trauma or neurosurgical procedure or with CSF shunt: vancomycin plus ceftazidime
- Vancomycin should be added if *S. pneumoniae* cannot be excluded If there are identifiable bacteria on the Gram stain, therapy should be directed toward the presumptive pathogen.
- Gram-positive cocci: vancomycin plus cefotaxime or ceftriaxone
- Gram-negative cocci: penicillin G
- Gram-positive bacilli: ampicillin plus gentamicin
- Gram-negative bacilli: gentamicin plus cefotaxime or ceftriaxone

Steroids are often used to decrease meningeal inflammation and to modulate the inflammatory response caused by release of bacterial products from bacteria killed by antibiotics. Therefore, if steroid therapy is to be instituted, it should be started with or before the first dose of antibiotics. Steroids have been shown to reduce neurologic sequelae, especially hearing loss, in children aged greater than 2 months with meningitis caused by *H. influenzae*, but the decreased incidence of this infection due to the conjugate vaccine has made this pathogen uncommon, and the benefits for infections for other pathogens are not as clear.

Treatment with steroids has been found to be associated with a significant reduction in mortality and in neurologic sequelae of acute bacterial meningitis in adults.

Recommended dose is 0.15 mg/kg IV (10 mg in adults) given with or slightly before the first dose of antibiotics and continued every 6 hours for 2 to 4 days in patients older than 2 months of age, except in patients in septic shock, immunosuppressed patients, or patients with post-neurosurgical meningitis. Supportive care includes the following:

- Hypotension or shock should be treated with vigorous fluid resuscitation and pressors.
- Coagulopathy should be treated if present.
- Increased intracranial pressure (ICP) may develop in patients with meningitis as a result of cerebral edema, and may lead to life-threatening cerebral herniation. Hyperventilation may be employed to decrease the PaCO2, resulting in cerebral vasoconstriction. Hyperosmolar agents, such as mannitol may be used to decrease cerebral edema. Other measures, such as elevating the head of the bed to 30 degrees, antipyretics, controlling seizures, and giving lidocaine prior to endotracheal intubation are also helpful.
- SIADH may result in water retention and hyponatremia, contributing to cerebral edema. It is treated with fluid restriction and hypertonic sodium.
- Seizures: correction of hyponatremia or hypoglycemia, and anticonvulsants should be used for seizure control.

Prevention

In addition to universal precautions, droplet precautions should be used until meningococcal disease is ruled out. Household contacts of patients with meningococcal meningitis should receive rifampin (600 mg for adults, 10 mg/kg for children older than 1 year, and 5 mg/kg for children less than 1 year of age) orally every 12 hours for 4 doses, ciprofloxacin 500 mg orally for 1 dose, azithromycin 500 mg orally for one dose, or ceftriaxone 250 mg IM (125 mg for children) for one dose.

Healthcare workers do not need prophylaxis unless they have had direct mucosal contact with the patient's secretions. Meningococcal vaccine is recommended for travelers to epidemic areas, military recruits, college freshman, and in established epidemics. Apneumococcal conjugate vaccine is now part of the routine childhood immunizations, though the impact this will have on pneumococcal meningitis is not yet known. The polyvalent pneumococcal vaccine should be considered for elderly or immunocompromised patients.

Epidemics

Epidemics of meningitis have been documented in areas of overcrowding due to disasters, such as refugee camps, since *N. meningitides* has airborne transmission. Mass immunization may help prevent disease.

The CDC reports periodic epidemics in Sub- Saharan Africa, and an epidemic occurred in Saudi Arabia during the Hajj in 2000. Anthrax is listed by the CDC as a potential biological weapon and can cause meningitis after inhalation. The widely publicized cases of inhalational anthrax in the United States in 2001 that were disseminated through the mail are an example of how this could be used.

ASEPTIC MENINGITIS

Aseptic meningitis is an inflammation of the meninges that occurs in the absence of growth on routine culture media. The signs and symptoms are similar to those of bacterial meningitis, but are usually not as severe. The neurologic exam is usually normal. The prognosis for viral meningitis is very good.

Causes

Causes include viruses, unusual bacteria (such as TB), fungi, spirochetes, and parasites. Enteroviruses are the most common cause of aseptic meningitis, especially in the summer months. Tuberculous and fungal meningitis are more common in immunosuppressed patients.

Diagnosis

Diagnosis is similar to that of bacterial meningitis, though other CSF studies such as India ink stain, VDRL, Lyme titer, stain for acid-fast bacteria, PCR for herpes, cryptococcal antigen, or cultures for anaerobic bacteria, viruses, mycoplasma, and fungi may be required. A PPD should be placed on all patients with meningitis from areas where TB is endemic, or if history or symptoms suggest TB infection. Lyme disease may be suggested by history or characteristic rash, and should be considered in endemic areas.

Management

Management is supportive for viral infections, though antibiotics should be started until bacterial culture results are obtained if the diagnosis is not clear. Treatment for tuberculosis, fungi, parasites, or Lyme disease should be instituted if appropriate. Some experienced clinicians may choose not to hospitalize clinically stable patients with a clear diagnosis of aseptic meningitis, but hospitalization is necessary for more ill patients or those in whom the diagnosis is not certain.

ENCEPHALITIS

Encephalitis is an inflammation of the brain parenchyma. It can be caused by infectious (usually viral) agents or due to immunologic mechanisms, as in post-infectious encephalitis. Approximately 20,000 cases occur per year in the United States, most of them mild. Viruses enter the host through the skin or through the respiratory, gastrointestinal or urogenital tracts. The virus then enters the CNS either by hematogenous spread, by retrograde transmission along neuronal axons, or by direct invasion following infection of the nasal mucosa. Viral replication in neural cells leads to cell dysfunction and death, with resulting cerebral edema and increased ICP.

Causes

Herpes simplex virus (HSV) is the most common cause of viral encephalitis in the United States (about 10% of cases). Disease in neonates is often caused by HSV type 2 acquired from perinatal transmission, but HSV type 1 is the most common cause in all other patients. The mortality rate is greater than 70% if left untreated, but is approximately 30% with treatment. Survivors commonly have significant neurologic sequelae. Other viruses include arboviruses (such as St. Louis encephalitis, eastern or western equine encephalitis, West Nile encephalitis, LaCrosse encephalitis), rabies, mumps, measles, and varicella. The arthropod-borne encephalitides are transmitted by mosquitoes from a host, such as wild birds, to horses or humans. Outbreaks occur periodically in the United States in the summer and fall.

Post-infectious encephalomyelitis may follow infection with various viruses, most commonly varicella and influenza in the United States, but measles is the most common cause worldwide. It often follows a vague viral syndrome, usually of the respiratory tract, and occurs days to weeks after the preceding illness. It is thought to be an autoimmune phenomenon that is initiated by the viral pathogen. Demyelination is a prominent pathological finding of this disease.

Diagnosis

Clinical manifestations include headache, fever, altered level of consciousness, disturbances in behavior and speech, and generalized seizures. Focal neurologic findings generally indicate HSV infection and include ataxia, cranial nerve defects, hemiparesis, or focal seizures. Skin lesions such as the characteristic exanthem of varicella or vesicles that suggest HSV type 1 or 2 may be present. History may reveal the bite of a potentially rabid animal, and knowledge of disease outbreaks in the community (such as mosquito-borne viruses) may help to guide diagnosis. Differential diagnosis includes metabolic diseases, toxic disorders, mass lesions, and acute demyelinating disorders.

Laboratory Evaluation

Cerebrospinal fluid must be obtained to exclude bacterial meningitis. CSF should be sent for cell count, protein, glucose, Gram stain, bacterial and viral cultures, and HSV PCR. In viral encephalitis, CSF cell count usually shows fewer than 500 cells/mm3, with a mononuclear prominence, though the cells may be predominantly polymorphonuclear early in the course of illness. CSF protein is normal to moderately elevated and glucose is usually normal. Detection of herpes virus by polymerase chain reaction (PCR) of CSF leads to a rapid diagnosis of HSV infection. Viral isolation from other body sites, such as the nasopharynx, skin lesions, urine, and feces may aid in diagnosis. Blood samples for CBC with differential, platelet count, electrolytes, BUN, creatinine, glucose, blood culture, and viral titers should be obtained. Detection of viral antibodies does not aid in acute diagnosis or management, but may be useful later to clarify the cause of the infection.

CT or MRI may show focal parenchymal involvement or temporal lobe edema in HSV encephalitis. EEG shows characteristic periodic spike wave temporal lobe activity and slow wave complexes in HSV encephalitis. It is usually normal in other encephalitides.

Management

Management of non-herpes viral encephalitis is supportive, though herpes simplex virus and varicella-zoster encephalitis are treated with acyclovir, 30–60 mg/kg/day divided q 8 h, in addition to supportive measures. Acyclovir should be administered until the virus is identified, especially if there is evidence of focality on physical or neurodiagnostic evaluation. Antibiotics should also be given until a bacterial etiology is excluded. Medical management of rabies is prevention of infection by the administration of rabies vaccine and rabies immune globulin after an exposure to a potentially rabid animal. Once infection occurs, it is uniformly fatal. Arboviral infections can be prevented by using insect repellents and protective clothing to avoid mosquito bites. Treatment of infection is supportive.

Epidemics

Epidemics of arthropod-borne encephalitis can occur during natural disasters if heavy rainfall and flooding lead to increased numbers of mosquitoes, or if insect control measures are disrupted. There have been recent epidemics of West Nile virus in the United States. In addition, the CDC lists Venezuelan, eastern, and western encephalitis as potential biological weapons. An unexplained large number of cases should raise suspicion for a potential act of bioterrorism.

TUBERCULOSIS

Although tuberculosis (TB) is not a top priority in initial disaster response, healthcare providers need to be familiar with the disease. Many disasters occur in regions of the world where the disease is endemic and contributes significantly to morbidity and mortality. TB has been called by many names throughout the centuries and notoriously is known as the disease of consumption (progressive wasting away of the body). In the last twenty years, the disease has gained significant attention with the problem of multi-drug-resistant TB and co infection with HIV.

EPIDEMIOLOGY

Tuberculosis has a global distribution and is highly prevalent throughout the tropics. The World Health Organization estimates that an individual in the world is newly infected with TB every second and that, overall, one-third of the world's population is currently infected. Factors that increase the transmission or incidence of TB include: the global trend of urbanization, overcrowding (prisons, low-income housing, and institutions), immigrants relocating from endemic regions, HIV, noncompliance with treatment, and multi-drug-resistant strains of TB.

PATHOPHYSIOLOGY

TB is caused by the bacteria *Mycobacterium tuberculosis* and occasionally from *Mycobacterium bovis* and *Mycobacterium africanum*. The infective agent is the tubercle bacilli, which can remain dormant in the body for many years. Infection typically occurs when the bacilli are dispersed into the air when an individual with active pulmonary TB coughs. The droplet nuclei remain suspended in the air for a prolonged period of time and can survive in a dark environment. The bacilli are small enough that they escape being trapped by the protective respiratory mechanisms and end up in the terminal alveoli. Five minutes of direct sunlight kills the bacilli. Therefore, infection usually occurs in a closed environment.

During primary infection the bacilli multiply within the lung and form a Ghon focus. The primary complex is the Ghon focus along with the hilar lymphadenopathy that occurs. In the normal immunocompetent individual, the body mounts a significant hypersensitivity/cellular reaction against the primary complex to kill the bacilli and contain the infection. This usually occurs within 4 to 6 weeks of infection. However, a few dormant bacilli may persist, with the only evidence being a positive tuberculin skin test. In some individuals the primary complex is not contained and they may develop tuberculous pneumonia that may be complicated by pleural effusions and collapse of the lung tissue. Cervical lymphadenopathy, meningitis, pericarditis, hypersensitivity reactions (e.g., erythema nodosum) and miliary spread may also occur in uncontained primary infection.

Post-primary TB occurs when there is reactivation and/or reinfection with bacilli. Reactivation may be triggered by a weakening of the immune system (age, HIV, other co-infections, malnutrition, as well as other causes). The immune reaction this time is localized and can be quite destructive. In the lungs extensive damage and cavitation may occur in the upper lobes. Pleural effusion, empyema, and pneumothorax are well-described complications. Extrapulmonary TB can potentially occur in any part of the body and hence the name the "great imitator."

CLINICAL

Pulmonary

The patient presenting with pulmonary TB often gives a history of fever, night sweats, weight loss, productive cough for more than 2 to 3 weeks, dyspnea, and sometimes hemoptysis. Patients who are HIV positive may have a nonclassic presentation.

Central Nervous System

TB meningitis is most commonly seen in infants and young children. It often presents in a more chronic nature than bacterial meningitis. There is the gradual onset of headache and meningeal signs with eventual decreased mental status. Secondary to the significant inflammatory reaction that occurs at the base of the brain, cranial nerve involvement is not uncommon, particularly of the optic and auditory nerves. Obstructive hydrocephalus may develop, leading to an increase in intracranial pressure. Spinal meningeal involvement may lead to paralysis. In infants the initial presentation may be failure to thrive. Diagnosis is made by lumbar puncture, where a high opening pressure may be noted, with white cells being predominantly lymphocytes (however, polymorphs may be noted in early infection), an elevated protein, and a low glucose. A fibrin web may develop if the CSF is allowed to stand. The CSF should be examined for evidence of AFB and cultured if possible. A lumbar puncture should never be performed in the patient with evidence of raised intracranial pressure, seizures, or focal neurological findings. Although a subject of much controversy, steroids appear to be of benefit in TB meningitis.

Tuberculomas may also develop and present with symptoms consistent with an intracranial lesion. Diagnosis is made with CT scan or MRI of the brain.

Lymph Node (Scrofula)

Tuberculous lymphadenitis occurs most commonly in the cervical region, but may present anywhere in the body. Initially the nodes are firm and tender and then become fluctuant and matted together. Sinus tracts may develop as the lymph node undergoes necrosis. Diagnosis is made by biopsy of the lymph node. In the clinical setting of TB; however, this may not be necessary.

Pericardium

In the tropics, TB is the most common cause for a pericardial effusion. Patients present with chest pain, shortness of breath, and dizziness. On physical exam, hypotension, elevated JVP, evidence of right-sided heart failure, a pericardial rub, and distant heart sounds may be appreciated. Cardiac tamponade can develop if untreated. Besides clinical findings, the diagnosis can be made by: an enlarged globular heart on chest x-ray, low voltage on ECG, and by echocardiogram. Pericardiocentesis should be performed only under experienced hands.

Spine (Pott's Disease)

Very common in the tropics and if unrecognized/untreated can result in devastating paralysis. The lower thoracic and lumbar regions of the spine are most commonly affected; however, it can occur anywhere. Patients present with chronic pain of the vertebral region involved, limitation of movement, and sometimes with an acute neurological finding. Tenderness to the affected spine and a gibbus deformity may be noted on physical exam. Diagnosis is made by plain films and biopsy/culture. Besides chemotherapy, surgical stabilization may be required.

Gastrointestinal

Intestinal involvement can occur from ingestion with *Mycobacterium bovis*. Peritoneal involvement occurs from post-primary spread. Patients may have nonspecific abdominal complaints: weight loss, anorexia, abdominal pain, nausea, vomiting, and diarrhea. Intestinal obstruction may develop secondary to stricture formation. Ascites is common as the disease progresses. Diagnosis can occasionally be made by paracentesis, but peritoneal biopsy is preferred.

Genitourinary

Involvement of the kidneys can lead to dysuria, nocturia, hematuria, flank pain, and less commonly acute renal failure secondary to tuberculous interstitial nephritis. On examination of the urine, a sterile pyuria is found. It is uncommon to find AFB in the urine. Cultivation of the bacilli confirms the diagnosis. In males chronic epidymitis or orchitis may develop. Female genital tract involvement presents with pelvic pain, possible vaginal bleeding, and infertility. It may be mistaken for pelvic inflammatory disease. In both sexes the diagnosis is made by biopsy and culture.

Miliary

Can potentially go anywhere in the body affecting any or multiple organ systems.

HIV Co-Infection

Infection with both rapidly accelerates the disease process of both HIV and TB. It is important to remember that atypical presentations of TB may occur and miliary disease is more common. A high index of suspicion for co-infection needs to be held for all patients with TB.

DIAGNOSIS

Microscopy

For individuals with suspicion for pulmonary TB, three sets of sputum samples should be obtained over a several-day period. Chest physiotherapy can be performed to improve sputum production. AZiehl-Neelsen stain can be used to look for evidence of the red-staining acid-fast bacilli. Asputum is considered positive when 10,000 bacilli per ml of sputum are noted. In an advanced facility a fluorochrome stain may also be used. Aside from sputum, other clinical specimens may be examined: bronchoalveolar lavage, gastric lavage (may be an alternative in children who cannot produce sputum), pleural effusions, peritoneal fluid, CSF, lymph node biopsies, and bone marrow aspirate. The classic histological findings in a tissue biopsy are a region of centralized caseous necrosis that may be surrounded by histiocytes, Langhans giant cells, and lymphocytes.

Culture

If facilities are available the gold standard for diagnosis is to culture the bacilli. The usual culture medium is Lowenstein Jensen; however, liquid culture and automated systems can be used if available. *Mycobacterium tuberculosis* is very slow growing, and it may take up to 8 weeks to develop a positive culture.

Molecular

Several molecular techniques using nucleic acid amplification have been developed. These tests are highly sensitive and specific, and several commercial kits are available.

Radiographic

Radiographic studies can be helpful in making the diagnosis of TB. Chest x-rays in post-primary TB may show apical/upper unilateral or bilateral infiltrates, cavitations, and calcifications. Pleural effusions can also be seen. Some patients (particularly HIV and immunocompromised) will have minimal changes or nonspecific findings on chest x-ray. Where CT scan of the chest is available, this may further help in the evaluation of questionable findings on a chest x-ray.

Tuberculin Skin Test

This test relies on a hypersensivity reaction that occurs 24–72 hours after intradermal placement. The test does not necessarily indicate active infection, just that the individual has been exposed to the bacilli. The test may be negative in infected individuals who have the following conditions: malnutrition, severe infection, military TB, HIV, cancer, or other immunosuppressive conditions. A test is considered negative in a normal immunocompetent individual if the induration measures less than 10 mm. In a child who has received the BCG vaccine, up to 15 mm is considered negative.

TREATMENT

The cornerstone of successful TB treatment is compliance, and this is best achieved by DOT (directly observed therapy/ treatment). To ensure successful treatment, a population needs to be stationary for 6 to 9 months. This can be a challenge in refugee camps and during the acute phase of an emergency. Therefore, treatment for TB should not be started unless one can adhere to DOT or ensure compliance and full completion of chemotherapy. Another principle of treatment is to use several agents for synergism and to decrease drug resistance. Treatment for TB is prolonged compared to many other infectious diseases. The common agents used for treatment will be briefly discussed. Several of these agents are available in a combination pill. *Streptomycin* was the first agent used to treat TB. It is bactericidal and belongs to the aminoglycoside family and is given intramuscularly. Adverse reactions include ototoxicity and nephrotoxicity.

Isoniazid is bactericidal and adverse reactions include peripheral neuropathy and hepatitis. Pyridoxine is given to avoid the neurotoxic adverse reactions.

Rifampin is bactericidal and adverse reactions include turning body fluids a pinkish color, hepatitis, and gastrointestinal upset.

Pyrazinamide is bactericidal and adverse reactions include joint pains and hepatitis.

Ethambutol is bacteriostatic and may cause optic neuritis.

Thiacetazone is bacteriostatic and may cause a life-threatening Steven Johnsonlike reaction in HIV positive individuals.

Regimens

Can vary depending upon availability of agents and drug resistance patterns. An initial phase is typically four agents for 2 months: isoniazid, rifampin, pyrazinamide, and ethambutol. Within 2 weeks of treatment most infectious patients become noninfectious. The continuation phase is usually from 4 to 6 months depending on the site and new vs. recurrent case. A typical regimen during this period may include isoniazid and rifampin. Supportive treatment for TB is also of great importance. Proper nutrition and weight gain take high priority. Other co-infections should be addressed and treated whenever possible.

PREVENTION

Whenever possible, respiratory and isolation precautions should be taken when treating actively infected individuals. Ideally, these patients should be kept in a separate ward until they have received at least 2 weeks of treatment. As mentioned earlier, direct sunlight kills the bacilli.

The BCG vaccine is a live attenuated vaccine derived from *M. bovis*, which is given intradermally. It should be part of the childhood vaccine series in countries with a high prevalence of TB. Children benefit the most from this vaccine when it can decrease the incidence of disseminated and severe TB. It affords little protection to adults.

HUMAN IMMUNODEFICIENCY VIRUS,TYPE 1, AND AIDS

In 1981 a previously unrecognized syndrome of oral candidiasis, severe ulcerative genital herpes, and repeated episodes of *Pneumocystis carinii* pneumonia was first described in North America and Western Europe. At the same time, a syndrome of chronic diarrhea and wasting, called "slim disease," was being reported from Sub- Saharan Africa. The original patients in North America and Western Europe were predominantly homosexual men, but cases had also been recognized in intravenous drug users and in hemophiliacs and others who had received transfused blood or blood products. In Africa women and infants appeared as likely as men to be affected, but the elderly and prepubescent children were spared. These observations strongly supported modes of sexual and blood-borne transmission of a newly prevalent but still unknown infectious agent.

By 1984, the etiologic agent of the acquired immune deficiency syndrome had been identified as a human T-lymphotropic retrovirus, the human immunodeficiency virus (HIV). In almost all cases, the cause of AIDS is HIV type-1, or HIV-1. HIV-2, another human retrovirus, first identified in Portugal and France, with origins traced to West Africa, appears to be a much less aggressive pathogen, though it has been occasionally associated with AIDS.

EPIDEMIOLOGY

The incidence and prevalence of HIV/AIDS vary widely by continent, with the highest number (and concentration) of cases found in Sub-Saharan Africa. Of note, in recent years there have been encouraging signs that a few hard-hit African countries (e.g., Uganda with a seroprevalence as high as 20%) have begun to lower the rate of new infections with education and increased availability and use of barrier contraception (condoms). HIV/AIDS has a well-established though relatively low and stable (<1%) prevalence in the Americas, Western Europe, and Australia/New Zealand, where an astonishing degree of progress has been made with respect to diagnosis, management, and treatment of the underlying viral infection. In Eastern Europe and many parts of Asia, reliable data are difficult to obtain. Given the increasing prevalence of intravenous drug use in some countries, the likely wide dissemination of HIV infection through sharing of needles and secondarily through sexual partners will set the stage for many new AIDS cases the coming decades.

PATHOGENESIS

HIV-1 is an enveloped virus, approximately 100 nm in diameter, with a coneshaped nucleocapsid containing a diploid, positive-, single-stranded RNA and multiple proteins. The virion contains a virus-encoded reverse transcriptase, which, once the virus has gained access to the host cell, synthesizes a DNA copy of the RNA genome. This DNA copy can then integrate into the host cell genome as a 9.7-kilobase segment and begin the process of viral replication. Crucially, this target cell is the primary regulatory agent of specific cellular immunity, the CD4 T-lymphocyte. The steady destruction of this CD4 T-lymphocyte population by repeated cycles of viral replication creates the immunodeficient state that manifests clinically as AIDS. Once the etiologic agent of AIDS was identified, the cornerstone of sound public health policy and appropriate medical intervention was the validation of reliable and specific diagnostic testing. This was the HIV-1 ELISA screening test followed by western blot confirmation. This technology, first licensed in 1984, coupled with a policy of "donor-at-risk" self-exclusion, has helped to eliminate HIV from the world's supply of blood and blood products.

CLINICAL

Since the process from infection to clinical disease can take as long as 14 years (average: about 7 years), knowing an infected person's CD4 T-lymphocyte count is invaluable in determining what treatments or interventions may be necessary or beneficial. If the patient's CD4 T-lymphocyte count is less than 150 cells/mm3, prophylactic therapy to prevent *Pneumocystis carinii* pneumonia is indicated, and multiple drugs are available for this purpose, including trimethaprim-sulfamethoxasole, dapsone, clindamycin, and atovaquone. When the CD4+ count declines below 50 cells/mm3, preventive therapy with a macrolide (azithromycin or clarithromycin) or rifabutin is also indicated to forestall the onset of disseminated *Mycobacterium avian*-complex (MAC), often heralded by fevers, night-sweats, weight loss, and weakness; and accompanied by anemia and sometimes pancytopenia and abnormal liver function tests. Fungal infections (such as thrush and cryptococcal meningitis) or viral infections (such as cytomegalovirus [CMV] retinitis or ulcerative genital herpes) are treated when diagnosed and then prevented with secondary prophylaxis, but primary prophylaxis, even at low CD4 T-lymphocyte counts (i.e., <50 cells/mm3), has not been deemed a cost-effective intervention.

Primary HIV infection is most often asymptomatic. Occasionally, an "acute retroviral syndrome" has been identified involving fever, morbilliform rash, acute mononucleosis-like symptoms (sore throat, lymphadenopathy) or sometimes aseptic meningitis. This acute illness occurs 1 to 6 weeks after infection, and seroconversion to positive HIV ELISA may take another 2 to 6 weeks after the acute syndrome. After exposure to HIV infection by the sexual or parenteral route, seroconversion takes place within 3 months, and a negative test at 3 months can be accepted as evidence that HIV infection has not occurred.

When an individual has been identified as HIV seropositive (whether asymptomatic or with clinical disease), medical management of the infection/illness involves a staging determination of the absolute CD4 T-lymphocyte count and the plasma HIV "viral load" (expressed as genome copies per microliter) by the branched-chain DNA (bDNA) or polymerase chain reaction (PCR) technology. These two laboratory values, considered in the context of the patient's clinical state and willingness to initiate antiinfective (including antiretroviral) therapy, help to determine which prophylactic medicines are indicated as well as the appropriate time to begin antiretroviral therapy. Initiation of antiretroviral therapy should be strongly considered when the patient's absolute CD4 T-lymphocyte count is between 200 and 350 cells/microliter and/or the viral load is greater than 60,000 genome copies/microliter on repeated determinations. Patients who do not meet these criteria, and do not have significant clinical disease, may be safely followed without antiretroviral therapy, having laboratory parameters determined serially at three to six month intervals.

AIDS must be considered in any of the following clinical presentations: oral candidiasis (thrush) with or without dysphagia and weight loss; large, painful genital or perianal ulcers (herpes simplex); dyspnea, dry cough, and fevers, often of gradual onset, associated with clear or diffuse interstitial pattern on chest x-ray, arterial blood hypoxia, and exertional arterial oxygen desaturation (*Pneumocystis carinii* pneumonia). Cryptococcal meningitis can be a very indolent disease with subtle symptoms of mild headache or photophobia and can present with fever and progress to profound obtundation. Asymptomatic cases of disseminated cryptococcosis have occasionally been diagnosed on the basis of a persistently positive serum cryptococcal antigen tests. Chronic unrelenting diarrhea with weight loss and wasting has long been identified as a classic presentation of AIDS, and the list of possible etiologies is extensive, with cryptosporidiosis, microsporidiosis, cytomegalovirus colitis as but a few prominent examples. The deadly synergy between AIDS and tuberculosis has been observed in Sub-Saharan Africa and the inner cities of North America, where HIV-infected persons with active tuberculosis harbor greater numbers of tubercle bacilli while others are rendered more susceptible to tuberculosis when exposed.

Clinically, the presence of diffuse lymphadenopathy in an individual with appropriate risk factors is considered a marker of recent or immunologically "controlled" infection, and rapid involution of lymphadenopathy (in the absence of highly active antiretroviral therapy) can be a harbinger of clinical AIDS. Elegant virologic and immunologic studies have subsequently provided a sound scientific explanation for what was once an ominous clinical finding. HIV-mediated destruction of CD4 T-lymphocytes in germinal centers has been shown to occur as the lymph nodes melt away. Visual changes of any kind should prompt an immediate and detailed retinal examination by an ophthalmologist skilled in the diagnosis of AIDS-related conditions, chiefly CMV retinitis.

The value of screening retinal examinations in asymptomatic patients with CD4 T-lymphocyte counts <50 is supported by many clinicians. Fortunately, the success of antiretroviral therapy (ART) has virtually eliminated the incidence of CMV retinitis in areas where ART is widely available.

TREATMENT

As mentioned above, screening for opportunistic infections and offering chemoprophylaxis when appropriate is important. Individuals should be screened for other common co-infections (hepatitis B and C, syphilis, and tuberculosis). Proper nutrition is of utmost importance and in poorer countries may be the only available approach. Antiretroviral therapy is a complex topic the details of which are beyond the scope of this summary account. However, the well-established and probably long-lasting (>10 years so far in some cases) benefits of ART make it imperative that the clinician who diagnoses, or strongly suspects, HIV/AIDS, initiate a care plan or refer the patient to a setting where such a plan can be devised.

Patient counseling, particularly with regard to risk reduction and contact notification, is a valuable component of clinician-supervised HIV-testing and can limit the spread of infection through identification of asymptomatic infected persons and modifying risk-related behaviors in both infected and uninfected persons. The US government, through its Department of Health and Human Services, has established guidelines for the use of antiretroviral therapy. Multidrug regimens are required, usually at least three drugs, used in combinations supported by reliable clinical trials data.

The efficacy of different recommended triple-drug regimens is really quite comparable, and in the overwhelming majority of cases success is determined by the patient's ability to tolerate and scrupulously comply with the prescribed regimen. Careful patient education is essential prior to initiation of ART, as is close follow-up in the early stages to mitigate the impact of misunderstandings or side-effects on ultimate treatment success. When treatment fails due to the emergence of resistance to antiretroviral drugs, genotype and/or phenotype testing of the patient's virus will sometimes assist the clinician in devising an alternative regimen.

SEXUALLY TRANSMITTED DISEASES

The most common and also curable "conventional" sexually transmitted diseases (STDs) within a disaster setting include chlamydia, gonorrhea, syphilis, chancroid, and trichomoniasis. HIV/AIDS has been addressed elsewhere in this text; however, HIV and other STDs are closely linked. Concurrent STD infection substantially increases one's risk of contracting HIV.

INCIDENCE AND PREVALENCE

Sexually transmitted diseases are among the most common yet underdiagnosed causes of morbidity throughout the world. An estimated 340 million curable sexually transmitted infections occur worldwide each year. In developing countries STDs rank among the top five reasons for seeking health care among adults. In fact, STDs and their complications are the second leading cause of morbidity and mortality among reproductive age women.

RISK FACTORS

STD epidemiology is not significantly impacted by acute terrorist attacks. However, STD infections thrive in disaster situations that lead to prolonged population dislocations and social disruption, such as within refugee camps. Social instability, poverty, and disintegration of stable relationships all contribute to increased STD risk by weakening sociocultural constraints that ordinarily govern sexual behavior. The break in social norms compounded by easy access to and perforation of commercial sex activity also increases STD risk. Women and children are at special risk of being victims of sexual coercion to obtain their most basic needs. Sexual violence is a well-documented aspect of civil conflicts. This is of particular importance, as approximately 75% of refugees worldwide are women and children.

PRESENTATION AND TREATMENT

The spectrum of sexually transmitted diseases, as well as their presentations and long-term complications, is notably broad. While simple diagnostic tests exist to confirm a specific infection, limited resources and disjointed medical care make this technique less feasible during a massive disaster. In general, however, early symptoms are largely genitourologic in nature. These common traits have led the World Health Organization (WHO) to advocate for the Syndromic Approach (SA) in treating STDs within refugee settings. SA has several potential benefits over traditional diagnostic modalities:

- SA focuses on the most common and curable STDs. WHO estimates that approximately 6 of every 10 STD patients harbor two or more co-infections. Syndromic approach allows the most common infections to be grouped together and targeted with the most effective drugs, ultimately saving cost and reducing morbidity.
- SA allows identification of infected individuals during their first visit. Within a setting of high population mobility, it is imperative that patients be identified and treated at the first opportunity.
- SA is appropriate for settings with limited diagnostic resources. This facilitates implementation in areas where medical services might otherwise be limited.
- SA is user-friendly. Personnel can be rapidly trained in its utilization, allowing recruitment from local populations. This is crucial for rapid mobilization of care. Using this method, the United Nations Populations Fund (UNFPA) estimates the pharmaceutical cost of effectively treating STDs in a population of 200,000 to be approximately $10,000.

DIFFERENTIAL DIAGNOSIS

Familiarity with other infectious etiology for similar symptoms would be beneficial if treatment based on SA fails.

PROGNOSIS

Sexually transmitted diseases have excellent prognosis if detected and treated early.

PREVENTION

Treatment of STD extends beyond diagnosis and medical treatment. The key to reducing STD infections among dislocated populations is prevention and early identification. During a disaster/ refugee crisis, it is imperative to treat sexually transmitted diseases as a public health issue. Local authorities must become involved in the formulation and execution of STD management protocols. Integration of STD services should be considered as standard components of refugee/disaster health care services.

The WHO describes an effective prevention strategy as encompassing "Information, Education and Communication" (IEC). Effective communication involves understanding not just the medical but also the complex social dynamics involved in displacement:

Assessment of risk: The prevalence of STDs in the host and home country should be obtained. It is wrong to assume the vector of transmission will be unidirectional.

Treating the invisible patient: Partners of STD patients should be encouraged to access care and empirically treated.

Education: Areas of high risk (e.g., bars), prostitution, and alcohol use should be identified and targeted for prevention and information campaigns. Patients should be educated about safe sexual habits. Access to discounted and/or free condoms should be widely publicized to both the host and refugee community.

Understanding local customs, beliefs, and attitudes concerning sexuality and STDs is pivotal. Identification and further training of people within the refugee population in STD prevention and education are also necessary.

Non-clinicians can be invaluable in working directly with the community to gather data and to disseminate information in a manner patients find comfortable and trustworthy. Also be aware that a refugee population is often not homogeneous. Disasters often throw together groups who have had minimal interactions in the past, altering disease epidemiology.

SPECIAL CONSIDERATIONS

One way to directly impact STD prevalence among displaced populations is to alter their landscape of powerlessness and chaos. Creating income opportunities for women and organized social events for adolescents contribute toward lessening the impact of displacement.

SCHISTOSOMIASIS

Schistosomiasis, a parasitic disease also known as snail fever or bilharziasis, afflicts nearly 200 million people worldwide and results in more than 200,000 deaths annually. Its clinical importance is underestimated because acute disease is seen in a minority of people and symptoms may only result after years of chronic infection. There are references to schistosomiasis dating back to 1500 BCE. Hieroglyphics from ancient Egypt portray men with scrotal edema, thought to be a complication of the disease.

Calcified *Schistosoma* eggs have been found in Egyptian mummy tissue. However, it was not until 1851 that the etiologic agent was identified by Theodore Bilharz, who lent his name to the disease. Over the next century, the complex life cycle was elucidated and specific antiparasitic therapy was developed to combat the disease. Transmission is limited by the need for appropriate snail populations, which can only be found in certain climates.

The disease is endemic in over 77 countries. *Schistosoma japonicum* is found primarily in China, Indonesia, and the Philippines. *Schistosoma mansoni* is endemic on the Arabian peninsula and in Africa, South America, and some Caribbean islands. *Schistosoma haematobium* is limited to Africa and southwest Asia. Several species are found in the large bodies of fresh water in the United States but cause only a self-limited dermatitis, their definitive hosts being ducks. An increase in prevalence of schistosomiasis has been seen recently and is thought to be due to an increased exposure to contaminated water by human populations living in endemic areas. Adolescents have the highest prevalence and highest intensity of infection due to increased exposure combined with immature immunity.

PATHOGENESIS/LIFE CYCLE

Schistosoma are trematodes. Humans are the definitive host for *S. japonicum*, *S. mansoni*, *S. haematobium*, *S. mekongi*, and *S. intercalatum*, but several other species can cause human disease. Twenty other species can penetrate human skin, but disease is limited to a dermatitis.

Each species differs in global distribution, snail host, and preferred organ within human hosts.

Cercariae are the infective form and are found in fresh water where there is an abundance of snails. They are released by infected snails at a set time of day depending on the schistosome species. These larval forms penetrate intact skin and invade the local microcirculation, eventually migrating to the heart, lungs and, finally, to the liver. This migration takes approximately 5–10 days. Maturation into sexual forms takes place in the liver, where the worms mate.

Four to six weeks after initial skin penetration, the worms migrate to the small venules of the intestine or the bladder, depending on species preference, and there they lay eggs. Worms of *S. japonicum* species seek out the mesenteric venules of the small intestine. *S. mansoni* prefers the veins that drain the colon. *S. haematobium* resides in the venous plexus that drains the urinary bladder. Some eggs flow back to the liver, while the rest lodge in the wall of the organ they are near. They eventually penetrate into the lumen where some die, calcify, and form granulomas. The rest are excreted into the stool or urine. If the excreta encounter fresh water the eggs hatch into miracidia, which are able to infect freshwater snails, the intermediate host. Direct human–human transmission is not possible.

Adult worms can survive 3–5 years within humans and do not multiply. Thus, intensity of infection depends solely on cercariae exposure. Immunocompromised hosts do not develop an overwhelming infection. The worms cause little direct damage to the host, taking small blood meals with little appreciable result. They are covered by a tegument that shields them from immune attack.

PRESENTATION

Penetration of skin by cercariae is usually asymptomatic, but some may report a tingling or itching at the site of entry. Occasionally patients can develop a self-limited pruritic, papular rash. Most of the pathology and symptoms result from egg deposition, which elicits a granulomatous response.

Larval Pneumonitis

Self-limited; results from migration of schistosomula through pulmonary vasculature; manifested by mild cough, fever, eosinophilia, bibasilar infiltrates on chest x-ray.

Acute Schistosomiasis (Katayama Fever)

Four to eight weeks after contact a serum sickness-like illness develops with fevers, malaise, arthralgias, myalgias, diarrhea, cough, and eosinophilia. May cause hepatic tenderness with normal liver transaminases. Usually resolves and enters chronic stage, but fatality rates can be as high as 25%, especially with *S. japonicum* infection.

Cercarial Dermatitis (Swimmer's Itch)

Intense papular dermatitis resulting from death of cercariae of schistosome species unable to complete life cycle within humans; parasites die as schistosomula within the dermis. Treatment usually not needed.

Chronic Schistosomiasis: most prevalent form of disease; results from granuloma formation and scarring.

Urinary schistosomiasis (*S. haematobium*): urethritis, hematuria, ureteral scarring with obstructive uropathy, recurrent urinary tract infections, recurrent gram-negative bacteremia

Intestinal Schistosomiasis (*S. japonicum*, *S mekongi*, *S. mansoni*, *S. intercalatum*)

- Either presents with bloody diarrhea, tenesmus, and abdominal tenderness or asymptomatic with occult blood positive stools
- Rare: obstruction (from large mass of eggs) or intussusception (granulomas can serve as lead point) Hepatosplenic schistosomiasis (same species as above)
- Symptoms secondary to portal hypertension from presinusoidal hepatic fibrosis (Symmer's pipestem fibrosis)
- Cirrhosis does not develop and hepatocyte function is intact

- No stigmata of hepatic insufficiency such as gynecomastia, testicular atrophy, or telangiectasias
- Usually manifested by esophageal variceal hemorrhage, hypersplenism Schistosomal nephropathy
- End-stage renal disease from infection with *S mansoni* or *S. japonicum* resulting from circulating immune complexes.

Neuroschistosomiasis

- Results from eggs within the vertebral venous plexus which embolize to brain and spinal cord
- Cauda equina syndrome
- Transverse myelitis
- Fatal schistosomal cerebritis
- Recurrent bacteremia: enteric bacteria enter circulation via inflamed colonic mucosa

DIAGNOSIS

Suspect schistosomiasis in a traveler returning from an endemic area with a history of freshwater exposure or in those living in endemic areas having the appropriate symptoms:

- Visualization of parasite eggs: via microscopy of urine or Kato-Katz smear of stool (not part of standard O&P test; must order separately). Very specific diagnostic tool but lacks sensitivity. Egg morphology aids in species identification.
- Urine specimens taken between 10:00 AM and 2:00 PM may yield higher concentration of eggs.
- Complete blood count: degree of eosinophilia roughly parallels intensity of infection; may also see mild anemia.
- Urinalysis: mild albuminuria, microscopic hematuria.
- Rectal or bladder mucosal biopsy: very sensitive method; limited by expense and invasiveness.
- Serology: Antibodies against schistosomes remain positive despite resolution of infection; most useful for tourists

coming from endemic areas as positive result confirms exposure. Tests can be obtained from the CDC (1- 770-480-7775). Antibodies to keyhole limpet antigen present in those with acute schistosomiasis; tests for these are more widely available but less sensitive.

- Antigen detection: circulating anodic antigen (CAA) and circulating cathodic antigen (CCA) are released by adult worms; very sensitive and specific. Levels can be followed to indicate success of therapy.
- Ultrasonography: to assess sequelae of chronic schistosomiasis.

TREATMENT

- Praziquantel: 20 mg/kg orally every 4 hours for total of 3 doses
- Oxaminiquine: 15 mg/kg twice a day orally for 2 days; not for treatment of *S. haematobium* or *S. japonicum*
- Metrifonate: 7.5–10 mg/kg every 2 weeks for 3 doses (max dose 600 mg) for treatment of urinary schistosomiasis
- Add corticosteroids for the treatment of severe acute systemic disease and neuroschistosomiasis

PROGNOSIS

The prognosis of schistosomal infection is very good assuming adequate chemotherapy and prevention of reinfection. Long-term hepatosplenic schistosomiasis may cause irreversible fibrosis and portal hypertension. Bladder cancer is a potential complication of untreated chronic *S. haematobium* infection.

PREVENTION

Since snails are necessary for the life cycle of schistosomes, eradication of snail populations would be helpful but has been relatively unsuccessful thus far. Most effort is being focused on proper sewage treatment since eggs are carried in excretory waste.

Unfortunately, these measures are expensive. Also, some schistosome species can infect nonhuman hosts so transmission can occur despite adequate sewage treatment. During situations of famine or war, sewage management becomes an even more formidable problem, and increased rates of transmission can be expected. Vaccines are not currently available.

TETANUS

Tetanus is an acute, often fatal disease, characterized by generalized increased rigidity and convulsive spasms of skeletal muscles. *Clostridium tetani*, the tetanus bacillus, is a spore-forming, anaerobic, Gram-positive bacillus. This organism is a wound contaminant that causes neither tissue destruction nor an inflammatory response.

The introduction of the first generation of tetanus vaccines in 1927 has led to the prevention of hundreds of thousands of deaths due to the disease. In the United States, where the percentage of the population vaccinated is greater than 90%, the incidence of tetanus has decreased from 3.9 cases per million in 1947 to 0.16 cases per million in 2000. However, the annual incidence of tetanus is estimated at 700,000 to 1,000,000 cases per year. The mortality rates due to tetanus are as high as 28 per 100,000 in developing countries.

Wounds, recognized or unrecognized, are the sites at which the organism multiplies and elaborates toxin. The Centers for Disease Control 2003 report lists acute trauma as the condition leading to tetanus in 73% of patients. No acute injury (i.e., patients with abscesses, ulcers, or gangrene) was reported in 26% of patients. Wounds do not need to be obviously contaminated for tetanus to develop, and in unvaccinated individuals or people with waning immunity, such as diabetics, intravenous drug users, and HIV-infected patients, even minor wounds can cause fatal disease. Neonatal tetanus is the most common form of tetanus in developing nations. The disease is caused by contamination of the umbilical stump, with spores following childbirth through cutting the cord with a nonsterile instrument or by application of animal dung or dirt to the cut cord.

Tetanus immunization and treatment become important in the setting of natural and mass casualty incidents, such as terrorist attacks. After the Oklahoma City terrorist bombing, the most common procedure performed on injury victims was wound care. Tetanus toxoid, antibiotics, and analgesics were the most common pharmaceutical agents used. Supplies of tetanus toxoid can be promptly depleted in the setting of a disaster.

PATHOGENESIS

Clostridium tetani is sensitive to heat and cannot survive in the presence of oxygen. The spores, in contrast, are very resistant to heat and the usual antiseptics. The spores are widely distributed in the soil and in the intestines and feces of many domestic animals. The organism usually enters the body through a wound. In the presence of anaerobic conditions the spores germinate and produce the toxin tetanospasmin. Tetanospasmin is disseminated via blood and lymphatics and acts at several sites within the nervous system, including peripheral motor end plates, spinal cord, brain, and sympathetic nervous system. Tetanospasmin diffuses to the terminals of inhibitory cells and prevents glycine and GABA secretion. This leaves the motor neurons without inhibition, producing muscular rigidity. The autonomic nervous system is affected as well, predominantly manifested as a hypersympathetic state induced by failure to inhibit adrenal release of catecholamines. Toxin binding is irreversible and recovery depends on sprouting a new axon terminal at the neuromuscular junction.

PRESENTATION

Onset of the disease is gradual. The incubation period varies from 3 to 21 days, usually about 8 days, but can last months. In general, the further the injury site is from the central nervous system, the longer the incubation period. Shorter incubation periods have been associated with more heavily contaminated wounds, more severe disease, and a worse prognosis. Tetanus is classically subdivided into four clinical types: localized, cephalic, generalized, and neonatal. In neonatal tetanus, symptoms usually appear 4 to 14 days after birth, averaging about 7 days. Localized tetanus manifests as local muscle spasms in areas contiguous to a wound. Local tetanus may precede the onset of generalized tetanus, but is generally milder and often resolves spontaneously.

Cephalic tetanus is a rare form of the disease, occasionally occurring with otitis media or following injuries to the head. It affects the cranial nerve musculature. It may also be seen preceding generalized tetanus.

Generalized tetanus is the most commonly recognized form. The disease usually presents with a descending pattern. It often begins with trismus (masseter rigidity or "lockjaw") and risus sardonicus (increased tone of the orbicularis oris). Rigidity of the abdominal muscles may also be present. The generalized spasm can resemble decorticate posturing and consists of opisthotonic posturing. Spasms are often triggered by sensory stimuli. During the spasm, the upper airway can be obstructed or the diaphragm may participate in the general muscle contraction, causing airway obstruction and respiratory compromise. Spasms continue for 3–4 weeks and complete recovery may take months. Autonomic dysfunction usually occurs after several days of symptoms with sweating, elevated blood pressure, and episodic rapid heart rate and, in the modern era of intensive care, is the leading cause of death.

Neonatal tetanus is the most common form of tetanus in developing countries. It occurs in infants born without protective passive immunity, because the mother is not immune. It usually manifests as generalized weakness and failure to nurse. Rigidity and spasms occur later. Convulsions occur with increasing frequency and intensity and its mortality rate exceeds 90%.

DIAGNOSIS

The diagnosis of tetanus is made clinically by excluding other causes of tetanic spasms. Tetanus is defined by the acute onset of hypertonia or by painful muscular contractions (usually of the muscles of the jaw and neck) and generalized muscle spasms without other apparent medical cause. *C. tetani* is recovered from the wound in only 30% of cases. Aprotective serum antitoxin concentration should not be used to exclude the diagnosis of tetanus.

Obtain blood samples in patients suspected of tetanus to test for antitoxin level, strychnine, electrolytes (including calcium), blood urea nitrogen, creatinine, creatinine kinase, and urinary myoglobin determination. These will help rule out other causes of tetanic spasms and determine the presence of complications from tetanus, such as rhabdomyolysis.

DIFFERENTIAL DIAGNOSIS

- Strychnine poisoning
- Dystonic reaction
- Hypocalcemia
- Dental infections causing trismus
- Rabies

TREATMENT

Treatment strategies involve three management principles: neutralizing tetanospasmin present in the body, removing the source of the toxin, and providing supportive care for muscles spasms, respirations, and autonomic instability.

Neutralizing Tetanospasmin

Tetanus immune globulin (TIG) is recommended for persons with tetanus. TIG can only help remove unbound tetanus and has no effect on toxin bound to nerve endings. A single total dose of 500 IU given IM is recommended for children and adults and has been found to be as effective as higher doses. Some authorities recommend infiltrating part of the dose around the wound if it can be identified. Intravenous immune globulin contains antibodies to tetanus and can be used if TIG is not available.

Removal of the Source of Toxin

All wounds should be cleaned and debrided of necrotic material. To prevent ongoing production of toxin, antibiotics are administered. Metronidazole is the drug of choice. It is superior to penicillin in recovery time and mortality. Begin 30 mg/kg/day (maximum of 4 g/day) of metronidazole intravenously divided every 6 hours for 10 to 14 days.

Supportive Care

Attention to the airway and to ventilation is paramount at the time of presentation. In the acute phase, death results from acute respiratory failure caused by diaphragmatic paralysis or laryngeal spasms. Administration of a benzodiazepine intravenously such as diazepam or lorazepam will help to control spasm and decrease rigidity. When benzodiazepines fail, other treatments that have been used with varying success include dantrolene, intrathecal baclofen, and propofol. Ultimately, in severe cases, long-acting non-depolarizing paralytics may be needed.

With patients surviving beyond the acute phase, autonomic instability becomes the major cause of death. It occurs several days after the onset of spasms and manifests as labile hypertension, tachycardia, and pyrexia. No therapeutic regimen has proven to be universally effective. Labetalol provides alpha and beta blockade and is recommended for blood pressure control. Morphine can be beneficial, as it can provide cardiovascular stability without cardiac compromise. Other agents that modulate sympathetic output have been tried with variable success. Clonidine and magnesium have given mixed results. Alpha adrenergic blocking agents, such as phentolamine, have been successfully used with propranolol in some studies.

Supportive care should include placing the patient in a quiet, dark environment and minimizing patient manipulation. Complications such as rhabdomyolysis, weight loss, and infections should be monitored and treated. It is important that all survivors receive a tetanus immunization series as the amount of tetanospasmin produced in clinical tetanus is small and an immune response does not occur.

PROGNOSIS

Prognosis of tetanus depends on the facilities available. In developing countries without facilities for prolonged intensive care, the case-fatality ratio can increase to over 50%, with more than half of the deaths occurring in neonates.

With patients surviving the initial acute phase of the illness, autonomic dysfunction and hospital-acquired pneumonias become the most common causes of death.

Other complications of tetanus include weight loss, gastrointestinal hemorrhage, pressure sores, and thromboembolism. Mortality varies with patient. In the United States,

75% of tetanus patients who died between 1998 and 2000 were aged greater than 60.

PREVENTION

- Immunization
- Proper wound toilet

BITEWOUNDS AND RABIES

Humans can be injured by the bites and stings of many animals, including mammals, snakes, spiders, and insects. The most common wounds are those from larger companion animals, most frequently dog, cat, and human bites.

MAMMALS

Overview

Bites from dogs, cats, other mammals, and humans are a common problem seen in the developed and developing world. Most bites are of low severity.

Presentation

Dog bites may contain a large amount of crushing force. Tissue may be crushed, torn, or lacerated. Resultant infections will likely be polymicrobial. It is estimated that most bites worldwide are from domestic dogs.

Cat bites are often puncture wounds on the extremities. Needle-like teeth penetrate more deeply to tendon and bone. Such wounds are more likely to present a few days after with infection.

Human bites are usually on fingers, but may be on arms, breasts, genitals, or other regions. Secondary bites can occur from a closed clenched fist, also known as a fist-tomouth injury.

MICROBIOLOGY

Dogs

- Usually polymicrobial oral flora, including staph, strep, and *eikenella.*

Cats

- Similar to dogs, but frequent *Pasturella* bacteria.

Humans

- All of the above; considered more infectious, also Hepatitis B and C, and HIV.

DIAGNOSIS

For all bites, get circumstances surrounding the bite wound: where, when, appearance, and medical status of biting animal, and current location of animal if known. Evaluate wound with attention to tendon, nerve, and vascular supply. Consider x-ray if available to look for underlying fractures or retained foreign bodies/teeth fragments.

There is a high risk of tendon injury/tenosynovitis with cat bites to the hand and also a very high risk of tendon infection with clenched fist bites.

DIFFERENTIAL DIAGNOSIS

Human

- In any laceration to the hand, especially knuckles, strongly consider the possibility that the patient acquired it in a fight.
- Consider empiric treatment of lacerations over the 4th and 5th knuckles.
- Consider possibility of abuse in patients with human bites.

TREATMENT

General

- Control bleeding with direct pressure.
- Irrigate all wounds copiously with sterile water if possible; tap water otherwise.
- Anesthetize wound if able.
- Mechanically cleanse wound with removal of foreign debris.
- Consider debridement of dead or damaged tissue.
- Update tetanus prophylaxis.
- Consider rabies vaccine; most domestic animals are not immunized in the third world and any bite by domestic or wild animals there should be considered high risk of rabies transmission (see next section).
- Suturing is controversial. Unless the wound is gaping or the face is involved, wounds are left to heal by secondary intention.
- Bite wounds to the hand should not be closed primarily.
- All wounds should be rechecked in 1–2 days.
- Antibiotic choice is usually a penicillin, penicillase-resistant penicillin, a cephalosporin, or amoxicillin clavulanate.
- Quinolones or bactrim/clindamycin combination may be used in penicillin allergic patients.

Dogs

Treatment as above.

Cats

- Scratches require no treatment unless already infected or immunocompromised.
- Always leave wounds open.
- Cover *pasteurella* with antibiotic choice (amoxicillin clavulanate).

Humans

- If the joint space or tendon is involved strongly consider at least 24 hrs of IV antibiotics.
- If wound is >24 hours old strongly consider above and exposure and drainage.

Other Mammals

- For bites by other species, follow the general guidelines as listed above.
- Bites by large herbivores will involve more crushing injury and should prompt concern about underlying tissue.
- Monkey bites should be treated as human bites, and every attempt made to capture the biting animal. Old world monkeys may carry Herpes B in the oropharynx and bitten individuals are at risk of acquiring infection. Chemoprophylaxis for Herpes B should be started.
- Large cats (lions, tigers, leopards) and wild canines should be treated as above with the caveat that bites by larger animals will involve much more force, and associated injuries should be assessed as well.

SPIDERS

Overview

While there are many types of spiders that may bite, not all are venomous. Actual spider bites are rare occurrences. There are the forms of spider envenomations: neurotoxic and cytotoxic.

Diagnosis

Spider bites are hard to identify definitively. Every attempt should be made to identify the biting spider. Usually a white area appears around the lesion.

Treatment

- Apply ice to area for short periods of time.
- Local wound care.
- Update tetanus.
- Consider antibiotics.
- Antihistamines for local irritation.
- Antivenin is available for bites by spiders of the *Loxosceles* and *Latrodectus* genera and is somewhat effective if given soon after the bite. Spider antivenin is rarely available.
- Consider benzodiazepines for severe muscle cramps.
- Pain management as necessary.

SNAKES

Overview

Although most snakes are not venomous, any snakebite should be evaluated thoroughly.

Diagnosis

Most patients will be able to relate the history of snakebite. Every attempt should be made to identify the type of snake involved.

Treatment

- Local wound care: wash the wound with soap and water.
- Bandage firmly.
- Keep the injured area still and lower than the heart.

- Monitor the patient's condition and watch for signs of shock or airway compromise.
- Support ABCs.
- Consider antibiotics, similar to cat bites.
- If evidence of systemic envenomation (bleeding, DIC or neuromuscular involvement) antivenom should be given. Ideally, monovalent if the species of snake is known. The dose is the same in adults and children. A test dose is given first.
- Pain management as necessary.
- Do not apply tourniquet, apply electricity to the bite, or attempt to suck out the venom!

RABIES

Overview

Rabies is an acute, progressive, incurable viral encephalitis, caused by the bite of a rabid animal. The World Health Organization (WHO) reports that more deaths occur worldwide from rabies than from other common infections such as dengue fever, polio, meningococcal meningitis, or Japanese encephalitis. Of the 50,000 human rabies deaths reported annually, more than half occur in the Indian subcontinent, with most of the remaining cases occurring in Southeast Asia, Africa and Latin America. In developed countries, rabies is mostly in wild animals, while in Africa, Asia, and Latin America infected dogs are directly responsible for most of the rabies deaths.

Presentation

- Incubation period may range from 20 to 90 days.
- Incubation longer for more distal sites of inoculation (hands, feet).
- Initial symptoms are nonspecific: fever, fatigue, chills, headache, flu-like symptoms.

- Acute symptoms follow in 5–10 days, one of two types.
- Furious rabies: anxiety, confusion, insomnia, agitation, psychosis and hyperactivity, throat spasms, hypersalivation.
- Dumb rabies: depression, intermittent periods of arousal, coma.
- Acute symptoms are followed in 2–10 days by paralysis and death.

Diagnosis

- Direct fluorescent antibody test of brain tissue (postmortem).
- PCR tests on serum, spinal fluid, skin biopsy and saliva.

Differential Diagnosis

Differential diagnosis should include multiple other forms of encephalitis, including bacterial encephalitis or meningitis, hysterical reaction to animal bites (pseudohydrophobia), polio, allergic reaction to rabies vaccine, Guillain-Barré syndrome, psychotic break, lupus, or stroke.

Treatment

There is no treatment once the disease has developed except supportive care. The disease is almost always fatal.

Prevention

The primary method of prevention in humans is post-exposure prophylaxis. In many developing countries, immunization of domestic animals plays a large part in rabies prevention.Post-exposure prophylaxis consists of two components:

1. Passive immunization with antirabies antiserum (either 20 units/kg human rabies immune globulin (HRIG) or 40 units/kg equine antiserum).
    - Infiltrate up to 50% of the total dose locally to the bite wound.
    - The rest administered IM gluteally.

2. Antirabies vaccine should be administered.
   - Multiple types of vaccine, multiple methods of administration.
   - Classic: one dose of 1 ml IM (deltoid) vaccine on days 0, 3, 7, 14, and 28.
   - There are also alternative intradermal methods in areas where vaccine is scarce.
   - Additionally, initial local wound care including irrigation may lessen the risk of rabies.
   - WHO recommends disinfection of wound with iodine or alcohol.

Special Considerations

Who should receive rabies vaccination?

- Any bite wound by a dog in an endemic or third world country.
- Any bite wound in a developed country by wild animals.
- Any bite wound in any country by an unknown or unobservable animal.
- May defer vaccine in species unlikely to be infected with rabies or dog bites where the dog is observable and has a record of receiving two rabies vaccines within its first year.
- Bats: in the United States it is recommended to empirically vaccinate if patient is in close proximity to bats while asleep or debilitated.
- Occupational risk or potential exposure.

TICK-BORNE DISEASES

Ticks are excellent vectors for disease transmission, and more than 800 species of these obligate blood-sucking creatures inhabit the planet. They are second only to mosquitoes in worldwide transmission as vectors of human disease, both infectious and toxic. In the United States, ticks are the most common vectors of vector-borne diseases. Ticks can carry and transmit a vast number of pathogens, including bacteria, spirochetes, rickettsiae, protozoa, viruses, nematodes, and toxins. Asingle tick bite can transmit multiple pathogens, which can also lead to atypical presentations of some classic tick-borne diseases; additionally, secondary infections and allergic reactions to proteins in tick saliva are also possible.

It is especially important to discuss prevention of tick-borne diseases for relief workers and others at risk. Clinicians should be aware of the signs and symptoms of tick-borne illness because increased morbidity and mortality are associated with delay in treatment.

Ticks are arthropods of the class Arachnida. Of the three families of ticks, only the hard ticks (*Ixodidae*) and soft ticks (*Argasidae*) have medical importance. Hard ticks have a hard shell or scutum. Ticks have two main body parts: the capitulum (sucking structure) and the body. When a tick attaches to a host, it digs a barbed structure called a hypostome into the skin of the host, and release several substances including: a cement to anchor the attachment; enzymes; vasodilators; and antiinflammatory, antihemostatic, and immunosuppressive substances. These facilitate feeding, and an anesthetic in the saliva makes the bite relatively painless. In addition, the saliva also contains neurotoxins that can lead to tick paralysis.

The life cycle of most ticks lasts between 6 months and 6 years and includes three stages (larvae, lymph, and adult). Hard ticks usually attach for long periods of time but only feed one time at each stage. After its meal, the tick detaches, drops from the host, finds a resting place where it can digest its blood meal and molts to the next feeding stage. In contrast, soft ticks can feed much more rapidly and many times on the same host.

LYME DISEASE

Lyme disease, named after the town Old Lyme, Connecticut, where the disease was recognized in 1975, is the most common vector-borne disease in the United States. It is caused by the spirochete

Borrelia burgdorferi. It is most common in children, but also effects adults. It occurs worldwide but is endemic in three US areas: the coastal Northeast (MA to MD), Midwest (MN, WI), and West (CA, OR, UT, NV). The vector is the *Ixodes scapularis* (Northeast) and *I. pacificus* (West).

Presentation

Less than a third of infected patients recall a tick bite. This is likely due to the small size (1–2 mm) of the nymph tick that usually causes transmission. The nymph stage is most active from May to August. After a tick attaches, transmission does not usually occur until 2 days later during the blood feeding. This is important because ticks that are noted can be removed soon after attachment, resulting in a much lower transmission rate. If transmission of *B. burgdorferi* occurs, the incubation takes between 1–36 days. During this time, *Borrelia* spirochetes migrate hematogenously to synovial tissue, skin, and nervous system tissue.

Signs and Symptoms

There are three described stages of Lyme disease. During stage one, a "bull's-eye" rash (erythema migrans) at the site of the bite may develop. Constitutional symptoms that may develop include: low grade fever, lymphadenopathy, splenomegaly, myalgias, and headache. During the second stage when hematological spread occurs, neurologic (seventh cranial nerve palsy), joint (monoarticular arthritis with the knee being most commonly involved), and cardiac symptoms (AV block) predominate. During stage three, chronic arthritic and neurologic abnormalities (including encephalopathy) may manifest.

Diagnosis

Primarily based on clinical and epidemiologic features with serologic testing (ELISA confirmed by western blot). Although bacteria can be seen in body fluids, arthrocentesis and CSF analysis are generally non-diagnostic. The classic rash known as erythema migrans is present in most patients, but only a third report tick bite.

Treatment

Oral antibiotics are the treatment of choice for most cases of Lyme. Recommended dose is Doxycycline 200 mg/day x 21–30 days for men, nonpregnant woman, and children greater than 8. Amoxicillin is used for pregnant or lactating women and children less than 8. It is important to know that a Jarish-Herxheimer type reaction can occur in the first 24 hours of treatment. Treatment is generally extended to 30 days for associated mild neurologic symptoms. However, prednisone is not currently recommended for facial nerve palsy.

IV antibiotics are recommended if cardiac or neurological abnormalities such as meningitis, encephalitis, or peripheral neuropathies occur. The antibiotic of choice is Ceftriaxone for up to 4 weeks.

Prevention

In the United States a commercial vaccine is no longer available. Measures to avoid tick bites is the best means of protection: proper clothing, DEET repellant, and permethrin-treated clothes. Although debatable, an empiric dose of Doxycycline may decrease transmission if the bite is noted within 72 hours.

TICK-BORNE RELAPSING FEVER

Tick-borne relapsing fever is a spirochete disease caused by at least 13 different *Borrelia* species and is present worldwide. The vector is the soft tick *Ornithodoros*, and rodents are commonly infected. The soft tick bite is usually painless. The incubation period is 4–18 days. Relapsing fever presents as a viral-like illness with high fever, myalgias, chills, and headache, and many patients have an eschar at the bite site. The clinical course will usually involve the initial syndrome for 3 days followed by an asymptomatic period of 7 days then another relapse. Neurologic symptoms are common. Diagnosis is made by demonstration of *borreliae* in peripheral blood during a febrile episode (thick and thin smear preparation, Wright or Giemsa stain can be used). Treatment is with Doxycycline, Penicillin, Erythromycin, or Ceftriaxone.

ROCKY MOUNTAIN SPOTTED FEVER (RMSF)

RMSF is an acute febrile systemic tick illness with significant mortality caused by the organism *Rickettsia rickettsii.* The infection is most commonly seen in the southeast United States. The incubation period is between 2 and 14 days. The symptoms are nonspecific, with fever, severe headache, myalgias, prostration, and nausea/vomiting. The characteristic maculopapular rash usually appears on the fourth febrile day on the wrists, ankles, palms, soles, and forearms. A vasculitis may develop that can cause hypotension, edema, and petechiae. Specific organ involvement includes: cardiac (cardiomegaly, myocarditis, EKG changes), pulmonary involvement (interstitial pneumonitis), and neurologic (mild headache to lethargy, seizures, coma, transient deafness, tremor, rigidity, paralysis, ataxia, aphasia, blindness). The initial diagnosis is often made clinically. Confirmation is obtained by: serology, skin biopsy, or direct isolation and identification of the organism. Treatment is with Doxycycline or Chloramphenicol.

EHRLICHIOSIS

There are two forms of human ehrlichioses: HME (human monocytic ehrlichiosis) and HGE (human granulocytic ehrlichiosis). The organism is a rickettsia-like coccobacilli called *Ehrlichiosis*. There are multiple species that cause disease and are transmitted by different ticks, including the brown dog tick. The organisms invade monocytes in HME and neutrophils in HGE. Both are identified as emerging diseases by the Centers for Control and Prevention (CDC). Infection peaks from June through August, and those at risk are similar to those at risk for Lyme. HME is found in the south central and southeast United States, while HGE is found in the upper Midwest and Northeast.

Reservoirs include the white tailed deer and white-footed mouse. The incubation period ranges from a week to a month. Common symptoms are fever, headache, and myalgias. Leukopenia, thrombocytopenia, and elevated liver function tests can be seen in anywhere from 50 to 90% of patients. Rashes occur in approximately a third of patients with HME but in only 2–11% of those with HGE. Other findings such as ARDS, meningitis, pancarditis, renal failure, and DIC have been reported. Fatality rates have been reported at 2.7% for HME and 0.7% for HGE. Diagnosis is usually clinical with serologic analysis. Most test results are retrospective. Sometimes microscopic identification of mulberry-like clusters, called morulae, inside leukocytes on peripheral blood smears can be visualized. The most common mode of diagnosis is confirmation of IgG antibodies with IFA. Treatment is with Doxycycline or Tetracycline for 7–14 days and is curative.

BABESIOSIS

Babesiosis is a tick-borne, malaria-like, acute febrile illness caused by the intraerythrocytic protozoan parasite *Babesia.* Since the late 1960s, more than 200 cases have been documented in the United States. Almost all of these cases were caused by *B. microti* and occurred in the coastal regions of southern New England (Cape Cod, Nantucket, Martha's Vineyard, Block Island). Babesiosis has also been reported in Maryland, Virginia, Georgia, Wisconsin, Minnesota, California, and Washington. The mammalian reservoirs are deer and mice and the tick vector is the same as Lyme, *Ixodes dammini.* the Highest incidence is from May to August. After an incubation period of 1 to 4 weeks the clinical presentation is with nonspecific flu-like symptoms, including fever, chills, headache, fatigue, and anorexia. Other less common symptoms are nausea, diaphoresis, depression, photophobia, myalgias, arthralgias, dark urine, emotional lability, and hyperesthesias. Unlike Lyme disease, rash is not a feature of the illness. Splenomegaly is present on exam in patients. More severe disease occurs in splenectomized patients. The diagnosis is established by examination of thick and thin Giemsa-stained blood smears. Characteristic intra-erythrocytic forms may be present.

Recovery without specific therapy is the rule for otherwise healthy patients. Antibiotic therapy is recommended only for patients with severe disease and those who have had splenectomies. Treatment with the combination quinine and clindamycin is the treatment of choice.

COLORADO TICK FEVER

Endemic to the Rocky Mountain area, Colorado tick fever (CTF) is an acute tickborne viral infection characterized by headache, back pain, biphasic febrile course, an occasional maculopapular rash (around 10%), and leukopenia. The etiologic agent of CTF is an arbovirus in the genus *Orbivirus*. CTF occurs in altitudes from 4,000 to more than 10,000 feet, in the Canadian provinces of British Columbia and Alberta and the western parts of the United States. The tick vector is *Dermacentor andersoni*, the same vector as RMSF. It is important to contrast CTF and RMSF because the treatments are different. Even though RMSF was described in the Rockies, it is actually less common than CTF, which is twenty-fold more common in Colorado.

Diagnosis is clinical suspicion confirmed by serologic testing. Leukopenia and thrombocytopenia may be seen. The diagnosis can be confirmed by serologic testing. Treatment for CTF is entirely supportive and generally has a good prognosis. Most patients do not require hospitalization, but if RMSF remains a diagnostic possibility, initial treatment with Doxycycline or Chloramphenicol and a period of observation are necessary until the diagnosis of RMSF can be ruled out.

TICK PARALYSIS

Tick paralysis is a condition that occurs when an adult female tick attaches and releases a neurotoxin that can produce cerebellar dysfunction or an ascending paralysis in the host. It occurs worldwide, but most cases occur in the southeastern and northwestern regions of the United States, western Canada, and Australia. Both hard ticks and soft ticks have been implicated. Tick paralysis usually occurs in the spring and summer months, and most cases occur in children. Onset of symptoms occurs 4 to 7 days after the tick attaches. Symptoms include weakness in the lower extremities, which ascends within hours or days to involve the trunk musculature, upper extremities, and head. Patients may present with ataxia or respiratory distress, and mortality rates of up to 10% have been reported. Analysis of CSF samples usually reveals no abnormalities, and the diagnosis is clinical and depends on a history of tick bite or finding a tick on the body of the patient. The differential diagnosis includes Guillain-Barré, Eaton-Lambert syndrome, myasthenia gravis, poliomyelitis, botulism, diphtheritic polyneuropathy, or any disease with an ascending flaccid paralysis or acute ataxia.

Treatment consists simply of removing the tick and supportive therapy; improvement is generally seen within a few hours and complete recovery within 48 hours. Supportive care, including mechanical ventilation, may be necessary. The mortality rate is approximately 10%; nearly all those who die are children. Tick paralysis in Australia is often more severe than in the United States. Hyperimmune serum is available in Australia and is often needed because symptoms may worsen up to 48 hours after removal.

PREVENTION OF TICK-BORNE DISEASES

Personal prevention of tick-borne disease involves removal of ticks from the body, prophylactic antibiotics, and prevention of tick bites. Ticks prefer to attach to the head, neck, and groin of humans, although they can be found anywhere. Removal of ticks is described below.

Second, there is the question of prophylactic antibiotics after finding a tick. If the tick has not been attached for 24 hours, the likelihood of disease transmission is low. Third, prevention of tick attachment is important, especially in those people traveling in endemic areas.

Strategies to prevent tick exposure include wearing appropriate clothing and applying tick "repellant." Both topical DEET and clothing impregnated with permethrin have been shown to be effective in field trials when used alone. Wearing protective clothing treated with permethrin, in addition to using DEET on exposed skin, provides the greatest degree of protection against tick bites.

RECOMMENDED METHOD FOR TICK REMOVAL

1. Remove an embedded tick by grasping it with blunt forceps or tweezers as close to the point of attachment as possible and applying gradual but firm steady upward traction.
2. Do not use bare fingers to remove ticks from animals or humans; when tweezers are unavailable, fingers should be shielded with a tissue, paper towel, or rubber glove.
3. Do not handle the tick with bare hands. After removing the tick, thoroughly disinfect the bite site and wash hands with soap and water.
4. Dispose of ticks by placing them in a container of alcohol or flushing them down the toilet.

LEPTOSPIROSIS

Leptospirosis is a zoonotic disease caused by pathogenic spirochetes from the genus *Leptospira.* This febrile illness occurs worldwide, with the majority of cases occurring in underdeveloped tropical regions. Leptospirosis is likely the most common zoonosis worldwide. Exact incidence rates are difficult to determine due to the nonspecific nature of most leptospiral infections; however, lifetime prevalence as ascertained by seropositivity can be as high as 40% in certain subpopulations. Leptospirosis was first described in 1886 by Adolf Weil, who observed four cases of "acute infectious illness with spleen tumor, jaundice, and nephritis." Over 200 serovars of pathogenic *Leptospira* have been identified. Recently the genus *Leptospira* has been subdivided into several species based on DNA-relatedness. However, for clinical purposes it is more useful to divide *Leptospira* based on serologies, so the serovar and serogroup designations continue to be used.

At-risk populations include those who have direct contact with the urine of carrier animals or contact with contaminated materials, such as fresh water or soil. Occupational risk includes: farm workers, veterinarians, adventure seekers, butchers, sewer workers, soldiers, hunters, hikers, miners, dog owners, inner-city dwellers, disaster survivors, and lab workers.

PATHOGENESIS

Leptospires are carried by a wide variety of wild and domesticated animals, most commonly rodents, dogs, cows, pigs, sheep, goat, and horses. Animals may experience active infection or be asymptomatic carriers, in which case the organism resides in the proximal tubule of nephrons and is shed in the urine. Humans contract the disease through direct contact with infected urine, or indirectly via infected urine deposited in the environment. Environments where exposure typically takes place include freshwater bodies, swamps, floodwaters, cane fields, rice fields, farms, mines, and the inner-city. Leptospires can persist in warm water, moist soil, or mud for many months. Leptospires enter the human body via lacerated or abraded skin, and intact mucous membranes. It is uncertain whether they can enter via intact skin. Once inside, *Leptospira* diffusely disrupt the cell membranes of small-vessel endothelial cells, which explains the varying clinical manifestations that can encompass nearly all organ systems.

PRESENTATION AND CLINICAL COURSE

The presentation and clinical course of leptospirosis can be highly variable, ranging from asymptomatic infection to the extreme of hemorrhagic fever with hepatorenal failure, cardiac conduction abnormalities, and cardiovascular collapse. Broadly, leptospirosis may be split into two syndromes.

Anicteric Form

After an incubation period of 2–20 days (10 days on average), patients typically experience the sudden onset of fever, chills, nausea, vomiting, headache, and myalgia. This corresponds to the septicemic phase, which lasts 3–7 days. Physical exam findings at this time are relatively nonspecific, and include maculopapular skin rash, pharyngeal injection, lymphadenopathy, organomegaly, and muscle tenderness. The presence of conjunctival suffusion or muscle tenderness involving the calves and lumbar region should raise the suspicion of leptospirosis.

The illness may progress to a second stage, after a 1- to 4-day asymptomatic period, resulting in a biphasic illness. This immune phase, characterized by the appearance of IgM antibodies, is again difficult to distinguish from other febrile illnesses, and is thought to result from the host immune response rather than the pathogen itself. Fever is generally lower than in the septicemic phase. Signs and symptoms of meningitis are often present, including severe headache, nausea, vomiting, photophobia, neck stiffness, and mental status changes. Even in those with no signs or symptoms of meningitis, CSF examination reveals aseptic meningitis. In addition, patients may develop ocular manifestations 3–8 weeks after initial onset of symptoms, including iritis, iridocyclitis, or chorioretinitis. Ocular manifestations, which can be unilateral or bilateral, may resolve or become chronic.

Icteric Form (Weil's Disease)

Weil's disease is the most severe form of leptospirosis, occurring in approximately 5–10% of symptomatic infections. It is usually a progressive monophasic illness, although it can sometimes present as a biphasic illness. Initially, Weil's disease is indistinguishable from the anicteric form of the disease, but around 3–9 days after the onset of symptoms, jaundice, renal failure, and bleeding diathesis may become apparent. In addition to the signs and symptoms present in the anicteric form, severe and persistent fever, abdominal tenderness in the right upper quadrant, organomegaly, cough, chest pain, hemoptysis, epistaxis, petechiae, and ecchymoses commonly occur. Renal failure may occur. Adult respiratory distress syndrome, and multiple organ system failure can also occur in severe cases.

DIAGNOSIS

General Laboratory Tests

The general laboratory values cannot make the diagnosis of leptospirosis, but they can help raise the suspicion.

- White blood cell (WBC) counts may be normal or slightly elevated in mild disease, with marked elevation in severe disease.
- Creatine phospokinase (CPK) is elevated in approximately 50% of patients.
- Acute renal failure (ARF) may result in elevated blood urea nitrogen (BUN) and creatinine.
- In Weil's disease serum bilirubin is elevated, infrequently reaching 60–80 mg/dl. Alkaline phosphatase and hepatic transaminases are also slightly elevated, with the transaminases rarely exceeding 200 U/L.
- Urine may show proteinuria, pyuria, microscopic hematuria and hyaline or granular casts.
- Cerebrospinal fluid (CSF) shows normal glucose and normal or elevated protein levels. Total CSF WBCs are generally <500/¼l.

Diagnostic Tests

Adefinitive diagnosis of leptospirosis can be made through direct detection of the organism or serological tests that detect antibodies to the organism. If suspicion is high, treatment should not be delayed pending definitive diagnosis.

Direct Detection

- Leptospires can be cultured, although this test is slow and insensitive. The organisms grow best at a neutral pH at 28-30°C on selective media: Elinghausen- McCullough-Johnson-Harris (EMJH), Korthof's, and Fletcher's. Growth is typically observed in 2–6 weeks. During the first 10 days of illness,

CSF and blood are more likely to yield positive cultures. Blood samples should be collected in heparin or oxalate, as citrate is inhibitory to the organism's growth. Leptospires can be cultured from the urine from week 1–3.

- Polymerase chain reaction (PCR) is extremely sensitive and can give a very early diagnosis, even when the patient has already been started on antibiotics.
- Dark-field microscopy and staining should be avoided as there are many falsepositives and false-negatives with these tests.

Indirect Detection

- Serologic tests for leptospires require clotted blood or serum. Regardless of the specific test, either a fourfold increase in titer or seroconversion in paired samples makes the diagnosis. Ahigh IgM titer can also be diagnostic, but in endemic areas the cutoff needs to be adjusted based on local population studies.
- The microscopic agglutination test (MAT) is the gold standard serologic test.
- IgM ELISA is also sensitive and specific, but less so than MAT. It is positive earlier than the MAT. ELISA makes an excellent screening test, and many commercial kits are available.
- Numerous other serologic methods exist. Among those that are commercially available in some form, LEPTO Dip-S-Tick (an IgM-detecting enzyme-linked dot immunoassay) and the indirect hemagglutination test (IHA) have the highest sensitivity and specificity.

DIFFERENTIAL DIAGNOSIS

- Influenza
- Malaria

- Primary HIV infection
- Infectious mononucleosis
- Rickettsiosis
- Borreliosis
- Brucellosis
- Hantavirus
- Dengue fever
- Yellow fever
- Viral hepatitis
- Viral meningitis

TREATMENT

Some controversy exists as to the effectiveness of antimicrobial treatment in leptospirosis as very few randomized controlled trials exist, some with contradictory results.

Jarisch-Herxheimer reactions have rarely been reported. Besides antibiotics, supportive care may be necessary.

Mild

- Doxycycline 100 mg PO BID for 7 days

Severe

- Penicillin G 1.5 million U IV QID for 7 days
- Ceftriaxone 1 g IV or IM QD for 7 days

Chemoprophylaxis

- Doxycycline 200 mg PO once weekly for duration of exposure

PROGNOSIS

Anicteric leptospirosis has an excellent prognosis. The mortality of Weil's disease is estimated to be 5–15%. Leptospirosis during pregnancy is associated with high fetal mortality.

PREVENTION

- Identification of reservoir species in a particular environment
- For domestic animals, antibiotics, vaccination and isolation can be used
- Improvements in sanitary conditions and sealed storage of food, so as not to attract reservoir animals

Preventing contact with infected urine can decrease transmission. Important measures include:

- Wearing protective clothing in high risk environments, such as fresh water bodies and floodwaters, or when contact with known carrier animals is anticipated
- Improving sanitation and hygienic measures
- Providing access to clean water

At the level of the human host:

- Chemoprophylaxis with doxycycline, for short-term heavy exposure
- Limited quantities of inactivated vaccines are available in Italy, France, Spain, Japan and China; several trials have shown various inactivated vaccines to have a limited efficacy: however, no long-term efficacy studies exist
- Dissemination of outbreak control information after disasters to the public via the press, and to physicians via public health agencies

WOUND CARE MANAGEMENT

Historically, wounds are a significant cause of mortality and morbidity during war. Most are caused by either blunt or penetrating trauma.

Acutely, wounds may present with pain, bleeding, and direct visualization of soft tissue injury. Late presentation includes erythema, warmth, pain, swelling, purulent drainage, and ascending lymphangitis.

DIAGNOSIS

History

P AMPLE history: allergies, medications, PMHX (past medical history), last meal, events leading to injury

- Inquire about tetanus immunization status
- Ask about remote injuries

Physical Exam

- Physical exam
- Primary survey: assess airway, breathing, circulation
- Secondary survey including evaluation of the wound; determine integrity of underlying major blood vessels, major internal organs, nerves, tendons, and joints as appropriate
- Assess motor and sensory function and pulses distal to the injury before and after wound management

GENERAL WOUND MANAGEMENT

The goals of wound care are to: control bleeding, prevent infection: even trivial wounds are at risk for infection, and promote healing. Control of severe bleeding is a higher priority than wound cleaning.

Direct Pressure

The best method for the control of bleeding. Use the heel of your hand and the most sterile material available. Large wounds, in which your hands cannot cover the injury site, require that the wound first be packed with an absorbent material. Most blood loss will slow appreciably within 10 to 20 minutes.

Pressure Bandage

If >20 minutes of bleeding with direct pressure, apply a pressure dressing. Use a bulky dressing on the wound, and an elastic wrap or a clean strip of cloth wrapped securely around the extremity and tied with the knot over the wound. Blood flow should be assessed regularly by checking distal pulses and sensation. Do not remove even if the dressing becomes blood soaked.

Pressure Points

Use digital pressure on a pressure point to slow arterial bleeding. Maintain pressure points by placing a round stick in the joint, bending the joint over the stick, and then keeping it tightly bent. Elevation: whenever possible the wound should be immediately elevated above the patient's heart.

Tourniquet

Use a tourniquet only when all other methods do not control the bleeding. A tourniquet left in place too long can damage the tissues and progress to gangrene, with eventual loss of the limb. Never place a tourniquet directly over the wound or a fracture. Use a blood pressure cuff or a stick to tighten the tourniquet; tighten only enough to stop blood flow. After securing the tourniquet, identify the location of the torn vessels. Apressure dressing should be applied in this location. Release the tourniquet every 10 to 15 minutes for 1 or 2 minutes so blood can flow to the rest of the extremity and prevent limb loss.

Infection Prevention

All wounds should be regarded as contaminated. If the area is hairy, clip the hair adjacent to the wound with a pair of scissors. Shaving may increase the chance of infection and is not recommended. Disinfectants (alcohol, hydrogen peroxide, and soaps) should be used to wash the area around a wound and should not be poured into wounds, where they damage viable tissue and may increase the incidence of wound infection. Use a high-pressure irrigation syringe to clean the wound. Simply rinsing or soaking a wound is inadequate to remove bacteria. Irrigate with at least 100 ml of water per inch. Wound irrigation is the single most important factor in preventing infection. Deeply imbedded, visible debris not removed by irrigation may be removed carefully with sterile forceps.

Motor and sensory function and pulses distal to the injury should be checked after wound management.

SPECIFIC WOUND MANAGEMENT

Contusions

Only large bruises require emergency care.

Abrasions

1. Irrigate and scrub using a sterile gauze pad to remove residual debris and prevent tattooing of the skin. Keep moist with antibiotic ointment.
2. Dress with sterile gauze.
3. Change the dressing twice a day and any time the gauze gets wet.

Lacerations

Superficial

1. For small lacerations, adhesive strips (or whatever tape is available) may be applied perpendicular to the wound.
2. Can use benzoin or cyanoacrylate glue to aid in adhesion.
3. Suture.

Heavily Contaminated

1. Clean thoroughly.
2. Suturing a heavily contaminated wound may lead to a higher risk of infection.
3. Use wet to dry dressings by loosely packing the wound with moistened gauze and cover with dry dressing. Change every 12 hours.
4. Antibiotic use may be considered.

Amputations/Avulsions

1. Control bleeding

2. Irrigate and bandage the stump and detached body part.
3. Wrap in moistened sterile gauze.
4. Place in a plastic bag.
5. Place the plastic bag in a bucket of ice or the coldest water possible. Do not apply ice directly to the body part or frostbite may ensue.
6. Treat an avulsion as a laceration without completing the separation.

Puncture Wounds

- Particularly high risk of infection
- Uncontaminated
  1. Irrigate
  2. Dress
  3. Monitor for infection
- Contaminated
  1. Irrigate thoroughly
  2. Start antibiotics since infection is almost certain: make sure to cover for Pseudomonas

Impaled Wounds

- Large objects: leave in place and transport to a medical facility. Before transport stabilize object with padding as high as the object to prevent movement during transport. Remember that metal objects that are impaled can conduct heat out of a cold patient.
- When removing an impaled object, remove it slowly and gently, but firmly, pulling out along the line the object entered. Stop if resistance or pain is encountered.
- If the object endangers the airway, remove it.
- If the object is in the eye, protect the object against movement, cover both eyes, place the patient at 45°, and carry the patient out.

ABDOMINAL TRAUMA

The accurate and timely assessment of abdominal trauma is paramount to reduce patient morbidity and mortality. Patients with abdominal trauma are generally divided into two classes: blunt and penetrating. While attention is often easily drawn to a penetrating wound of the abdomen, blunt abdominal trauma can be subtler. Abdominal pain may be absent in the setting of intoxication or other distracting injuries. Furthermore, patients may lose a significant amount of blood into the abdominal cavity before a change in the appearance of the abdomen occurs. The diagnostic challenge of blunt injuries, along with the higher likelihood of multi-organ involvement, results in a higher mortality compared with penetrating injuries.

ANATOMY

On inspection, the abdomen is divided into three regions: the anterior abdomen, flank, and back. The anterior abdomen is bounded by the anterior axillary line laterally, the symphysis pubis inferiorly, and the trans-nipple line superiorly. The anterior and posterior axillary lines make up the lateral borders of the flank. The sixth intercostal space defines the superior border, and the iliac crests define the inferior border. The back contains the entire space between the two posterior axillary lines, bordered inferiorly by the iliac crests and superiorly by the tips of the scapulae. Upon exhalation, the diaphragm may rise to the level of the fourth intercostal space, increasing the risk of associated abdominal injury if penetration occurs below the nipple line.

The internal anatomy of the abdomen is also divided into three regions; the peritoneal, retroperitoneal, and pelvic cavities. The peritoneum, bordered superiorly by the diaphragm, contains the liver, spleen, stomach, most of the small bowel, as well as the transverse and sigmoid colon. Organs of the retroperitoneum include the kidneys, ureters, much of the duodenum, and the ascending and descending colon. The abdominal aorta and the inferior vena cava are also located within the retroperitoneum. Enclosed by the pelvic bones, the pelvic cavity contains the rectum and bladder, and in women the internal reproductive organs.

PATHOPHYSIOLOGY

Blunt trauma injuries result from compression, crushing, or shearing forces often occurring at the junction of fixed and mobile structures. Penetrating injuries result from cutting or lacerating forces. The most commonly injured organs in blunt abdominal trauma are the spleen and liver. Stab wounds and other impalement injuries most often injure the liver, followed by the small bowel, diaphragm, and colon. Gunshot wounds and other missile injuries most often injure the small bowel, followed by the colon, liver, and abdominal vasculature.

Depending on the condition or level of impairment of the patient, the history may be either unobtainable or unreliable; however, when possible, it should be obtained, as it may facilitate the assessment of injury patterns. Pertinent information to obtain following a motor vehicle crash includes the type of impact (e.g., frontal, roll-over), vehicular speed, the patient's location within the vehicle, the use or deployment of passenger restraints, the presence of passenger-space intrusion, and the condition of other passengers in the vehicle. In falls it is important to inquire about the height of the fall, the surface that the victim landed on, and if the fall was broken by any objects (i.e., trees).

For impalement injuries, it is helpful to know the length of the object (i.e., knife). In gunshot injuries, the patient or witnesses should be asked about how many shots were heard, the type of weapon used, and the approximate distance between the victim and the assailant. It is important to ascertain from pre-hospital providers or witnesses the amount of extracorporeal blood loss at the scene.

PHYSICAL EXAM

After the patient has been fully disrobed, examination of the abdomen should proceed in an organized fashion as part of a comprehensive secondary assessment. Unexplained hypotension and/or tachycardia must be assumed to emanate from intrathoracic or intraabdominal hemorrhage, until proven otherwise. The abdomen should be inspected for abrasions, ecchymosis, distention, lacerations, and puncture wounds.

It is imperative to log-roll the patient and examine both the back and perineum. While decreased or absent bowel sounds are common with intraperitoneal injuries, their presence does not rule out significant intraperitoneal injury. Abdominal tenderness is frequently elicited in the presence of intraabdominal visceral injury, but may be absent with retroperitoneal injuries. The presence of rebound tenderness on exam suggests peritoneal irritation; however, its absence does not exclude significant injury. The abdomen should also be palpated for a mass, which could represent a ventral wall hernia or a hematoma. Serial examinations facilitate the early discovery of occult intraabdominal injury.

Arectal examination is mandatory, looking for gross blood, subcutaneous emphysema, and rectal tone. The likelihood that the rectal exam will detect these is low, but their presence is highly specific for significant intraabdominal pathology. Urethral catheterization is standard; however, if upon inspection of the urethral meatus blood is found, or a high-riding prostate is elicited on the rectal examination of a male, urethral catheterization should be preceded by a retrograde urethrogram.

IMAGING

Various radiographic imaging studies—including plain film, ultrasound, and computerized tomography (CT)—may be used to evaluate the trauma patient. It is important, however, that imaging not take precedence over initial resuscitation and stabilization.

Ultrasound is rapidly becoming customary in the initial evaluation of abdominal trauma. The FAST exam can provide valuable information regarding the presence of free fluid in the abdomen. It is quick, noninvasive, and highly sensitive. Some shortcomings include an inadequate evaluation of the retroperitoneal space, poor sensitivity for the detection of bowel injury, and the failure to detect a bleeding source.

The use of CT is noninvasive and can provide a myriad of information. In addition to being highly sensitive for intraperitoneal blood, CT can also evaluate the retroperitoneal space, identify the organ injured or source of bleeding, and determine the extent of injury. It is invaluable for defining injuries that may be treated conservatively, without operative intervention. Furthermore, CT can accurately detect injuries to the bony structures of the pelvis and vertebral column. Among the limitations of CT are its poor sensitivity for detecting bowel, pancreatic, or diaphragmatic injuries. The major disadvantage of CT relates to the logistics of moving a critically ill patient from the resuscitation area. Therefore, CT is usually contraindicated in hemodynamically unstable patients.

Plain films of the abdomen are rarely useful in the evaluation of abdominal trauma. In penetrating trauma, they may be used to search for foreign bodies or missile tracks; however, CT is the preferred imaging modality. The chest x-ray, aside from being essential for identification of potential intrathoracic injury, may help to demonstrate free air. A pelvic x-ray may identify pelvic fractures, which could be a source of significant occult blood loss.

DIAGNOSTIC PROCEDURES

Diagnostic peritoneal lavage (DPL), once the standard of care in the pre-CT era, is a rapidly performed, invasive procedure to detect intraabdominal injuries. Similar to ultrasound, DPL screens for intraperitoneal blood but cannot identify the source of bleeding. It is now generally reserved for patients in whom there is unexplained hemodynamic instability, and ultrasound is unavailable or the results equivocal.

Local wound exploration can be performed in patients who have sustained a penetrating wound and have no evidence of hemodynamic instability or peritoneal signs. Following local wound exploration, if the wound tract does not violate the peritoneum, the patient may be managed conservatively. If there is penetration, a DPL may be performed or the patient, most often, is taken for celiotomy.

MANAGEMENT

The fundamental principles of emergency care apply in the management of abdominal trauma; the ABCs are the first priority.

Once all identified threats to life are managed, patients should have two large-bore Ivs initiated. Routine trauma labs should be obtained at this time. While hemodynamically unstable patients often require prompt operative intervention, one must never overlook other potential lifethreats. For example, patients with upper abdominal penetrating trauma may be hypotensive due to intrathoracic emergencies, such as a tension pneumothorax or cardiac tamponade.

Blunt trauma patients are rarely operative candidates based solely on clinical grounds. These patients typically require CT or other diagnostic modalities prior to defining management and disposition options.

The absolute indications for celiotomy in blunt trauma are listed in Table 1. Relative indications in the hemodynamically stable patient include solid visceral organ injury, and a positive FAST/DPL or hemoperitoneum on CT with no clear etiology. While the blood may ultimately be from a minor liver or spleen laceration that is not seen on CT, it could represent a perforated hollow viscous. A completely asymptomatic blunt-trauma patient with normal studies may be discharged home or kept for serial examinations.

Except for long-distance shotgun blast wounds, all patients with a gunshot to the anterior abdomen require celiotomy. All hemodynamically unstable stab wounds require operative management. In the hemodynamically stable patient. All other patients can be observed with serial exams for 24 hours.

The hemodynamically stable patient with penetrating trauma to the back or flank may require double or triple contrast CT, if wound exploration is non-diagnostic. If the patient becomes unstable, or there is high suspicion for diaphragmatic injury, surgical intervention is indicated.

THORACIC TRAUMA

Of all trauma-related deaths, approximately one quarter are attributed to thoracic injury. Less than 10% of blunt chest injuries and up to 30% of penetrating injuries require thoracotomy. The majority of patients with thoracic trauma can be managed by simple maneuvers and do not require surgical treatment. Immediate deaths are essentially due to either major disruption of the heart or great vessels. Early deaths due to thoracic trauma are as a result of hypoxia, hypercarbia and acidosis secondary to airway obstruction, pulmonary contusion, cardiac tamponade, exsanguination, or aspiration.

The extent of internal injuries cannot be judged by the appearance of a skin wound. Blunt forces applied to the chest wall cause injury by three mechanisms: rapid deceleration, direct impact, and compression. The degree of external trauma may not fully predict the severity of internal injuries, and clinical suspicion of cardiac and vascular trauma should be heightened. Direct impact by a blunt object can cause localized fractures of the ribs, sternum, or scapula with underlying lung parenchyma injury, cardiac contusion, or pneumothorax.

Compression of the chest by a very heavy object, which prevents respiration and causes marked increases in blood pressure within veins of the upper thorax, may result in traumatic asphyxia. Anterior–posterior compression forces place indirect pressure on the ribs, causing lateral mid-shaft fractures. More than respiratory insufficiency, thorax trauma can cause hemorrhagic shock due to hemothorax. Hemothorax is common in both penetrating and non-penetrating injures to the chest.

If the hemorrhage is severe, it may not only cause hypovolemic shock but also dangerously reduces vital capacity by compressing the lung on the involved side. Persistent hemorrhage usually arises from an intercostal or internal thoracic (internal mammary) artery and less frequently from the major hilar vessels.

Bleeding from the lung generally stops within a few minutes, although initially it may be profuse. In some cases hemothorax may come from a wound of the heart or from abdominal structures such as the liver or spleen if the diaphragm has been lacerated. Hypovolemic shock and hemomediastinum can derive from a thoracic great vessel injury that may be the result of penetrating or blunt trauma. The most common etiology is penetrating trauma; however, the descending thoracic aorta, the innominate artery, the pulmonary veins, and the vena cava are susceptible to rupture from blunt trauma.

CLINICAL ENTITIES

Causes of Respiratory Distress

- Rib fractures/flail chest
- Pneumothorax
- Tension pneumothorax
- Hemothorax
- Pulmonary contusion
- Open pneumothorax
- Aspiration

Causes of Hemorrhagic Shock

- Hemothorax
- Hemomediastinum

Rib Fractures

Fractured ribs generally occur at the point of impact. Their presence indicates a need for examining the underlying lung for pulmonary contusion, laceration, hemoor pneumothorax. Multiple or anterior and posterior rib fractures may cause a flail segment. Fracture of the relatively protected first through third ribs indicates severe impact and mandates careful search for associated vascular injury. In the elderly patient, fractured ribs may result from simple trauma; while in the young significant forces can be applied to the thoracic cage without a resulting fracture.

Flail Chest

A flail chest occurs when a segment of chest wall does not have continuity with the rest of the thoracic cage. This condition is present when two or more contiguous ribs are fractured in two or more places. The resulting flail segment causes severe disruption of normal chest wall movement contributing to serious respiratory distress. The unstable segment wall moves separately in a paradoxical manner to the rest of the chest cage during the respiratory cycle.

The pathophysiologic effects of flail chest are evidenced by a decrease in vital capacity, reduction in functional residual capacity, and hypoxia due to the underlying pulmonary contusion. Often patients exhibit ventilation-perfusion imbalance, decreased compliance, increased airway resistance, and increased breathing effort. Initial therapy includes adequate ventilation, administration of humidified oxygen, analgesia, and fluid resuscitation. The injured lung is sensitive to both under-resuscitation of shock as well as fluid overload.

Appropriate patient management involves selective use of endotracheal intubation and mechanical ventilation. The primary indication for endotracheal intubation and mechanical ventilation is respiratory decompensation. Aggressive pulmonary physiotherapy with suctioning, incentive spirometry, early mobilization, and humidification of air is appropriate for all patients. Intermittent positive pressure breathing, postural drainage, and therapeutic fiberoptic bronchoscopy to suction retained secretions and treat atelectasis are often necessary. Stabilization of the chest wall rarely requires external surgical fixation.

Pneumothorax

Ahigh index of suspicion for the presence of a pneumothorax must be maintained in all blunt trauma victims. Pneumothorax usually results from a penetrating wound of the chest that creates a communication between the pleural space and external environment. As the size of this defect approaches two-thirds the size of the tracheal diameter, air passes preferentially through the lower-resistance injury tract rather than through the normal airways. This severely compromises oxygenation and ventilation and is immediately life threatening.

In an open or "sucking" wound of the chest wall, the lung on the affected side is exposed to atmospheric pressure, which results in the lung's collapse and a shift of the mediastinum to the uninvolved side. Because of the profound ventilation-perfusion inequality, the patient becomes cyanotic and has serious respiratory distress. The open pneumothorax must be treated rapidly using one of two approaches. In the spontaneously ventilating patient, application of a sterile occlusive dressing with vaseline gauze large enough to cover the wound entirely taped on three sides is the treatment of choice. Tube thoracostomy at a remote site to the injury should be placed.

If the chest wall defect is relatively small, the pleura may soon seal and no further intervention is necessary. A second approach is to simply intubate the patient and initiate positive pressure ventilation. Often surgical repair is required.

Tension Pneumothorax

Tension pneumothorax develops when air enters the pleural space via a penetrating chest wound with a valve-like opening but cannot exit. This leads to progressively increasing intrathoracic pressure in the affected hemithorax, resulting in impaired central venous return and mediastinal shift to the opposite side. Clinically the patient exhibits dyspnea, tachycardia, hypotension, tracheal deviation, unilateral absence of breath sounds, neck vein distention, and cyanosis, and may complain of chest pain. The hemodynamic instability is secondary to decreased venous return due to endopleural hypertension. The presence of hyperresonance and the absence of breath sounds are useful in differentiating a tension pneumothorax from cardiac tamponade. Tension pneumothorax is an emergency requiring immediate decompression using a large-bore needle placed into the second intercostal space in the midclavicular line of the affected hemithorax. This converts the injury into a simple pneumothorax.

Definitive treatment requires the insertion of a thoracostomy tube with underwaterseal drainage. If the lung does not fully re-expand after tube thoracostomy and there is a large ongoing air leak, the airways should be evaluated bronchoscopically to exclude a major bronchial injury. However, in most cases, no further treatment for tension pneumothorax will be required after thoracostomy tube insertion.

Hemothorax

Hemothorax is more common in penetrating than in non-penetrating injures to the chest. If the hemorrhage is severe, hypovolemic shock will occur as well as respiratory distress due to compression of the lung on the involved side. Patients who sustain acute hemothorax are at risk for hemodynamic instability due to loss of intravascular volume and compromised central venous return due to increased intrathoracic pressure.

Lung compression due to massive blood accumulation may also cause respiratory compromise. Sources of hemothorax are: lung, intercostal vessels, internal mammary artery, thoracoacromial artery, lateral thoracic artery, mediastinal great vessels, heart, and abdominal structures (liver, spleen) with an associated diaphragmatic hernia.

The diagnosis is readily made from the clinical picture and x-ray evidence of fluid in the pleural space. Optimal therapy consists of the placement of a large (36 french) thoracostomy tube. A moderate size hemothorax (500–1500 ml) that stops bleeding after thoracostomy can generally be treated by closed drainage alone.

However, a hemothorax of greater than 1500 to 2000 ml, as with continued bleeding of more than 100 to 200 ml, per hour is an indication for emergency thoracotomy or thoracoscopy.

Pulmonary Contusion

Pulmonary contusion is common after any form of blunt chest trauma and frequently manifests itself as hypoxemia. The goals for treatment are oxygen therapy, positive pressure either with a Continuous Positive Airway Pressure (CPAP) mask or by intubation and mechanical ventilation with Positive End Expiratory Pressure (PEEP). Splinting from the pain associated with rib fractures requires adequate pain management. The contused lung is prone to capillary leak, and therefore careful fluid management is paramount. It is a potentially life-threatening condition unless recognized early and treated aggressively. The onset of symptoms may be slow and may progress over 24 hours post injury.

Open Chest Wounds

In open or "sucking" wounds of the chest wall, the lung on the affected side is exposed to atmospheric pressure, resulting in lung collapse and a shift of the mediastinum to the uninvolved side. This clinical entity must be treated rapidly. A nonocclusive seal taped on three sides and applied over the wound is sufficient, and can be applied until reaching definitive care. In compromised patients, thoracostomy tube placement, intubation, and positive pressure ventilation are often required.

Rupture of Trachea or Major Bronchi

The trachea and major bronchi because of their similar anatomic position are subject to the same mechanisms of injury for either blunt or penetrating trauma. It is a serious injury with an estimated mortality of 30%. More than 80% of the ruptures of bronchi are within 2.5 cm of the carina. Injuries to the main bronchi and intrathoracic trachea are more prevalent than those to the cervical trachea because the latter is protected by the mandible and sternum anteriorly and by vertebrae posteriorly. The intimate anatomical relationship of the trachea to the great vessels, lungs, and heart explain the high incidence of serious associated injuries in blunt and penetrating trauma.

The clinical picture appears in two patterns, depending on whether or not there is free communication between the rupture of the trachea-bronchial tree and the pleural cavity. If there is free communication, a large pneumothorax results. The usual signs of tracheobronchial disruption are the following: hemoptysis, dyspnea, subcutaneous, and/or mediastinal emphysema, and occasionally cyanosis. Tube thoracostomy shows continuous bubbling of air in the water seal, and suction fails to re-expand the lung.

The chest x-ray may demonstrate pneumothorax, pleural effusion, pneumomediastinum, or subcutaneous air. Overall, 90% of these patients will have an abnormal chest x-ray.

Bronchoscopy should be carried out promptly when tracheobronchial rupture is suspected, since it is the most reliable means of establishing the diagnosis. If it indicates that the bronchial tear involves less than one-third of the lumen, the patient is stable, and if the thoracostomy tube underwater-seal drainage results in complete expansion of the lung, treatment may be conservative. However, in all other types of tracheobronchial injury, thoracotomy should be performed as soon as possible.

Myocardial Contusion

Myocardial contusion in blunt chest trauma may be associated with fractures of the sternum or ribs. The diagnosis is supported by abnormalities on ECG, frequently sinus tachycardia or frequent PVCs (premature ventricular contractions), along with potentially elevated cardiac enzymes, and wall motion abnormalities on echocardiogram. Cardiac contusion can simulate a myocardial infarction. The patient suspected of cardiac contusion must be admitted for cardiac monitoring. This type of injury is more common than generally realized and may be a cause of sudden death within 24 to 48 hours after the incident.

Pericardial Tamponade

Penetrating cardiac injuries are a leading cause of death in trauma. It is rare to have pericardial tamponade with blunt trauma.

Echocardiography or pericardiocentesis must be undertaken early if this injury is considered likely. Suspect it in patients with: shock/ hypotension, distended neck veins, muffled heart sounds, cool extremities, and no pneumothorax Initial treatment is pericardiocentesis. Removal of as little as 15 to 20 ml of blood will result in immediate hemodynamic improvement. All patients with this entity will require thoracotomy or median sternotomy for pericardiography, inspection, and repair of the heart.

Thoracic Great Vessel Injuries

Injury to the pulmonary veins and arteries is often fatal, and is one of the major causes of on-site death and accounts of 8–9% of vascular injuries seen in trauma centers. It may be the result of penetrating or blunt trauma. The patient with chest trauma may present with respiratory distress due to hemothorax. An initial "rush" of a large volume of blood after tube thoracostomy may indicate great vessels injury. The classic sign of pericardial tamponade may be present. Suggestive radiological signs include presence of a hemothorax, pneumothorax, widening of the superior mediastinum more than 8 cm, widened paratracheal stripe, apical cap, and depression of the left main-stem bronchus. CT angiography or aortography should be performed in the patient with moderate to severe injuries. The patient with signs of respiratory distress, hemodynamic instability and suspected pneumothorax should undergo immediate tube thoracostomy. If blood loss is greater than 1 liter, with continued bleeding along with hemodynamic instability, a thoracotomy must be performed in an attempt to repair the ruptured vessel.

Trauma to the Esophagus

Trauma to the esophagus is rare in patients following blunt trauma injury. Perforation of the esophagus is more frequently caused by penetrating injury. It is lethal if unrecognized because of mediastinitis. Patients often complain of sudden sharp pain in the epigastrium and chest with radiation to the back. Dyspnea, cyanosis, and shock occur, but these may be late symptoms.

Diaphragmatic Injuries

Diaphragmatic injuries occur more frequently in blunt chest trauma, and almost exclusively on the left side. They are frequently missed since rarely does the chest xray show any abnormality like an elevated hemidiaphragm or nasogastric tube in the left chest. Operation for other abdominal injuries often reveals diaphragmatic tears which require direct repair.

NEUROTRAUMA

Head Injury

Head injuries account for 50% of all trauma-related deaths. Traumatic brain injury (TBI) results from either direct or indirect forces to the brain and may occur both as an immediate consequence and from complications, e.g., hematomas (subdural, epidural, intraparenchymal) or cerebral swelling with herniation syndromes.

Initial Evaluation

The ABCs of trauma apply to the head-injured patient. If intubation is required, the orotracheal route with in-line C-spine stabilization should be used. A rapid sequence technique is preferred to help blunt an increase in intracranial pressure (ICP) seen during intubation. Cervical spine precautions should be maintained until injury is ruled out clinically or by x-ray. Important aspects of the history include: witnesses concerning onset and mechanism of injury, lucid intervals, seizure activity, past medical history including medication(s), and any recreational drug history. Physical exam should focus on the primary survey, followed by determination of the level of consciousness using the Glasgow Coma Scale (GCS). If the GCS is 8, the patient is considered unable to protect the airway and should be intubated. The initial neurological assessment should include: cranial nerves (including pupil size and reactivity), sensorimotor exam, and reflexes. Beware of a unilateral dilated pupil in the unresponsive patient, which may indicate increased ICP and impending herniation. Evaluate lacerations of the face or scalp and deep wounds and palpate with a sterile glove to check for any "step-off" deformities. Document any periorbital (raccoon sign), or postauricular (Battle sign) ecchymosis. Also, check for CSF leak, clear fluid from ear (otorrhea) or nose (rhinorrhea), and look for blood behind the tympanic membrane (hemotympanum). These three signs suggest a basilar skull fracture and mandate a CT scan.

Palpate the neck posteriorly for C-spine tenderness or deformity. Finally, complete the rest of the physical examination. For those patients who cannot respond, it is imperative to obtain radiographs of the complete axial skeleton from the base of the skull to the sacrum in at least two views. A head CT should be performed on all patients with acute head injuries and a history of loss of consciousness or focal neurological deficits.

PATHOLOGICAL CONDITIONS AND MANAGEMENT

Skull Fractures

May be obvious or subtle. Isolated linear non-displaced fractures with an intact scalp require no specific treatment and may be discharged with appropriate analgesic and head injury precautions. Open or depressed fractures require urgent neurosurgery consultation and admission, and may require operative debridement and/or elevation. Basilar skull fractures require admission for neurologic observation; if CSF leak, monitor for meningitis.

Epidural Hematomas

Are usually associated with temporal bone fracture and tear of the middle meningeal artery. They may have a "classic presentation" of head trauma and loss of consciousness followed by lucid interval with a typical hyperdense lens (biconvex) shape appearance on CT. They are less common than subdural hematomas, but require emergent neurosurgical evacuation.

Subdural Hematomas

Usually result from tears of cortical bridging veins. Alcoholic and elderly patients are at increased risk. Acutely, there is typical hyperdense crescent appearance on CT; however, in the subacute phase (2 day to 2 weeks) they may be difficult to visualize. Neurosurgical consultation is mandated since evacuation may be necessary (evidence of increased ICP, >5 mm midline shift, focal neurologic findings, posterior fossa location).

Intraparenchymal Hemorrhages

Often occur in the frontal or temporal lobes when brain strikes bone during deceleration. Clinical findings depend on the size and location of the hematoma, which can be seen on CT as a hyperdense focal area. Edema can result in rapid increased ICP. Treatment includes admission, control of ICP, and possible neurosurgical evacuation.

Diffuse Axonal Injury

Is a result of a shearing force causing microscopic hemorrhages, which may not be visible on CT and are best seen on MRI. Clinical findings range from mild neurologic impairment to coma. Treatment includes admission, control of increased ICP if necessary, and expectant management.

Subarachnoid Hemorrhages

May present with severe headache and nuchal rigidity. CT reveals blood within the ventricles, cisterns, or sulci. Treatment includes prompt neurosurgical consultation, admission, seizure prophylaxis with Phenytoin (load 20 mg/kg IV) and possible shunt placement. Is a diffuse head injury that may occur following blunt trauma to the head. It is associated with brief altered mental status or transient loss of consciousness. Initial symptoms of headache, dizziness, nausea, amnesia, and confusion are usually present but complete recovery is the rule.

Classification of TBI based on the GCS

The best score from each of the categories is used as a method to judge severity (Table 1). An overall score is made by summing the score from the 3 areas assessed. The total score may range from 3 to 15, and severe injury, GCS = 8; moderate injury, GCS 9-12; minor injury GCS 13-15.

SPINAL TRAUMA

Cervical spine (C-spine) injuries are present in around 1–2% of all blunt trauma patients and 5–10% of patients with head trauma.

It is important to maintain C-spine precautions, document a complete neurologic exam, and assess the respiratory status frequently since high spinal injuries can impair breathing.

Evaluation

The patient may be cleared clinically if there is no C-spine pain, a full range of motion, no tenderness to palpation, no intoxication or altered mental status, no distracting injury, and no neurologic deficits.

In all other cases, C-spine x-rays must be obtained and the full cervical spine seen, including C7-T1.

In patients with a fracture on plain films or those with a neurologic deficit, neurosurgery should be called immediately. Extensive diagnostic investigations, including CT or MRI, may be required.

SPINAL CORD INJURY (SCI) SYNDROMES

Anterior Cord Syndrome

Compression of the cord or spinal artery occlusion results in loss of all motor and sensory function below the lesion other than position sense which is preserved.

Posterior Cord Syndrome

Rarely traumatic; usually related to vitamin deficiencies and infections (e.g., syphilis); results in loss of position and vibratory sense.

Central Cord Syndrome

Typically seen in elderly patients following hyperextension injuries to the neck, often without x-ray abnormality; weakness in hands, arms greater than legs; with loss of pain and temperature sensation.

Brown-Sequard Syndrome

Hemisection of the cord producing ipsilateral paralysis and loss of proprioception below the injury, with contralateral loss of pain and temperature; typically results from penetrating trauma.

SCIWORA (Spinal Cord Injury Without Radiographic Abnormality) Syndrome Typically seen in pediatric trauma; neurologic deficits may be subtle, transient, and/or delayed (mean 1.2 days); MRI is normal in up to 50%, with atrophy of cord evident 1–3 months post-injury; the vast majority (83%) involve the cervical cord.

Complete Cord Injury

Flaccid below injury level and distal areflexia; vasomotor instability from loss of sympathetic vascular tone results in peripheral vasodilation with hypotension, warm/dry extremities and paradoxical bradycardia; decreased anal tone on rectal exam; and priapism.

Spinal Shock

In contrast, is defined as a temporary loss of spinal reflex activity below a total or near-total SCI.

Management

There are three priorities in the care of patients with potential SCI:

1. Airway management involves in-line stabilization (not traction), cricoid pressure, and rapid sequence intubation (RSI) for patients unable to ventilate adequately or protect

their airway. Fluid resuscitation also is important; obvious bleeding must be controlled and occult hemorrhage ruled out.

2. Patients must have constant full spine immobilization, including C-spine stabilization with a hard collar and sandbags or other similar devices to prevent further spinal injury.
3. Aside from fluid resuscitation and oxygenation, neurogenic shock usually responds to low-dose Dopamine at 2.5–10 ¼g/kg/min. However, in the trauma patient, this diagnosis should be one of exclusion. Closed SCIs with neurologic deficits should be treated with IV high-dose Methprednisolone, 30 mg/kg IV bolus followed by an infusion at 5.4 mg/kg/h for 24 hours, which may improve neurologic recovery.

8

Biological Wars and their Effects

In the past, blast injuries were usually associated with conventional warfare or unintentional accidents occurring in the workplace or at home. Over the last several decades, terrorism and landmines have increasingly contributed to the amount of injuries seen. Currently, worldwide there are over 120 million active landmines, with 25,000 serious injuries or death occurring annually. Proximity to an explosion and where it occurs (inside versus outside) both impact the extent of injury that occurs. The physical effects of blast injuries may be divided into primary, secondary, tertiary, or miscellaneous injuries.

PRIMARY BLAST INJURY

Results as a direct effect of changes in atmospheric pressure caused by a blast wave. Air-filled organ systems are mostly infected and include the ear, lung, and bowel. Injuries seen include: tympanic membrane rupture, pulmonary contusions, bronchopleural fistulas, arterial air embolism, pneumothorax, hemothorax, ARDS, and hemorrhage/perforation of the bowel. The physician must have a high index of suspicion and be able to identify the unique three "killers" of primary blast injury: pulmonary barotrauma (the most common), acute arterial or venous gas embolism, and intestinal barotraumas (a major source of delayed mortality).

SECONDARY BLAST INJURY

Results when objects accelerated by the energy of the explosion strike a victim, causing either blunt or penetrating ballistic trauma. These may include total body disruption and traumatic amputations. Head injuries are a common cause of death in this as well as in tertiary injuries.

TERTIARY BLAST INJURY

Results from a victim's body being displaced by expanding gases and high winds; trauma then occurs from tumbling and impacting objects. Common injuries include abrasions, contusions, lacerations, and miscellaneous blunt trauma. Children are especially prone to tertiary blast injury.

MISCELLANEOUS INJURY

Miscellaneous blast-related injuries include: inhalations and exposures of toxic substances such as asbestos dust, carbon monoxide, cyanide, white phosphorus, and phosgene gas; burns from direct flashes and burning buildings; and crush injuries from the collapse of buildings. Oxygen therapy is the main treatment for most of the miscellaneous blast-related injuries. Patients exposed to cyanide would be expected to have an anion gap metabolic acidosis, and sodium thiosulfate therapy would be indicated as it causes less hypotension compared to sodium nitrite.

Phosgene gas is a unique exposure because it may cause severe delayed pulmonary edema. It was the most lethal of the World War I gases. Phosgene is currently used in the manufacture of dyestuffs, pharmaceuticals, polyurethanes, and metallurgic applications, with an estimated worldwide production of five billion pounds. Treatment is mainly supportive, with oxygen, steroids, and inhaled beta-2 agonists. The key point is to first suspect phosgene gas exposure and then admit the patient for close monitoring for 24 hours.

White phosphorus is also a unique chemical exposure because it is found in munitions, industrial accidents, and fireworks. White phosphorus ignites on contact with air, creating heat and releasing phosphorus pentoxide, a pulmonary irritant. In addition, it can cause severe hypocalcemia and hyperphosphatemia. Treatment involves copious lavage of any exposed areas and placing any raw particles in water to prevent further combustion. Additionally, a 1% copper sulfate solution should be applied to the skin to neutralize the white phosphorus.

INITIAL ASSESSMENT

Important aspects of the history include: where the patient was in relation to the explosion; was it indoors, outdoors, or underwater; and was the explosion industrial related, accidental, or from a terrorist event? One should also get an idea of the number injured, so an appropriate disaster plan can be activated if needed. If necessary, proper decontamination measures should be taken by the staff, before a patient potentially exposes others or contaminates an area of the hospital. Physical exam should start with checking the vital signs and the ABCs. Aside from obvious physical exam findings, careful attention should be placed on the pulmonary and abdominal exam. The tympanic membranes should always be examined, for perforation indicates the presence of a high-pressure wave (greater than 40 kilopascals, 6 psi) and may correlate with other significant organ injury. Any individual with suspicion of significant injury or abnormal vital signs should have venous access established with a large bore intravenous catheter.

MANAGEMENT

After initial assessment, injuries should be treated appropriately. As mentioned before, a high index of suspicion must be held for pulmonary and abdominal injuries. Laboratory tests that may be helpful include a complete blood count, type, and screen or crossmatch for transfusion, basic electrolytes, creatine kinase (in crush injuries) carboxyhemoglobin and/or cyanide level (if indoors), arterial blood gas, urinalysis, and chest x-ray. Other tests may be ordered based upon injuries noted. Pulse oximetry can be helpful, but it needs to be remembered that readings can be reassuringly normal in carbon monoxide poisoning. In managing pulmonary injuries, oxygen, bronchodilators, and ventilators should be available. Obvious acute abdominal injuries require acute surgical care; otherwise, further radiological studies for evaluation or serial exams may be warranted. Portable emergency department ultrasound use can detect blood in the abdomen or intraabdominal fluid using the focused assessment with sonography for trauma (FAST) examination, and it can improve outcomes in penetrating cardiac injury. Based upon the pattern of injuries seen, the attention of a pulmonologist, general surgeon, orthopedist, neurosurgeon, or burn specialist may be required.

CRUSH INJURIES

Crush Injury/Crush Syndrome

Earthquakes and manmade disasters are the leading causes of crush injuries and an increased incidence of crush syndrome. The estimated incidence are ~20% and ~2–5%, respectively. However, given the global climate of war and acts of terrorism, we should anticipate a rise in manmade disasters in the future. Bywaters and Beall offered the first classic description of crush syndrome in Londoners treated during the German Blitz in 1940–41. Zhi-Yong described its devastation in one of history's worst natural catastrophes, the 1973 Tangshan earthquake in China, where the death toll was 242,769 and the additional injured 164,851. The mechanism of injury is entrapment of victims under collapsed structures for periods of 4 hours or longer. In crush-injured victims, deaths within the first hours are caused by shock and hyperkalemia, while deaths days later are from myoglobinuric acute renal failure.

The pathogenesis of all crush injuries begins with rhabdomyolysis, whereby increased and prolonged pressure on skeletal muscle leads to cellular death and the release of its intracellular contents. While generally resistant to ischemia, muscle tissue is very sensitive to pressure. It impairs the cellular Na+,K+-ATPase pump and calcium transport, resulting in a rise in intracellular free calcium, which in turn activates neutral proteases that disrupt myofibrils and leads to cellular damage and death. This cascade of events leads to the clinical features of myoglobinemia, hyperphosphatemia, hyperkalemia, hyperuricemia, hypocalcemia, metabolic acidosis, DIC, and hypovolemic and hemodynamic shock, the hallmark of crush syndrome.

Hyperkalemia with acute renal failure is the most immediate and life-threatening complication, occurring hours to days after a patient's extrication. An oxygen-binding heme protein found in skeletal and cardiac muscle, myoglobin is rapidly cleared from plasma primarily through renal excretion. With massive muscle destruction, the release of myoglobin surpasses its clearance, resulting in the typical discoloration of pink spun plasma and reddish brown urine. The urine dipstick will test positive as it reacts with the heme-containing myoglobin.

To differentiate between heme and myoglobin as opposed to hemoglobin, a microscopic examination of the brown urine will reveal an absence of red blood cells. The direct renal toxic effect of myoglobin and its secondary obstructive effects as it precipitates in the renal tubules play a critical role in the development of acute renal failure. An estimated 50% of the crush-injured patients with severe rhabdomyolysis will develop acute renal failure secondary to myoglobinemia. It is important to note that the degree of creatine phosphokinase elevation and the presence of myoglobinemia do not predict those who will go on to develop ARF. Other important factors include hypovolemia, metabolic acidosis, and age.

Presentation

Patients with crush injury will typically present with flaccid paralysis and sensory loss in the affected limbs. While they can appear like victims of spinal cord injury, their deficits do not correspond to a nerve distribution. On neurologic examination, their rectal tone and urinary-bladder function will also be preserved. Initially, extricated patients appear relatively well and without systemic signs metabolic derangement. The compressive force that entrapped the limbs in effect acts as a tourniquet, preventing systemic return of metabolic byproducts of cellular ischemia and necrosis. With rescue and decompression, a paradoxical acceleration to shock and hemoconcentration may develop. This may account for reports of victims dying immediately after extrication from collapsed structures.

Management

Anticipating and preventing the systemic and renal complications of crush syndrome is essential. Aggressive fluid resuscitation should begin during patient rescue, since a delay of 12 hours or more is associated with up to 100% incidence of acute renal failure. A large-bore intravenous line should be established as soon as a free limb is available and normal saline infused at a rate of 1.5 liters per hour. It is generally expected that 4 to 8 hours are needed to fully free an entrapped victim and remove them to the medical treatment area. Postponement of full extrication has been suggested until adequate fluid resuscitation has been achieved.

With stabilized blood pressure and urine flow, forced mannitol alkaline diuresis should be initiated to prevent hyperkalemia and acute renal failure. This therapy generally occurs in the medical facilities, where input and output are strictly monitored. Alkaline urine prevents the precipitation of myoglobin in the renal tubules while mannitol aids in the osmotic diuresis of myoglobin. The fluid of choice is D5 0.5NS, with each liter containing 10 g of mannitol as a 20% solution and 40 mmol of bicarbonate. The goal is to maintain a urine output of ~300 ml/h and urine pH >6.5 until myoglobinuria resolves.

This aggressive fluid management usually leads to a positive fluid balance of 4 liters per day. While well tolerated in young adults, this therapy must be tailored to the elderly. If the patient becomes oliguric, a bolus of 20 g of mannitol along with 120 mg of furosemide may be used. The theoretical disadvantage of urine acidification by loop diuretics is outweighed by its benefits. It is important to note that mannitol in excess of 200 g/d may produce acute renal failure and thus should be avoided. If anuria and renal failure develops despite treatment, daily hemodialysis must be instituted.

COMPARTMENT SYNDROME

The mechanism of crush with entrapment is the ideal setting for compartment syndrome. It is defined as elevated pressure within a closed tissue space that impairs neurovascular function, leading to tissue death. Compartment pressure can rise either from external compression or from internal volume expansion (hematoma or third spaced fluid). Normal tissue pressure is usually less than 10 mm Hg. At 20 mm Hg, capillary blood flow diminishes. Above 30–40 mm Hg, tissue will be at risk for ischemic necrosis, with nerve being more susceptible than muscle. Since all skeletal muscle groups are invested in fascia, compartment syndrome can occur anywhere in the body. The compartments most frequently involved by this syndrome are those in the forearm and the lower leg.

The classic presentation of those with compartment syndrome will be muscle weakness and pain that is out of proportion to their injury or examination. On inspection, there might be swelling, ecchymosis, and deformity suggesting an underlying fracture. On palpation of the muscle, severe pain will be elicited. Active contraction or passive stretching of muscle within the compartment will also worsen the pain. Hypoesthesia in the distribution of the nerves that traverse the involved compartment can occur. Do not wait for the classic description of pain, pallor, paresthesia, pulselessness, and paralysis (the 5Ps), as they are late findings and suggest irreversible damage. To confirm the diagnosis, compartment pressures must be measured.

Controversy exists regarding absolute criteria that mandates fasciotomy, a surgical procedure that carries high morbidity of bleeding, infection, and loss of limb. Pressures that exceed 40 mm Hg are generally accepted as indications for surgery. Some authors recommend a trial of intravenous hypertonic mannitol first to decompress compartment pressures. When effective, relief of symptoms, size of swollen limb, and compartment pressures are expected within approximately 40 minutes of treatment. Should conservative management fail, emergent fasciotomy is needed. This entails longitudinal incisions over the skin, and then the fascia of the affected compartment to release the swollen and injured muscle. In a disaster setting where the crush victim might be neurologically impaired, a high index of suspicion in needed. Early and multiple repeat compartment pressures might be needed to make the diagnosis. Treatment initiated within 4 hours of the onset of symptoms has an excellent prognosis to full recovery of function.

MISSILE INJURIES

Many authors previously devoted considerable effort to differentiating between the magnitude of injury caused by "ordinary" versus "high-velocity" missile wounds. As a result of experience gained in recent conflicts and to a greater extent based on wound ballistic research performed over the past decade, new and somewhat different concepts are evolving. One very fundamental concept is that the high-velocity wound is not necessarily a totally different entity, as had been previously thought. From a military perspective, the switch to high-velocity rounds is based on a practical standpoint. The automatic weapon, with its increased requirement for ammunition, necessitated lighter-weight ammunition. To compensate for the loss in missile mass, if wounding power was to be maintained, it was necessary to increase missile velocity. The lighter cartridge allowed the individual infantryman to carry the increase in basic load of ammunition (more rounds, same weight) and allowed for greater and more sustained firepower.

The penetrating missile or fragment destroys tissue by crushing it as it punches a hole through the tissue. This hole or missile track represents the so-called permanent cavity. The cross-sectional area of the missile track is comparable to the presenting area of the missile, and its dimensions are roughly the same for all soft tissues. After passage of the projectile, the walls of the permanent cavity are temporarily stretched radially outward. The maximum lateral tissue displacement delineates the temporary cavity. Any damage resulting from temporary cavitation is due to stretching of the tissue. Resistance or vulnerability to stretch damage depends mostly on tissue elasticity. The same stretch that causes only moderate contusion and minor functional changes in relatively elastic skeletal muscle can cause devastating disruption of the liver. The result of temporary displacement of tissue is analogous to a localized area of blunt trauma surrounding the permanent cavity left by the projectile's passage.

If one presented at the average large city hospital with a gunshot wound in the thigh (entrance and exit holes of less than l cm in diameter) and gave the history of being shot with a 22 Long Rifle bullet, the surgical treatment rendered would be minimal. The same would probably apply if the history were of a wound from a 38 Special or a 45 Automatic. If, however, the history was given that the wound had been made by an M-16, the victim would most likely be subjected to an excision of the entire bullet track and possibly even several cm of tissue on all sides of the track. Comparing the first 12 cm of penetration on the M-16 wound profile with that of the other examples shows that in such a wound the M-16 is unlikely to cause any more tissue disruption than the 22 Long Rifle. The reason for this is that the M-16 round does not fragment or yaw in the first 12 cm of soft tissue it traverses, nor does it develop its very significant temporary cavitation effects prior to 12 cm of penetration. The widespread belief that each and every wound caused by "high-velocity" projectiles must be treated by "radical debridement" is incorrect and results from failure to recognize the role of other variables, such as bullet mass and construction, in the projectile-tissue interaction.

PHYSICAL PROPERTIES

Penetrating missiles include both munition fragments and bullets (which are often divided into "high" and "low" velocity). Velocity is not as important as the amount of kinetic energy transferred to tissues. Kinetic energy transfer depends on: velocity, presenting area of fragment, and the mechanical properties of tissue.

FRAGMENT INJURIES

Fragments are usually small and numerous. They are of low velocity (100–500 m/s) and low energy (10–100 J), and have poor tissue penetration. Although injuries are often numerous, they are usually limited to the fragment track.

BULLET WOUNDS

Hand-gun bullets are of low velocity (<250 m/s) and low energy (200–300 J). Rifle bullets are of high velocity (750–1000 m/s) and high energy (2–3 kJ). Physiological effects depend on degree of energy transfer. High-velocity bullets can result in lowenergy transfer wounds.

PATHOPHYSIOLOGY

The effects of bullets can result from both direct and indirect effects. In low-energy transfer wounds, injury results from direct effects along the bullet track. In highenergy transfer wounds, indirect effects are more important: radial forces perpendicular to the track may result in cavitation, which in turn may generate contusions and lacerations away from the track, and negative pressure within the cavity can suck in environmental contaminants.

Rifle bullets also tumble (yaw) within the wound, which may increase the presenting area and increase energy transfer, which in turn can result in small entry and exit wounds but a large wound cavity. Radial-energy transfer can also cause indirect fractures. Bullet and bone fragmentation can cause secondary tracks and further unpredictable damage

TREATMENT

Low-Velocity Injuries

- Debride the wounds superficially.
- Lavage the wound with sterile fluid.
- Do not close the skin.

- Administer intravenous antibiotics such as Penicillin for 1–3 days.
- Give tetanus prophylaxis.
- Treat fractures by closed means with a cast, traction or external fixation.
- If bullet fragments remain in a joint cavity, arrange to have them removed within a few weeks.

High-Velocity Injuries

- Debride the wounds in the operating theater, using adequate anaesthesia.
- Lavage each wound after removing all dead tissue and foreign material.
- Lavage between the entrance and exit wounds, passing gauze through the track if necessary.
- Do not close the wound. Re-debride in 2–5 days and close or skin graft when clean.
- Administer antibiotics such as Penicillin and Gentamicin along with tetanus prophylaxis.
- Treat fractures with a cast or, preferably, external fixation or traction.

Wound Debridement/Excision

Debridement should be rational rather than radical. The recommendation is not to excise the wound to the extent that viable muscle is intentionally excised circumferentially, but rather to open the wound such that drainage is assured, while at the same time excising that muscle which is severely damaged or disrupted and therefore devitalized. The physician must aggressively incise the wound, but should not empirically excise tissue more widely than clinical judgment would normally dictate. The majority of combat surgeons continue to utilize the 4 Cs for identifying nonviable muscle: Color—dark; Consistency—"mushy"; Contraction—lack of failure when pinched with forceps; and the Cut—noted is the absence of brisk bleeding from the cut surface. The single most important principle in the management of battle wounds is their nonclosure following debridement. The physician must not give in to the temptation to primarily close certain "very clean appearing" war wounds. Such closure is ill advised and inappropriate and can only be condemned. All wounds must be left widely open with the following exceptions: sucking chest wounds, joint capsules, wounds of the dura, and some head and neck wounds; however, with severe contamination it may be safer to leave these open.

In some circumstances, delayed primary wound closure may be performed 4–10 days after debridement. The indication for delayed primary closure is the clinically clean appearance of the wound. Whereas most wounds are closed in the operating room utilizing the interrupted wire technique and local or general anesthesia, some may be very amenable to tape closure.

BURN MANAGEMENT

An evaluation of the Airway, Breathing, and Circulation (the ABCs) should receive first priority. The history should include the time, location, and circumstances of the injury, where the patient was found, and their condition. Past medical and social history, current medication usage, drug allergies, and tetanus status should be rapidly determined.

Smoke inhalation causes more than 50% of fire-related deaths. Patients sustaining an inhalation injury may require aggressive airway intervention. Most injuries result from the inhalation of toxic smoke; however, superheated air may rarely cause direct thermal injury to the upper respiratory tract. Patients who are breathing spontaneously and at risk for inhalation injury should be placed on high-flow humidified oxygen. Patients trapped in buildings or those caught in an explosion are at higher risk for inhalation injury. These patients may have facial burns, singeing of the eyebrows and nasal hair, pharyngeal burns, carbonaceous sputum, or impaired mentation. A change in voice quality, stridorous respirations, or wheezing may be noted. The upper airway may be visualized by laryngoscopy, and the tracheobronchial tree should be evaluated by bronchoscopy. Chest radiography is not sensitive for detecting inhalation injury.

FIRST AID AT SCENE

1. Stop the burning process and remove the patient to a safe area.
2. Place patient in a supine position and initiate CPR if indicated. The same general principles of cardiopulmonary resuscitation apply, and are a priority.
3. Cover patient (clean sheet and/or "space blanket").
4. If possible, start large-bore (16 ga) IV with lactated Ringer's solution (LR).
5. Oxygen: intubate if necessary. Carbon monoxide poisoning is the most frequent cause of death in the first hours after a fire.

ADDITIONAL CONSIDERATIONS

- Rapidly remove burning clothing.
- Electrical burns: ensure patient is clear of electrical source prior to rescue.
- Chemical burns: remove soaked clothing, and irrigate with copious amounts of water.
- Ensure that the patient and the medical team are completely clear of the fire area for their protection and to avoid interference in fire fighting efforts.

EMERGENCY DEPARTMENT TREATMENT

1. Reassess ABCs of Basic Life Support. Begin fluid resuscitation per the Parkland formula.
2. Oxygen by high-flow mask, nasogastric tube, and Foley for all serious burns. Intubation if indicated.
3. Assess extent and severity of burns (rule of 9s or mapping; patients hand = 1% body surface).

4. IV analgesics titrated to reduce pain to tolerable levels during initial cleaning and debridement.
5. Gently clean and debride wounds; cover wounds with Silvadene or Sulfamylon. Keep patient warm; clean and re-cover wounds daily.
6. Evaluate the eyes using fluorescent instrumentation.

SPECIAL SITUATIONS

Chemical Burns

- Alkali powder (lime): brush the powder from the skin before lavage is begun.
- Phenol: instead of lavage and in any case after lavage as well, the skin should be washed with a solvent such as polyethylene glycol, propylene glycol (anti-freeze), or glycerol to remove residual phenol.
- White phosphorous: must be kept moist to prevent ignition of the retained phosphorous particles. Wash the involved area with an 0.5 or 1.0% solution of copper sulfate. This will cause formation of a blue-black film of cupric phosphide on the surface of the retained particles. Debride the particles and keep them moist or you will have another fire.

ESTIMATING SURFACE AREA WITH THE RULE OF 9S

Child

- Head: 18%
- Torso back: 18%
- Torso front: 18%
- Leg left: 14%
- Leg right: 14%
- Arm left: 9%
- Arm right: 9%

Adult

- Torso front: 18%
- Torso back: 18%
- Leg left: 18%
- Leg right: 18%
- Head: 9%
- Arm left: 9%
- Arm right: 9%
- Genitalia: 1%
- Size of patient's palm: 1%

BURN ASSESSMENT

After completion of the primary survey, a secondary survey should assess the depth and total body surface area (TBSA) burned.

First-Degree Burns

First-degree burns involve the epidermis layer of the skin, but not the dermal layer. These injuries are characterized by pain, erythema, and lack of blisters. These burns heal without scar formation. First-degree burns are not considered in calculation of the TBSA burned.

Second-Degree Burns

Second-degree burns are subdivided into superficial and deep partial-thickness burns.

Superficial Partial-Thickness Burn Injury

Superficial partial-thickness burn injury involves the papillary dermis, containing pain-sensitive nerve endings. Burn management, burns, burn blisters, or bullae may be present, and the burns usually appear pink and moist.

These burn management, burns, and burn injuries heal with little or no scarring.

Deep Partial-Thickness Burn Injury

Deep partial-thickness burn injury damages both the papillary and reticular dermis. These injuries may not be burn management, burns, or burn painful, and often appear white or mottled pink. Deep partial-thickness burns can produce burn management, burns, and burn with significant scarring.

Full-Thickness or Third-Degree Burns

Full-thickness or third-degree burns involve all layers of the epidermis and dermis and may destroy subcutaneous structures. They appear white or charred. These burns are usually insensate because of destruction of nerve endings, but the surrounding areas are extremely painful. Third-degree burns are best treated with skin grafting to limit scarring.

Fourth-Degree Burns

Fourth-degree burns involve structures beneath the subcutaneous fat, including muscle and bone.

Note circumferential, or near-circumferential, burn wounds because they may cause progressive extremity ischemia or interfere with ventilation as burn wound swelling increases. In such situations, timely escharotomy is essential. Perform extremity escharotomies as soon as peripheral perfusion is threatened. Do not wait until the extremity is overtly ischemic. Perform torso escharotomies as soon as ventilation appears compromised.

MANAGEMENT OF MODERATE TO SEVERE BURNS

Initial Fluid Resuscitation:The Parkland Formula

Initiation of fluid resuscitation should precede initial wound care. In adults, IV fluid resuscitation is usually necessary in second- or third-degree burns involving greater than 20% TBSA. In pediatric patients, fluid resuscitation should be initiated in all infants with burns with 10% or greater TBSA and in older children with burns with greater than 15% TBSA.

Two large-bore IV lines should be placed. Lactated Ringer's solution is the most commonly used fluid for burn resuscitation.

The Parkland formula is used to guide initial fluid resuscitation during the first 24 hours. The formula calls for 4 cc/kg/TBSA burn (second- and third-degree) of lactated Ringer's solution over the first 24 hours.

Half of the fluid should be administered over the first 8 hours post-burn, and the remaining half should be administered over the next 16 hours. The volume of fluid given is based on the time elapsed since the burn.

Urine output should be used as a measure of renal perfusion and to assess fluid balance. In adults, a urine output of 0.5–1.0 ml/kg/h should be maintained. Patients with significant burns should have a Foley catheter inserted in order to monitor urine output.

Anasogastric (NG) tube should be placed in patients with burns involving 20% or more TBSA in order to prevent gastric distention and emesis associated.

Second 24 Hours

P 5% albumin in LR @ 0.5 ml/kg/%burn (200 cc of salt-poor albumin placed in 800 cc of LR).

Plus

- D5W (or 1/4 normal saline (1/4 NS) primarily for children) to yield the same hourly infusion rate as the first 24 hours.
- Adjust D5W or the 1/4 NS rate, not the 5% albumin solution, in order to maintain urine output of 30–50 ml/hr.

GENERAL CONSIDERATIONS

1. ALL medications must be given IV during the resuscitation because of the dramatic changes in capillary permeability. Otherwise, the patient can receive an overdose when fluid mobilization occurs.

2. Sodium shifts can cause serious hyponatremia. The rate of fall of serum sodium levels is very important, especially in young patients. Serum sodium must be carefully monitored when giving large volumes of IV fluids.
3. Transfusion is indicated for hematocrit under 30. Packed RBCs are preferred.
4. Insulin infusion may be instituted for serum glucose over 200 mg%.
5. Histamine (H2) blockers and antacids should be used to keep the gastric pH at 7.0.

AMERICAN BURN ASSOCIATION BURN CENTER TRANSFER CRITERIA

- Second- or third-degree burns greater than 10% TBSA in patients younger than 10 years or older than 50 years.
- Second- or third-degree burns greater than 20% TBSA in persons of other age groups.
- Second- or third-degree burns that involve the face, hands, feet, genitalia, perineum, or major joints.
- Third-degree burns greater than 5% TBSA in persons of any age group.
- Electrical burns, including lightening injury.
- Chemical burns.
- Inhalational injury.
- Burn injury in patients with preexisting medical disorders that could complicate management, prolong recovery, or affect mortality.
- Any patients with burns or concomitant trauma (e.g., fracture) in which the burn injury poses the greatest risk of morbidity or mortality. In such cases, if the trauma poses the greater immediate risk, the patient may be treated initially in a trauma center until stable before being transferred to a burn center. Physician judgment is necessary in such situations

and should be in concert with the regional medical control plan and triage protocols.

- A lack of qualified personnel or equipment for the care of children (transfer to facility with these qualities).
- Burn injury in patients who require special social/emotional and/or long-term rehabilitative support, including cases involving suspected child abuse or substance abuse.

Bibliography

Alexander, Yonah, and Paul A. Leventhal: *Preventing Nuclear Terrorism: The Report and Papers of the International Task Force on Prevention of Nuclear Terrorism*, Lanham, MD: Rowman & Littlefield, 1987.

Allison, Graham: *Nuclear Terrorism: The Ultimate Preventable Catastrophe*, New York: Times Books, 2004.

Arend, A.: *International Law and the Use of Force*, London, Routledge, 1993.

Basrur, Rajesh M., and Hasan-Askari Rizvi: *Nuclear Terrorism and South Asia*, Albuquerque, NM: Sandia National Laboratories, February 2003.

Bellamy, C.: *Knights in White Armour: The New Art of War and Peace*, London, Random House, 1997.

Bernauer, Thomas: *Genes, Trade, and Regulation: The Seeds of Conflict in Food Biotechnology*, Princeton, Princeton University. 2003.

Brandwein, P.F.: *Sourcebook for the Biological Sciences*, San Diego, Harcourt Brace JOvanovich, 1986.

Bukharin, Oleg: *The Threat of Nuclear Terrorism and the Physical Security of Nuclear Installations and Materials in the former Soviet Union*, Monterey, CA: Center for Russian and Eurasian Studies, Monterey Institute of International Studies, 1992.

Chrispeels, Maarten : *Plants, Genes and Crop Biotechnology*, Sudbury MA, Jones and Barlett Publishers, 2003.

Dixit, Prabla: *Communalism: A Struggle for Power*, New Delhi, Orient Longman, 1981.

Fransman M, Junne G, Roobeek A: *The Biotechnology Revolution?*, Oxford, Blackwell, 1995.

Fumento, Michael: *Bioevolution: How Biotechnology is Changing Our World*, San Francisco, Encounter Books, 2003.

Hoffman, Bruce: *Inside Terrorism*, New York: Columbia University Press, 1998.

Huntington, S.P.: *The Soldier and the State*, N.Y., Vintage Books, 1964.

Janowitz, M.: *The Professional Soldier: A Social and Political Portrait*, N.Y., The Free Press, 1960.

Kaplan, David: *The Cult At the End of the World*, New York: Crown Publishers, 1996.

Laquer, Walter: *The New Terrorism: Fanaticism and the Arms of Mass Destruction*, Oxford: Oxford University Press, 1999.

Morholt, E. : *Sourcebook for the Biological Sciences*, San Diego, Harcourt Brace JOvanovich, 1986.

Norris, James A.: *The First Afghan War 1838-1842*, Cambridge, University Press, 1967.

Norton, Augustus R., and Martin H.: *Greenberg, Studies in Nuclear Terrorism*, Boston: G.K. Hall & Co., 1979.

Potter, William C.: *Nikolai Sokov, Harold Müller, and Annette Schaper, Tactical Nuclear Weapons*, Options for Control, Geneva: United Nations Institute for Disarmament Research, 2002.

Retzer, W.J.: *Biotechnology Workbook*, Englewood Cliffs, Prentice Hall, 1991.

Rhodes, Richard: *The Making of the Atomic Bomb*, New York: Simon and Schuster, 1988.

Rosen, P.: *Societies and Military Power: India and its Armies*, Ithaca, Cornell University Press, 1996.

Sayler, G.S., Fox, R., and Blackburn, J.W.: *Environmental Biotechnology for Waste Treatment*, Plenum Press, New York, 1991.

Schroeer, Dietrich*: Science, Technology, and the Nuclear Arms Race, Ontario: John Wiley & Sons, 1984.*

Switzer, R.L.: *Experimental Biochemistry*, New York, W.H. Freeman and Company, 1977.

Index

R

S

T

W

□□□

Def. Studies